SUSTAINABILITY OF WATER AND SANITATION SYSTEMS

SUSTAINABILITY OF WATER AND SANITATION SYSTEMS

Selected papers of the 21st WEDC Conference
Kampala, Uganda, 1995

Edited by John Pickford,
Peter Barker, Bob Elson, Cath Ferguson,
Jeremy Parr, Darren Saywell, Rod Shaw and Brian Skinner

Intermediate Technology Publications
in association with
The Water, Engineering and Development Centre
1996

Published by ITDG Publishing
The Schumacher Centre for Technology and Development
Bourton Hall, Bourton-on-Dunsmore, Rugby, Warwickshire CV23 9QZ, UK
www.itdgpublishing.org.uk

in association with WEDC, Loughborough University, Leicestershire LE11 3TU, UK

© WEDC, Loughborough University of Technology 1996

First published in 1996
Print on demand since 2004

ISBN 1 85339 339 8

All rights reserved. No part of this publication may be reprinted or reproduced or utilized in any form or by any electronic, mechanical, or other means, now known or hereafter invented, including photocopying and recording, or in any information storage or retrieval system, without the written permission of the publishers.

A catalogue record for this book is available from the British Library

ITDG Publishing is the publishing arm of the Intermediate Technology Development Group.
Our mission is to build the skills and capacity of people in developing countries through the dissemination of information in all forms, enabling them to improve the quality of their lives and that of future generations.

The Water, Engineering and Development Centre (WEDC) is concerned with education, training, research and consultancy for the planning, provision and management of physical infrastructure for development in low- and middle-income countries.

Conference secretary: Rowena Steele
Papers produced by: Karen Betts

Printed in Great Britain by Lightning Source, Milton Keynes

ACKNOWLEDGEMENTS

The editors would like to acknowledge the commitment
of the Local Organizing Committee whose arrangements helped to ensure
the success of the 21st WEDC Conference.

CONTENTS

INTRODUCTION   xi

Section A   MANAGEMENT

Peter Barker, Cath Ferguson, Ian Smout and Max Wade   *WEDC*
Management of irrigation maintenance   3

Ms Agnes Bitature   *Uganda*
The nze ndi kano communication campaign   7

Geoff Bridges   *UK*
Motivation for NRW control   10

Edward Bwengye-Kahororo   *Uganda*
Women, water, sanitation in south west Uganda   13

F. Mawuena Dotse, Nii Odai Laryea and Betty Yankson   *Ghana*
Can rural women manage water?   15

David Kane   *Uganda*
Skills and management training for sustainability   17

J.G.B. Mitchell, T. Borotho and D.S. Barraclough   *Lesotho*
Parastatal development — institutional strengthening   20

Patrick A. Okuni and John P. Rockhold   *Uganda*
An approach for community-based sustainability   23

Dr F.A.O. Otieno   *South Africa*
Role of industries in sustaining water quality   26

Dr J.V. Pinfold   *Uganda*
Participatory techniques and didactic methods   29

Ms Anu Saxén-Rosendahl   *Kenya*
Demand-driven approach for sustainability   32

Rod Shaw   *WEDC*
The World-Wide Web and sustainable development   35

Michael Wood and Negash Dina   *Ethiopia*
Buying into rural water systems   39

Section B   WATER AND THE ENVIRONMENT

Moses Bagbiele, Elizabeth Kidd and S. O-Sarpong   *Ghana*
Community-oriented hygiene and sanitation   45

Mrs C. Binder, R. Schertenleib, J. Diaz et al.   *Switzerland*
The early recognition of environmental impacts   48

Eka I. Braide and Oka M. Obono   *Nigeria*
Sustainability in guinea worm eradication programme   52

Steven A. Esrey *USA*
Sustaining health from water and sanitation systems — 55

Malcolm Farley *UK*
Reducing water losses in Vietnam — 60

Geoff Folkard, John Sutherland and Reya Al Khalili *UK*
Natural coagulants — a sustainable approach — 63

Richard Mtonga and Theron Scott Robson *Tanzania*
Pump and engine maintenance scheme — 66

Fati Mumuni *Ghana*
Dam maintenance — 68

P.G. Nembrini *Kenya*
Water supply in Rwanda (1995): from war to sustainability — 70

Dr Abimbola Odumosu *Nigeria*
Sustainable community water supply in Nigeria — 73

Cyril H.A. Ratnam *South Africa*
With water only metres away — 76

Richard G. Taylor and Dr Ken W.F. Howard *Canada*
Averting shallow well contamination in Uganda — 80

Section C RURAL WATER SUPPLY AND SANITATION

Rob Burgess and M. Slabbert *South Africa*
Reconstruction development plan — Hlanganani — 87

Brian Copeland *Uganda*
Sustainability with large communally-owned systems — 90

Claus R. Jesperson *Uganda*
Village-level operation and maintenance — 93

Peter H. Killewo, Pontian Ruta and Edward Lungwa *Tanzania*
Singida integrated rural development project — 96

John Situma Mukhwana and Jarmo J. Hukka *Kenya*
Sustainability of community water supplies — 99

James Mwami *Uganda*
Spring protection — sustainable water supply — 101

Brian H. Skinner *WEDC*
Ferrocement water storage tanks — 104

Mtwalib Walude *Uganda*
Sustainability of Kaborole shallow wells — 108

N. Wobusobozi, R. Glotzbach and H. Nuwamanya *Uganda*
The gravity flow schemes programme in Uganda — 110

George Aduko Yanore *Ghana*
Sustainable rural watsan management in Bolgatanga — 112

Section D SANITATION AND WASTE

Mansoor Ali and Darren Saywell *WEDC*
Community initiatives in solid waste — 119

Dr K. Alibhai, Arthur Boon, A. Vincent and J. Williams *UK*
Increasing sewer longevity by septicity control — 123

Paul Arnold *Ethiopia*
Solid waste management in Addis Ababa — 127

Derek Harrington and Dr Karim Alibhai *UK*
Sustaining quality by control of industrial discharges — 130

David Holmes *Venezuela*
Sustainability of rural sanitation in Venezuela — 135

Michael Jere, A.T. Dzotizei and M. Munjoma *Zimbabwe*
Pit-latrine-emptying using motorized equipment — 140

Dr (Mrs) T.V. Luong *Bangladesh*
Sanitation and hygiene, Bangladesh's action — 143

Paul B. Majura and A.F. Banda *Zambia*
Sustainability of Lusaka sewage works — 147

John K. Odolon *Uganda*
Participatory hygiene and sanitation programme — 150

INTRODUCTION

by John Pickford

Nearly 100 papers were presented at WEDC's 21st conference, held in Kampala in September 1995. Of these, 44 papers were selected for this volume. The conference theme — sustainability of water and sanitation systems — was very opportune. Developing countries experience special difficulties in maintaining systems in full working order, so maintenance was a recurring topic. Moreover, the topics covered were wide-ranging, from sustainable development of underground and surface water resources to sustainable hygiene education so that local communities are able to derive long-term benefits from new or improved facilities.

As is usual at WEDC conferences, the majority of the papers were based on practical experience. They recount what authors and their colleagues have actually done to ensure that the systems with which they are involved are planned for sustainability, are implemented in a sustainable way and have prospects for long-term sustainability. Difficulties are also described — what went wrong as well as what went well.

SECTION A

MANAGEMENT

Management of irrigation maintenance

Peter Barker, Cath Ferguson, Ian Smout and Max Wade, WEDC

THE PRINCIPLE REASON for maintenance is the avoidance of economic costs caused by failures in delivering and removing water from the system in accord with crop requirements. Failures may affect the quantity of water or the timing of water delivery and removal.

Secondly, failure to maintain to an adequate standard may result in the generation of external diseconomies of production. Diseconomies are the incidental, unwanted and costly by-products of economic activity. These are frequently associated with environmental degradation and in the context of irrigation are manifested by salinity build up and waterlogging.

Thirdly, poor maintenance may introduce conflicts and arbitrary redistributions of income between those dependent on the system. The interdependencies inherent in irrigation systems mean that individual neglect has implications for the welfare of other users. This consideration is important for the organizational design of maintenance programmes and the way in which incentives and sanctions are deployed in the design.

Typically an irrigation system is composed of canals, channels, drainage and civil works. Access roads, offices and subsidiary plants such as ginneries or mills may be part of the wider definition of the irrigation project. In the present study the area of interest is confined to water delivery and drainage and more particularly with management of weed and silt maintenance. The assets vulnerable to weed invasion and reduced performance are embankments, canal and channel beds and drainage channels.

Inadequate maintenance of these assets will eventually produce the inefficiencies and inequities outlined above.

The principle adverse effects of large amounts of weed in irrigation and drainage channels are as follows:

- weeds interfere with water flow in canals and drains, inhibiting water delivery to the crop and drainage from the fields;
- weeds entrap sediment, causing a progressive reduction in the capacity of a channel or reservoir;
- weeds reduce reservoir capacity by occupying useful volume and increasing water loss through evapotranspiration;
- weeds block pump intakes, interfere with the operation of regulator gates and weirs, and threaten structures such as canal linings and bridges;
- weeds assist the spread of diseases such as schistosomiasis and malaria by reducing flow velocities and providing habitats for the intermediate vectors of the parasites causing these diseases;
- weeds in irrigation and drainage channels provide a source of weeds which may spread into irrigated fields;
- weed control operations may require the drainage of canals and reservoirs, thereby interfering with irrigation schedules; and
- weed control operations utilize scarce resources including finance, labour and equipment.

Of these adverse impacts, weed growth-induced flow resistance and siltation may impose the most serious economic costs. The relationship between vegetation and hydraulic resistance (resistance to water flow) is of considerable importance to watercourse designers and managers. The most commonly used indicator of the reduction in discharge capacity caused by weed growth is Manning's roughness co-efficient (n) derived from the Manning equation:

$$Q = A.R^{0.67}.S^{0.5}/n$$

where:
- Q is the discharge;
- A is the cross-sectional area of flow;
- R is the hydraulic radius;
- S is the slope of the water surface;

and
- n is the roughness (retardance) coefficient.

The presence of weed in a channel increases the hydraulic resistance and raises the value of Manning's n above the design specification for the channel. The direct effects of reduced discharge capacity are inadequate water supplied at the far ends of irrigation canals and an inability of drainage channels to remove water from waterlogged areas.

Hydraulic performance and conditions

The management of weeds in irrigation and drainage channels can be analyzed by using the concepts of 'hydraulic performance' and 'condition'. The hydraulic performance of a canal or drain, at a particular time, can be expressed by reference to its hydraulic objective, i.e. to pass a target discharge along the channel while ensuring that the freeboard (distance from water level to bank top level) is not less than the design, or target, freeboard. On many irrigation schemes, the target discharge varies throughout the year according to irrigation requirements which, in turn, depend on the crop calendar and climate. By contrast, the target freeboard would normally be the same throughout the year, to provide a safety margin against water over-topping the bank.

Thus, hydraulic performance can be represented quantitatively by the 'delivery performance ratio' (DPR) and the 'freeboard ratio' (FBR), defined as follows:

$$DPR = \frac{\text{Actual Discharge}}{\text{Target Discharge}} \quad FBR = \frac{\text{Actual Freeboard}}{\text{Target Freeboard}}$$

For optimum hydraulic performance at a particular time, the DPR = 1 and the FBR = >1.

The actual freeboard at any time depends on both the actual discharge and the condition of the channel (Q, A and n in Manning's equation). Thus, at those times of year when irrigation requirements are low, and hence target discharge is low, a poorer channel condition can be tolerated because the optimal values for hydraulic performance parameters may still be attained (i.e. *DPR = 1*, and *FBR = >1*).

The condition of a canal or drain at a particular time depends on the degree of structural and dimensional deterioration, and the degree of weed infestation and siltation. Thus, the condition worsens over time, but it may be improved by maintenance operations.

The weed-related condition of a channel can be described in terms of the stages of hydroseral succession. The weed communities in irrigation and drainage channels pass through clearly recognizable stages of succession.

Weed clearance improves the hydraulic performance of a channel, recovering the weed-related condition from a 'poorer' to a 'better' state by returning it from a later to an earlier successional stage. The extent of the recovery is dependent on the degree of weed clearance. Dredging (or de-silting) operations, for instance, remove weeds and their root material as well as silt, thereby returning the channel to an earlier stage of succession than other weed clearance operations.

Following weed clearance, the successional process recommences. The rate at which it proceeds depends on the persistence of the remaining vegetation and the potential for invasion and colonization by new weeds as well as the frequency of weed clearance operations.

Economics

The central economic principle guiding weed and silt clearance effort is based on marginalist theory. The optimum amount of clearance effort is reached when the marginal benefit of clearance is greater than the marginal cost of clearance. Whilst marginal cost is less than marginal benefit, additional clearance is worthwhile. This condition is important because it underlines the fact that clearance is not an end in itself and that it is a costly business. Clearance can only be justified when additional benefits outweigh costs. Benefits may be thought of as additional crop values secured by improved yields, better quality produce, or both. They may also take the form of costs avoided, for example, costs attributable to bogged down machinery when drainage is inadequate.

The required amount of clearance is governed by the need to convey irrigation water to the fields and equally by the need to drain water away. Both of these imperatives require minimum levels of channel performance which vary according to season. At times when performance standards can be relaxed without jeopardising benefits less effort and cost can be put into clearance effort. The maintenance records at Mwea for 1992 indicate that the peak period for canal maintenance was May to July, and for drain maintenance, July to October. The records show that the allocation of labour and hydraulic machinery is consistent with the reported priorities of the management programme. The overwhelming requirement here is that rice-harvesting should commence in December and be completed as quickly as possible thereafter. All clearance effort is planned to secure this objective.

The works office at Mwea Irrigation Scheme prioritizes the maintenance programme in accordance with specific tasks required and the specific location of those tasks. Although decisions in the formulation of the maintenance programme are largely determined by system efficiency considerations, due consideration is also given to equity because of the interdependencies inherent in large irrigation systems. Fairness and farmer co-operation partly determine the timing and location of maintenance effort at Mwea.

Irrigation managers such as the works officer at Mwea Irrigation Scheme must formulate an efficient and fair maintenance programme which meets the requirements of the crop and geography. The current pattern of management at Mwea Irrigation Scheme is restricted to the achievement of short-term goals. It does not take account of the ecology of the succession of different weed communities which comprize the channel life-cycle in that, in some instances, maintenance at an earlier stage in the cycle could slow down the succession. This could reduce the necessity for maintenance over the medium or even long term.

The management programme in Mwea Irrigation Settlement Scheme is just one of a series of broad control strategies which are potentially available to execute the programme. They may include alternative mixes of capital (e.g. hydraulic machinery) and labour (e.g. manual cutting). Combinations of differing capital and labour intensity can be constructed to fulfil a given maintenance programme. Alternatively, the input mix may be of machinery and herbicides, labour and herbicides, or include biological control. The viability of such a change to the maintenance regime would depend on how it might affect the crop cycle and whether or not there would be an economic gain.

The array of potential broad strategies should be filtered down to a small number of two or three by consideration of local economic and technical conditions. In developing countries some of the more important conditions might be:

- availability of labour, bearing in mind other labour-intensive demands (e.g. planning and harvesting crops);
- availability of hydraulic equipment and the need for maintenance facilities, and the need to optimize machine utilization by spreading channel maintenance activities over time;
- availability of fuel, spares and skilled operatives for hydraulic equipment;
- availability of herbicides;
- public health and safety concerns (e.g. in the use of herbicides);
- weed type and growth characteristics which determine the frequency of maintenance operations;
- severity of silting;
- variation in target discharge and hence permissible channel condition during the year.

Consideration of these factors will frequently rule out potential strategies. For example, at Mwea Irrigation Settlement Scheme the use of irrigation water for drinking and bathing rules out certain types of herbicide application in irrigation channels and periodic labour shortages necessitates the use of machinery.

The identification of two or three feasible contender control programmes leads on to the more detailed specification of each maintenance programme and specifically the amount of each input e.g. labour and machinery, required to accomplish it. Knowledge of input requirement and input costs allows unit cost to be calculated. Specification of a programme facilitates the breakdown of costs into capital (fixed) and operation and maintenance (variable) cost categories and, importantly, identification of their incidence through time (Table 1). A maintenance programme should be viewed as a planning period (e.g. 15 years). Such a period allows for the inclusion of episodic components of a maintenance programme such as silt removal which may, in some cases, be necessary only at three-or four-year intervals.

With costs classified, laid out systematically and the years over which expenditure will occur identified, the selection of a single maintenance programme from the contenders can be accomplished by viewing each programme as an investment project with expenditures flowing through time. Some expenditures involve a bigger sacrifice to the agency than the same nominal amount of expenditures incurred later in the period. This is because early expenditures involve the loss of interest-earning potential whilst on delayed expenditures interest may be earned. Thus, a dollar's worth of expenditure in year one is a bigger burden than a dollar's worth of expenditure in year eight or 12.

To reflect the declining burden of later costs, decreasing weights ('discount factors') are applied to annual costs in order to bring the series of costs through time to their 'present value'. (Table 1 illustrates a calculation of the costs of dredging 90 km of primary and secondary canals once per year over a 15-year period of Mwea Irrigation Settlement Scheme). The 'discount rate' is typically taken to be the interest rate that the agency has to pay on borrowed funds, or the interest rate that it might have earned on invested funds. Application of the discount rate through time allows the present value of costs of alternative control programmes to be calculated and the selection becomes a matter of choosing the cheapest programme.

The investing agency may find it useful to know the constant sum of money required on an annual basis to fund the selected programme. This may be readily achieved by multiplying the present value of costs by the appropriate 'capital recovery factor' to determine the 'annualized cost'. (Table 1 illustrates the calculation of the annualized cost of dredging 90 km of primary and secondary canals once per year over a 15-year period at Mwea Irrigation Settlement Scheme). For a specified number of years and at a specified interest rate, the capital recovery determines the constant annual sum that must be recovered in order to finance capital borrowed plus interest charges incurred to implement a control programme. This annual sum of money has to be generated either through grants, loans or farmer payments to finance the selected programme. It makes a valuable contribution to the agency in that it indicates the affordability of a programme over the entire period.

Application of the model outlined above brings weed and silt control programme selection within the principles of engineering economy.

Conclusions

Economic efficiency requires that a specified standard of system performance is achieved with minimum use of resources.

To meet the objective of minimizing expenditure, maintenance programmes should be formulated to fulfil performance targets as required to meet the water needs of the agricultural cycle. Feasible programmes should then be subjected to least-cost analysis over a lengthy planning process.

Given the multiplicity of inputs and the size of irrigations systems, several overall programmes capable of fulfilling system objectives may emerge. Each of these overall programmes can then be subjected to the least-cost analysis as outlined above.

Irrigation managers report the importance of experience in the formulation and practice of maintenance programmes. Subjective evaluations of programmes can be greatly enhanced by systematic monitoring of individual programme performance. Realized input productivities can be recorded and compared with historical and expected performances. Targets can be set and in the wider context of system management, incentives and where necessary sanctions may be deployed to enhance system performance.

References

Bakry, M.F., Gates, T.K. and Khattab, A.F., 1992. 'Field measured hydraulic resistance characteristics in vegetation-infested canals.' *Journal of Irrigation and Drainage Engineering*, 118(2): 256-274.

Brabben, T.E. and Bolton, P., 1988. 'Hydraulic impacts of aquatic weeds in irrigation systems.' *Paper prepared for Joint TAA/ICID (British Section) Meeting on Weeds in Irrigated Agriculture*, 14 November 1988, Overseas Development Unit, Hydraulics Research, Wallingford, UK.

JICA, 1988. 'Feasibility Study on the Mwea Irrigation Development Project.' Japan International Co-operation Agency.

Table 1.

Year	Inputs	Input Costs (KSh)	Number of Excavators	Annual Total Cost (KSh)	20% Discount Factor	Present Value of Costs
1	Capital cost of excavator	6,650,000				
	Annual recurrent costs for excavator	276,989	5			
	Labour for cutting	120,322		34,755,267	0.833	28,951,137
2	Annual recurrent costs for excavator	300,989	5			
	Labour for cutting	120,322		1,625,267	0.694	1,127,935
3	Annual recurrent costs for excavator	327,869	5			
	Labour for cutting	120,322		1,759,667	0.579	1,018,847
4	Annual recurrent costs for excavator	357,975	5			
	Labour for cutting	120,322		1,910,197	0.482	920,715
5	Annual recurrent costs for excavator	391,693	5			
	Labour for cutting	120,322		2,078,787	0.402	835,672
6	Annual recurrent costs for excavator	429,457	5			
	Labour for cutting	120,322		2,267,607	0.335	759,648
7	Annual recurrent costs for excavator	471,754	5			
	Labour for cutting	120,322		2,479,092	0.279	691,667
8	Capital cost of excavator	6,650,000				
	Annual recurrent costs for excavator	276,989	5			
	Labour for cutting	120,322		34,755,267	0.233	8,097,977
9	Annual recurrent costs for excavator	300,989	5			
	Labour for cutting	120,322		1,625,267	0.194	315,302
10	Annual recurrent costs for excavator	327,869	5			
	Labour for cutting	120,322		1,759,667	0.162	285,066
11	Annual recurrent costs for excavator	357,975	5			
	Labour for cutting	120,322		1,910,197	0.135	257,877
12	Annual recurrent costs for excavator	391,693	5			
	Labour for cutting	120,322		2,078,787	0.112	232,824
13	Annual recurrent costs for excavator	429,457	5			
	Labour for cutting	120,322		2,267,607	0.093	210,887
14	Annual recurrent costs for excavator	471,754	5			
	Labour for cutting	120,322		2,479,092	0.078	193,369
15	Capital cost of excavator	6,650,000				
	Annual recurrent costs for excavator	276,989	5			
	Labour for cutting	120,322		34,755,267	0.065	2,259,092
	Sum of P.V. of costs					46,158,016

Calculation of annualized cost

Present value of costs (KSh)	× Capital Recovery Factor (20 per cent over 15 years)	Annualized Cost (KSh)
46 158 016	× .214	9 877 815

The nze ndi kano communication campaign

Ms Agnes Bitature, Uganda

IN 1994 AUGUST, the Rural Water and Sanitation East Uganda Project launched a 'wash your hands after using the latrine' campaign in two rural pilot villages. This was done because it was felt that more energy needed to be put into the hygiene education component of the Project. The water and sanitation programmes were progressing well; however, several studies showed that diarrhoeal diseases were still frequently experienced in the home.

The studies also showed that despite the good knowledge of causes of and methods of prevention of diarrhoeal diseases the actual practice of the relevant hygiene behaviours was minimal. The campaign approach was an attempt to present the hygiene messages in a way that is different from the conventional and orthodox hygiene education methods. Through this approach, the campaign would attract the people's interest amidst the cluttered health education market. The campaign would spark off curiosity and interest amongst the overloaded and fatigued audiences.

This paper describes the RUWASA experience of how an extra effort in terms of resources, especially manpower, can start off a chain of small actions that can lead to behaviour change. It is a story of how the people of the two villages participated in making the choice to reduce diarrhoeal diseases in their homes. It shows how the people monitored their own progress and achievements and illustrates the role of communication in the water and sanitation sector. It presents a challenge to policy decision makers, political leaders, donors, water and health sector officials who allocate resources to the information, education and communication components of their organizations.

Communication is not a panacea, but it can create the necessary atmosphere to trigger off the relevant behaviour which must be continually reinforced, so that adopters do not slide back into their old habits.

Problem definition and rationale

In Uganda today diarrhoeal diseases rank second among the five child killer diseases.

Over the years scientists have established that diarrhoea is transmitted mainly oral faecally i.e. through swallowing faecal germs.

Research has also shown that the most effective behaviours which discourage the transmission of diarrhoea are safe disposal of faeces, hand washing and protection of water sources.

'The provision of safe water sources and sanitation facilities is important— but constructing latrines and digging wells will have little effect on health unless people use these facilities, wash their hands and store drinking water hygienically in the home" Ahrtag (1993).

RUWASA Project has been providing people with safe water sources and encouraging them to build and use latrines, so far with some success. However, the Project had not done much about the third key behaviour, hand washing.

Communicators and health educators worldwide know that giving information to people alone is not enough to change their behaviour. And research has shown, and is increasingly showing, that campaigns are a viable means of starting the behaviour change process. Not only is it difficult to pass through an individual's information processing stages, but it is even harder to get a person to change their behaviour.

Campaigns use several media to reinforce one central issue which means that the target groups receive limited messages repeated over and over with slight differences, trying to persuade the target group to perform limited actions thus not exerting too much pressure on their ability to listen, understand and perform the change being advocated.

Although campaigns are relatively expensive in terms of resources used in planning and implementation, they often yield good results.

They have been reported to bring about rapid adoption of innovations and to produce high levels of motivation in staff because of the clear and specific targets which can be easily evaluated.

The strategy

The RUWASA hand washing campaign focused on the stimulation of 'Hand washing after the latrine' through encouraging and persuading the target groups to develop the hand washing habit through the process of practising a series of small actions.

These small actions included making a tippy tap, returning the coupon to the CCT to show that you have a facility and, the act of washing your hands. It was hoped these would eventually lead to habitual hand washing with a consequent reduction of diarrhoeal diseases.

The baseline survey (Asingwire 1994) revealed that before the campaign about 90 per cent of the sample interviewed knew the main causes and preventative actions to take to avoid diarrhoeal diseases.

The UNICEF KAP survey carried out in 1994 on diarrhoeal diseases also showed that knowledge levels are high.

But both surveys showed fewer than 10 per cent translated this information into actual practice or behaviour.

In retrospect, it was decided that the campaign should promote the adaptation of the practice rather than the acquisition of knowledge. The campaign chose to promote social arguments rather than health arguments like the germ theory.

The primary and priority target group were the mothers and children. Families with latrines were also considered because it was felt that families who had not yet responded to latrine building mobilization efforts would find it even more difficult to move a step higher to a more complex behaviour such as hand washing.

The multifaceted slogan 'ndi kano' which is taken to mean someone is special/smart/wise/modern/fashionable/clean/beautiful/a winner etc. depending on the context, was developed and pretested and survey proved it to be very popular.

The slogan was linked to other community values of respect, cleanliness, wisdom, happiness and modernity. The aim was to market hand washing using less scientific approaches and appealing more to the emotions of the audience rather than to reason/rationality.

Each time a message is repeated using a different channel or medium it gains power and credibility. Different media were used at different phases of the campaign and these included posters, serial dramas, t-shirts, flyers, music and interpersonal media.

The relationship between campaigns and sustainability appears paradoxical because of the very essence and concept of a campaign. A campaign is meant to be a concentrated motivation/persuasion effort, meant to last for a specific period of time, targeting a specific audience and message. It can be very resource consuming in terms of time, money, manpower.

- Then how can it be sustainable?
- What is sustainable about it?
- Is it the campaign methodology or strategy or the behaviour which is being promoted?

If you look at the strategy itself the answer lies in availability of resources and commitment especially committed human resources. The human resource needs to be highly motivated and the financial managers need to be well versed with the campaign concept in order to appreciate aspects of it especially the need for rewards.

However for our purposes we will look at the behaviour change aspect.

Our argument is that a behaviour like hand washing becomes sustainable when the target audience begins not only to reap benefits of practising the behaviour like good health but also when they begin to anticipate possible benefits.

This anticipation is seen at the stage when they decide to try out the behaviour: in our case, when they begin to wash their hands. The survey reports that at least 86 per cent tried out the behaviour.

Sustainability is also dependent on how successful the campaign is in achieving its objectives and the process that led to this success.

The campaign achieved the following:

- 78 per cent of the target sample were seen to have hand washing facilities, an increase from five per cent.
- 88 per cent of them showed evidence of use of the hand washing facilities e.g. wet soak pits and water in containers.
- Number of latrines built had increased from an average of 75 per cent to 90 per cent.
- The demand for sanplats increased. At the baseline the number of latrines with sanplats was on average 15 per cent but by the end of the campaign it had increased to 53 per cent.
- 83 per cent had been exposed to campaign messages and approximately 80 per cent increased their knowledge of diarrhoeal diseases.

Other less tangible effects were also reported:

- Spill over effects on the three neighbouring villages.
- Other health behaviours were adopted like building of dish racks, bathrooms, etc.
- The villages now have an increased human resource base with more knowledge about diarrhoeal diseases as a result of the training they received during the campaign.

Critical to sustainability was the involvement of the communities and their leaders from the onset. This gave rise to several village meetings and training sessions.

The campaign managers at village level were selected by their fellow village mates and trained.

The fact that the human resources responsible for the planning, implementation and monitoring aspects of the campaign were from within the community meant that a capacity had been built within that particular village and as we all know skills development and capacity building are essential ingredients of sustainability.

The training too contributed to sustainability in that it was highly participatory with activities like role plays, group discussions, physical drawing of maps of their villages indicating houses with handwashing facilities and latrines.

Using the diffusion of innovation theory, you can also argue that the campaign can trigger off enough behaviour change in the community such that when it ends the behaviour diffuses from the adopters to the laggards making the behaviour change process continuous and self sustaining.

The hand washing behaviour is also being reinforced by the existing structures in the form of community health workers, water user committees, traditional birth attendants and other health workers using the conventional hygiene education approaches. This is made simple because the difficult part is taking the first step.

During the campaign children were reported to be taking the practice as a game whereby they would spend the time washing their hands over and over again because of the fascination they had for the tippy tap.

The question is: *Is this a good or bad trend?*

Once children learn a behaviour they will practise it, it will become a habit and when they become parents tomorrow, they will teach it to their own children and so on.

How much more sustainable do we want behaviour change campaigns to be?

References

Dialogue on Diarrhoeal, Issue No. 54, Ahrtag 1993.

'Health Related Behaviours in Bukalimo village'...Report of a consultancy *Asingwire* March 1994.

Using Communication Campaign Theory - *Sven Windahl and Benno Signitzer.*

Designing health communication campaigns. What works: *Thomas E. Backer, Everett M. Rogers, Pradeap sopory.*

Communication campaign activities in Mpande, Iganga District. An Evaluation Study. *Asingwire, May, 1995.*

Motivation for NRW control

G. Bridges, UK

THE BENEFITS OF controlling non-revenue water (NRW), and especially the reduction of distribution system leakage, to improve service levels and water utility performance have been widely acknowledged for many years. However, despite the real financial benefits that accrue when such activities are undertaken as part of routine operation and maintenance (O&M) work, NRW levels in many water utilities are still unacceptably high, some even exceeding 50 per cent of water produced (Asian Development Bank, 1993).

Many initiatives have been implemented throughout the world by utilities, government water departments, etc., encouraged by the international lending agencies, to tackle high NRW levels through specific projects and programmes that frequently include the key elements of institutional development and training. There should therefore be no lack of technical comprehension of the problem and its solution within most utilities, even though internal resources and capabilities may be constrained. NRW control programmes must be economically justifiable (i.e. self financing) as it is pointless spending more on the control measures than the financial value of the benefits accruing from the implementation of those measures. Lack of the necessary resources internally to implement an NRW control programme, therefore, is no excuse for not utilizing the services of the numerous consultants, specialist contractors and even individual specialists, capable of undertaking the work on a period or maintenance contract basis. Based on the author's extensive worldwide experience gained through implementing NRW programmes with utilities, it is postulated that probably the prime reason for the widespread failure to control NRW effectively is the inadequate, or even the total absence of, motivation within the utility itself to tackle the problem effectively.

Motivating factors

Before developing strategies to improve the level of motivation it will be helpful to consider some of the factors that influence motivation. The following is not an exhaustive list, but covers areas that are considered likely to have a major influence on attitudes:

- Performance criteria (set by senior management).
- Definition and monitoring of responsibilities.
- Recognition of good performance.
- Financial remuneration of staff (salary, bonus, performance related pay, allowances, benefits, etc.).
- Work satisfaction (professional pride/ethics, patriotism, etc.).
- Team spirit.
- Career development (promotion, improved remuneration conditions).
- Status.
- Media profile (senior managers).
- Company/share value (mainly senior managers).
- Attitudes of superiors and colleagues.
- Fear (criticism, disciplinary action, reduced remuneration, demotion, job loss, etc.).

Different factors will motivate each level of staffing to various degrees. For instance, senior managers are more likely to be concerned with media profile and share values than technicians, the latter being motivated by remuneration and career development.

It is postulated that the whole ethos of the water utility, and in particular the attitudes of senior management, will heavily influence the motivation of staff. If senior management appear to be remote and uninterested in NRW control then other staff will similarly place little emphasis on it. The process of motivating staff must therefore adopt a top down approach for successful NRW control. Furthermore, each individual staff member must have a clear understanding of what constitutes his duties and responsibilities, and know that he is being monitored and will be called to task if he fails to fulfil them. This process should not be one of oppression, but of active support and encouragement designed to assist staff in using their full potential to achieve their responsibility targets. It is suggested that the failure of senior managers to take a keen interest in and to become involved with the activities of subordinate staff is a major cause of poor motivation in some utilities. For instance, how many senior managers job shadow their staff (such as during night tests) to experience the conditions their staff operate under, to show interest in their work, or to encourage them?

In public utilities there may be considerable pressure on senior staff to respond to political pressure and implement high profile capital schemes for short-term expediency. Such an approach can have exactly the opposite effect in the longer term than that desired. For example, the construction of a new treatment plant, pipeline, or booster pumping station may be adopted to improve an inadequate supply to consumers caused by high leakage levels or other system deficiencies. The provision of additional water or an increase in pressure, however, will only serve to increase the leakage. In fact, funds expended on the initial capital works scheme would have been better spent controlling the leakage, followed by determining the reduced need for capital works prior to commissioning them. This action, though, might not be sufficiently obvious to consumers to deflect ongoing criticism of the utility for inaction to resolve the situation, encouraging it to adopt the most expedient course of action. Capital works may be perceived as an 'easy' or 'instant' solution to the problem, whereas leakage control calls for long-term commitment, perseverance and dedication.

Motivation strategy guidelines

Although motivation is associated with individual personalities, there are two main categories under which motivation needs to be considered. These are:

- Motivation of the corporate body (water utility, government department, etc.).
- Motivation of individual staff.

Corporate motivation

Corporate motivation is dependent upon the motivation of individuals within senior management of the organization. Financial and professional/ethical aspects are clearly important at all staffing levels, but at this senior managerial level motivation is likely to be heavily influenced by perceptions of the public image of the utility. This is primarily because senior management see themselves as figureheads of the company who will be called to account by their board for poor performance or lack of achievement. For some, it will literally mean exposure in the media and promotion of their face as the personal image of the water utility. Few people welcome negative press coverage or criticism from the boardroom.

It can be argued that this type of motivation is political, as it is concerned with public image, social responsibility, obligations to shareholders (government or private), etc.. Motivation factors therefore have to be controlled and specified by the political or corporate masters of the senior management. This is generally achieved by setting targets for management to attain. These targets will typically be concerned with the following:

- Technical goals such as NRW level (overall or in specific areas).
- Financial performance (cost reductions, improved billing/collection, gearing ratio, etc.).
- Share value performance.
- Staffing ratios (number of staff per consumer).
- Media coverage (ratio of positive/negative reporting).
- Customer relations (number of complaints, response period, etc.).

Many of these criteria will be covered in an annual business plan or one designed to chart desired progress over a longer period, typically five years. Outside the privatized water industry, there are few examples of such business plans or target criteria being set. In public utilities it is the responsibility of the government, council, or whoever is politically responsible for the utility to set such criteria and hold individuals responsible for failure to achieve them. All staff must be made aware that they are accountable to their superiors for failure to achieve set targets or for poor performance. There may, of course, be good reasons or contributory factors towards such failures, and these must be taken into account. Performance reviews of all staff should be held regularly, typically annually, at which time individual performances are reviewed (both good and bad aspects!), aspirations and problems aired, revised targets and career progression reassessed. The aim of the review must be to encourage the person to realise his full potential within the organisation and to provide constructive criticism and remedial actions where performance is poor.

Probably the major factor contributing to high NRW levels in many utilities is the failure of senior management and board members to set clear targets and performance criteria for the utility, as well as staff incentives to achieve them. Some suggested initiatives that should improve NRW performance are as follows:

Board members

- Set (in conjunction with senior management) and regularly review performance targets.
- Publish performance (actual and target) in regular reports to government, shareholders, etc., or whoever has ultimate responsibility for or interest in the utility.
- Make continued membership on the board conditional upon achievement of realistic performance targets.
- Link board member remuneration directly to utility performance.
- Monitor and review senior management performance (collectively and corporately).

Senior management

- Advise board on performance targets.
- Regularly report to and discuss performance achievements with the board.
- Link remuneration to utility performance.
- Monitor performance of NRW section and staff, resource requirements and availability.
- Keep abreast of technological and other developments that could improve performance.
- Set high personal standards as an example to other staff through direct involvement in their activities.

Staff motivation

The motivation of staff directly implementing NRW activities on a daily basis will be heavily influenced by the attitudes of senior management and the board itself. If staff are aware that a keen interest is taken in NRW control at the top levels of the utility, that senior management are available and open to the discussion of problems and suggestions to improve performance, and that action will be taken if performance is not satisfactory, then a conducive atmosphere will be developed within which a corporate spirit will flourish and staff will respond positively to challenges made. This will be further consolidated through the implementation of financial reward or incentives for good performance or the achievement of targets. The aim should be that all involved persons benefit from improvements achieved within the utility.

Such improvements will automatically be passed on to consumers or shareholders through improved service levels or profitability.

Technician level staff are not generally motivated by corporate image, but primarily by job satisfaction and its associated rewards, as well as job security. Satisfaction of these criteria will usually develop a strong commitment to the utility and its goals.

A feature of some utilities who give a low priority to NRW control is that poor quality staff or even misfits are allocated to NRW activities to keep them occupied and 'out of the way'. Even where capable staff have been allocated to NRW work and trained in the application of relevant techniques, it is not uncommon for them to be subsequently reallocated to tasks deemed to have a higher priority, either because the task has a higher profile and more attractive image or due to staff shortages. Little thought appears to have been given to the impact this will have on the NRW section performance. In at least one utility known to the author, promotion is based solely on the number of years service, with an apparent total disregard of the abilities of the person promoted and his replacement to maintain and improve section performances. Although not wishing to deny a technically competent person a well-merited promotion, such an approach does not generally make the best use of staff capabilities. Some suggestions to improve NRW performance at the technical staff level are as follows:

- Establish clearly defined staff responsibilities and task descriptions.
- Regularly monitor and review performance (personal and divisional).
- Link remuneration with performance achievements.
- Run regular staff training sessions by senior management or outside organizations and individuals to update technical competence and provide refresher training.
- Encourage self-improvement through evening classes, self-learning and distance learning courses, etc..
- Establish career structure within the division.
- Encourage high calibre staff to join the division.
- Emphasize the high-tech. aspects of NRW activities.
- Encourage senior staff to demonstrate interest in the NRW control performance of technical staff.

Conclusions

The performance of many water utilities, especially in the developing world, to control NRW is far from satisfactory. Many utilities appear to pay lip service to NRW programmes, possibly because they feel coerced into them by lending agencies who make implementation of a suitable NRW programme one element of a large capital works scheme, or the undertaking of a suitable programme is made a covenant of the loan to fund the scheme. It is postulated that poor NRW performance is not generally as a result of lack of technical expertise or resources, but is due to lack of motivation and accountability for NRW performance from the highest levels of management within the utility.

It is recommended that all involved in NRW control programmes should be motivated through the setting of targets, clear definition of individual responsibilities, monitoring and review of performance at the corporate and personal levels, individual accountability, and the linking of remuneration with overall performance and the achievement of set targets. These actions will encourage the development of team spirit, a commitment to the goals of the utility and enhanced NRW performance.

References

'Water Utilities Data Book, Asian and Pacific Region', Asian Development Bank, Manila, November 1993.

Women, water, sanitation in south west Uganda

Edward Bwengye-Kahororo, Uganda

HITHERTO IN UGANDA, water and sanitation improvement interventions laid more emphasis on technical interventions, focussing on construction work. Communities were considered as users and beneficiaries. Since the mid-eighties possibilities to participate in planning, maintenance, management, effective use and financing were broadened for communities. However when projects reported working with communities, leaders and committees, they almost invariably dealt exclusively with the male population. In the nineties, a more gender-sensitive approach showed that women have several roles in water and sanitation interventions, by tradition and by necessity.

As individuals, women are the most directly affected by lack of water. They are the most directly concerned with water and sanitation matters in their households, and have a great interest in a reliable and perhaps good quality service. They also have more management experience in services at a neighbourhood level related to health and food.

The SWIP[1] programme recognized that community participation in planning, design, management and evaluation is central to sustainable water and sanitation interventions. Particular attention was given to include women and actions that increase possibilities for their empowerment at all levels.

Guidelines were developed and established for mainstreaming the roles of women in the interventions.

Why involve women?

Women in Uganda are largely responsible for all household tasks — all water and firewood collection and ensuring proper use and maintaining whatever form of sanitation exists.

Women play a leading role in carrying out household tasks in relation to domestic water and sanitation, as:

- acceptors of technologies such as safe water points and improved pit latrines.
- users of improved facilities.
- managers of water and sanitation interventions in households.
- agents of positive behaviour modification in use of improved facilities.

Similarly the SWIP programme strongly believes that given appropriate training, support and equipment, women can bring about changes in basic hygiene behaviour in daily activities.

Water alone does not bring about proper sanitation or health. Nor do both if households do not wash their hands after using pit latrines. As more water is made available, appropriate containers and proper use is central to increasing the desired health impact. Since women are the key influentials in behaviour changes, their involvement in the interventions was considered to be able to increase the impact.

Along with the introduction of improved community facilities there should be provision for new and appropriate equipment to maximize effectiveness acceptability and use. If the pit latrines continue to smell, nobody may use them. Women involvement in sanitation promotion and pit latrine improvement in particular would perhaps bring this effective acceptability and use closer.

If latrine use is accompanied by hand washing, the chance of realizing the health impact can be greatly increased. Women are, in the main, promoters of hygiene practices, and therefore, we need their involvement in order to bring this reality closer.

Women's active involvement in sanitation platform (sanplat) production was accorded high priority in the programme-supported interventions.

The process of involving women in water and sanitation

For the purpose of this discussion, women's involvement in water and sanitation intervention will be limited to sanitation platform, sanplat, promotion and management of water.

The programme employed the strategy of increasing involvement of women in water and sanitation promotion. Hygiene education and dialogue with a community and its leaders was therefore embarked upon. A decision was made to involve women in sanitation promotion with emphasis on sanplat casting, sale and use.

A latrine with a sanplat provided with a tight fitting cover, has a minimal smell, is fly-proof, inexpensive, safe and attractive to use, for all categories especially children. It is also culturally acceptable in this part of the country.

Pilot efforts revealed high rates of acceptability, need for flexibility and possibilities of sustainable village level operation and management.

Working with existing womens' groups was found to be one of the most feasible options.

District authorities identified very active womens' groups. They were sensitized in sanitation promotion, hygiene practices and the safe water chain. The groups selected representatives for training in slab/sanplat casting, marketing.

The process of establishing casting yards in the programme area includes the following tasks.

Extension staff working with local leaders identify and select an eligible community.

Work with community leaders to carry out sanitation base line survey. Analyze and discuss the findings in the community. Dialogue with the community on sanitation promotion and water improvement.

Mobilize the existing womens' groups for participation in sanplat production technology.

Benefitting women's group select manson for training at a convenient and suitable site.

Women's group construct a shelter, for casting.

Collect and provide local materials, sand and water for casting the sanplats.

Extension staff assist in transporting external inputs such as cement, chicken wire mesh, tools-molds.

Prepare the workplan for sanitation promotion and water improvement.

Cast, cure and sell the sanplats.

Training the women's group in management and safe water chain.

Support supervision by extension staff, community and women leaders.

Groups submit progress report to district administration.

Lessons learnt

Women work in shifts consisting of a minimum group of three for each of the working days in a week. This arrangement involves saving more time to do other household work.

Women are accorded opportunities to participate in sanitation promotion at decision-making levels.

The participation at this level increased their level of knowledge on what constitutes adequate hygiene and diarrhoeal diseases.

A fly-proof latrine improved with a sanplat and through safe water practices is now within reach of every household in the programme-supported area.

Women benefit from participation in water and sanitation interventions through savings in time, energy and financial resources.

Frequent contaminants and disease are spread rapidly via water. Human excreta contains pathogens that cause many diarrhoeal diseases and this poses a threat to the health of children and infants who are the main victims.

Sanitation platforms fit in user household operation, maintenance and management principles.

The scheme involves some elements of cost recovery from users.

It strengthens private sector involvement in sanitation promotion efforts.

Women's participation is very enthusiastic in most cases and has enhanced efficiency and effectiveness of the use, operation and maintenance of facilities.

Only a small fraction of management positions for water and sanitation is allotted to women. Even the few on management committees may be essentially shy and unable to influence key decisions.

A good number are caretakers of water points as compared to almost none in positions of community based workers — pump mechanics and gravity flow scheme attendants.

Women do not build pit latrines, especially in this part of Uganda. They are only users but are expected to ensure cleanliness and tidiness of the facility.

They are responsible for ensuring household hygiene which is a critical factor in diarrhoeal disease transmission. Once a child develops diarrhoea, women as mothers are expected to prepare and administer oral rehydration therapy.

Women's involvement in water and sanitation promotion is therefore a crucial factor in child survival and development efforts.

[1] South West Integrated Water and Health programme, SWIP, a programme of the Government of Uganda supported by UNICEF, SIDA, Sweden and CIDA, Canada

Can rural women manage water?

F. Mawuena Dotse, Nii Odai Laryea and Betty Yankson, Ghana

THE ADOPTION OF the International Drinking Water and Sanitation Decade has awakened consciousness in developing countries including Ghana on the need to focus attention on improving water and sanitation facilities. In Ghana, this awareness has facilitated the implementation of many rural water delivery programmes. In recognition of the significance of water to women, they are actively being encouraged to play key roles in the sector, particularly at the community (rural) level.

In the Ghanaian traditional society, it is a woman's responsibility to identify water sources, fetch, store and dispose of water. In communities experiencing acute shortage of water, women spend considerable time and effort searching for water. Findings from a district in Ghana indicate that:

'Before the introduction of potable water in the Bolgatanga District, about 96 per cent of women were known to be fetching water each day of their lives, spending 30 minutes to six hours and walking an average of 3.8 miles in search of water' (USAID, 1984).

The objective of this paper is to discuss the role which women are playing in the management of water facilities at the community level in Ghana and highlight the challenges and constraints which tend to impede their efforts.

It would be argued by the authors of this paper that caution must be exercised in involving women actively in the management of water facilities since the patriarchal system in the Ghanaian socio-cultural setting is not favourable.

It would be further argued that notwithstanding the socio-cultural limitations, women have the potential to be managers of community water facilities.

Women's involvement

Women's involvement in the management of rural water facilities in Ghana is manifested in their membership of water and sanitation (WATSAN) committees and as pump caretakers. As members of the WATSAN committees, women are expected to be involved in the planning, implementation, monitoring and evaluation of water programmes. For newly initiated water programmes, women members participate in resource mobilization activities to ensure the generation of adequate funds to meet the communities' contribution to capital costs of the water facility being provided. In the case of existing community water programmes, women WATSAN committee members either collect water user fees from residents or sell water at point sources and render accounts regularly. Given the trust reposed in women for their level of honesty, women have been elected as treasurers of most of the WATSAN committees. As community pump caretakers for sophisticated pumps such as the Ghana Modified Indian Mark II, women ensure pump site cleanliness, carry out routine inspection, repair and maintenance of the above ground components of the pump, liaise with area mechanics and keep proper records on the repair and maintenance of the pump. In the upper east and upper west Regions of Ghana, women caretakers have been trained to undertake below-ground repairs on the Afridev pump which is considered less sophisticated.

Challenges to women's involvement

A combination of socio-cultural, psychological and economic factors pose challenges to women's involvement in the management of water facilities. These factors are discussed in the following sections of the paper.

Socio-cultural

Traditionally, women are responsible for all domestic chores i.e. cooking, feeding of children, washing, fetching firewood, bathing children etc. (Melchoir-Tellier, 1981). Given this traditional role set for women, problems usually arise when women have to leave home either for short or long durations attending meetings and training workshops on water and sanitation. In a few cases, women WATSAN committee members have been physically prevented by their husbands from participating in workshops on the grounds that nobody would perform the woman's role when she is away from home. The intervention of project management and the district authorities have contributed to allaying the fears of husbands around the participation of their wives in meeting and training workshops.

Given the domination of men in the society arising out of the patriarchal system, the involvement of women in the management of water facilities is an issue in the community and its managers tend to enjoy some visibility and where they are women, the male non-WATSAN committee members feel marginalized in the development of their communities.

Psychological

In some societies in Ghana, women are considered as being inferior to men. This phenomenon is particularly evident in rural communities. Some women particularly the uneducated have readily accepted this position and do not therefore want to assert themselves by assuming new roles as managers of water facilities. This is because these roles are considered the preserve of men (Simpson Herbert, 1992). Against this background, women tend to discourage their fellow women from active participation. It can be said that ignorance and illiteracy are perpetuating the inferior status of women and hence their reluctance to play leading roles in the water and sanitation sector.

In a contrasting situation, some women have 'liberated' themselves from male dominance and plunged into active involvement in the management of water facilities. These women are very assertive and tend to override their male counterparts on the committee and other members of the society. This has produced negative feelings and antagonism against these women. In such circumstances, the co-operation and complementary support required from the community is absent.

Economic

Rather than consider active involvement in the management of water facilities as complementary to their working life, most women regard the activity as additional responsibility and therefore shy away from it. In some Ghanaian villages, by the age of 18, most women would have at least one child and therefore have responsibilities towards husbands and children.

Suggestions for improving women's involvement in managing water

A number of proposals are suggested towards promoting rural women's involvement in the management of water facilities. In the first place, implementors of rural water programmes require a great deal of time and effort to convince women that their public role is complementary to their domestic role. Secondly, it must be recognized that women cannot be dealt with in isolation; they should be considered as part of the entire village network. It should, in this connection, be realized that no intervention would be complete without the support of all villagers since participation in development is gender-neutral. This is because working towards a partnership of all community members to promote a sustainable water delivery programme is more realistic than focusing all attention on women (Asaad et al., 1994).

A crucial factor to note in this proposal is that communities should be made to realize the important role of women in managing water facilities. This recognition would enable the community residents to be more willing to offer the women the needed encouragement in their new roles as managers of water. Thirdly, the introduction of women into formal structures concerning their new roles should be done gradually and cautiously. If it is made suddenly and foisted on the people, the males in the society would kick against the idea and render the women ineffective. If women are pushed into playing new key roles in their communities' water needs, the men can be likened to a baby who is weaned abruptly and left without a foster parent; the psychological imbalances can be disastrous in the society.

Finally, women and the entire society should also be helped to understand their role not only in narrow perspectives such as water projects but in general community development work.

Conclusion

Even though women's participation in the management of rural water facilities is important, it is becoming increasingly clear that a plethora of factors pose barriers to the attainment of this objective. Awareness and sensitization workshops should be organized for both male and female opinion leaders. It is recognized that where only females are sensitized through workshops, male resistance hardens and the women are not allowed to put into practice the ideas obtained from the workshops.

References

Assaad, Marie, Samiha el Katsha and Susan Watts (1994): 'Involving Women In Water And Sanitation Project In An Egyptian Village', *Water International* Vol. 17 No. 3 pp 113-120.

Melchoir-Tellier, Siri, (1991): 'Women, Water And Sanitation', *Water International*, Vol. 16 pp 161-168.

Simpson-Herbert, Mayling (1992): *Women And Water*, World Health, Geneva pp.20, 21.

USAID, (1984): *Helping Ghana Search for Water*, WASH Technical Report No. 132, Arlington, Virginia.

Skills and management training for sustainability

David Kane, Uganda

NATIONAL WATER AND SEWERAGE CORPORATION (NWSC) provides water and sewerage services to over 600 000 people in nine urban areas throughout Uganda including Kampala, the capital. The NWSC workforce totals 1700 people covering all levels from senior management to unskilled labour. The distribution of the workforce is typical of most public utilities and is shown in Figure 1.

Since 1984 NWSC has embarked on an expansion programme to reinforce and extend existing services. The capital works programme has been accompanied by corresponding programmes of institutional development and legal reform. In December 1992 Mott MacDonald, who had previously acted as consultant to NWSC on legal reform, were awarded a contract to prepare and manage a training programme for NWSC for the five-year period 1993 to 1997. The programme will provide training for all levels of the workforce including senior management.

Over the five years Mott MacDonald will provide 90 man months of specialist input. This includes a resident training manager and a team of seven visiting specialists with a mix of expertise in project administration, finance, management, water quality, water and sewerage treatment, electrical and mechanical maintenance, instrumentation, water distribution and sewerage collection systems.

The programme has two main objectives. Firstly, to develop technical and management skills within NWSC so that the capital programmes currently being implement will be sustainable. Secondly, to develop a training capacity within NWSC that will continue to meet the training and skills development needs of the corporation.

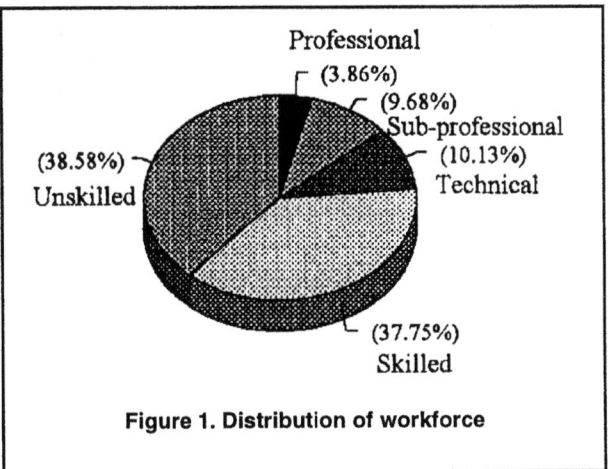

Figure 1. Distribution of workforce

Approach

The approach used in developing a training programme for NWSC broadly followed that presented by Carefoot and Gibson in *Human Resources Handbook* published in 1984 as a contribution to the International Drinking Water and Sanitation decade.

A key step in the process is the identification of training needs. Contractual time constraints prevented a full agenda of manpower analysis, performance deficiency analysis and task analysis as suggested by Carefoot to determine where performance deficiencies resulted from lack of skills or knowledge rather than other environmental or attitudinal factors. To overcome these constraints a dual approach using interviews and workshop sessions to identify areas of poor performance was adopted.

This ensured that training proposals were not prepared in isolation from other factors contributing to poor performance.

Through their involvement in donor-funded projects, NWSC managers were well acquainted with the technique of Objectives Oriented Project Planning (OOPP). To build on this strength an OOPP workshop was held to identify the causes of poor performance within NWSC. The workshop was attended by senior and middle managers and through the OOPP process the group identified *insufficient utilization of human resources* as the core problem within NWSC. Four major causes contributing to the core problem were identified as:

- staff inadequately skilled;
- inadequate management;
- inadequate grading and testing;
- unplanned allocation of resources.

It was clear from the results of the OOPP workshop that there was a need for skills and management training to accompany the ongoing programmes of institutional development and legal reform if the capital works being constructed by NWSC were to be sustainable.

To identify areas where training was required an extensive series of interviews with selected supervisors and managers was conducted. The face to face interviews were supplemented with questionnaires. The interviews were carried out by members of the consultant's team, each a specialist in his own field, and through interaction with the interviewee it was possible to identify performance shortfalls that could be corrected through training.

The interviews and questionnaires were considered adequate to identify skills and knowledge training needs for functionalists. The interview process itself contributed to an understanding of the areas where management skills were lacking or needed to be reinforced.

The results of the training needs analysis showed that there was a need for training in three broad areas:
- skills training;
- professional training;
- management training.

To meet these needs several approaches were adopted.

Skills training

The skills required within NWSC reflect those common to all water utilities. These skills cover a wide range of disciplines ranging from plumbing and mains laying to administration and bookkeeping and include specialized support services such as chemistry and public relations. The workforce is also representative of that found elsewhere in that most skilled workers are adequately qualified in their functional fields but have progressed to supervisory and administrative positions for which they are ill-equipped.

To correct these deficiencies two approaches were adopted: to develop the present in-house training capacity of NWSC and to use local training institutions. Where large numbers were to be trained or training needs were specific to NWSC, in-house courses were adopted as being the most suitable vehicle. Where numbers to be trained were small and the skills were not peculiar to NWSC then local institutions were seen as appropriate.

Separate in-house training programmes were prepared to cover the main groupings of:
- finance, accounting, audit and administration;
- operations and maintenance supervisors;
- operations and maintenance artisans;
- support services including laboratory, and workshop services.

Each programme included a progressive plan of skills training for a five-year period and a detailed plan of in-house courses for the first 12 months. Course outlines were developed for nearly 50 short courses and were categorised into seven main groups:
- treatment
- pipeline systems
- plant operations and maintenance
- supervisory skills
- customer relations
- computer applications
- finance, accounting and audit

Previous training programmes at NWSC had concentrated on basic technical skills and a core group of trainers and basic facilities were available as a foundation from which to develop a well equipped and well staffed training centre. The core group of trainers already had basic skills in plumbing and mains laying, distribution networks including waste control, water and waste water treatment, and mechanical and electrical maintenance. A training manager was recruited to provide administrative and managerial support and a qualified accountant was assigned to the centre to provide support for finance training. Line staff from NWSC and external trainers from local institutions or professional firms are hired to augment the teaching staff when the permanent training staff do not have the skills required for specific courses.

Former site offices were converted to provide offices for trainers and administrative support staff and a new building comprising two lecture rooms, a resource centre, store rooms and toilet facilities was constructed. A multi-purpose block was constructed shortly afterwards to provide additional space and canteen facilities. The resource centre has recently been equipped with a four-station computer network and will shortly be stocked with a comprehensive reference library.

Four demonstration units will shortly be installed on the site for use in training programmes. The four units are:
- water pipe network;
- water treatment unit;
- pumping unit;
- pipe flow unit.

In the first year of the in-house programme 33 in-house courses were run at the training centre and at NWSC area offices. Courses varied in duration from three to five days and were attended by 435 participants. This represents 1743 days of in-house training for NWSC personnel. Subsequent years of the in-house programme will continue at the same level of output.

The in-house programme of skills training was supplemented by the attendance of 29 employees at local training institutions offering courses of various durations covering such topics as car mechanics, project planning, high voltage supply, electronics, welding and fabrication.

Professional training

Professional training is offered to selected NWSC staff to enable them to gain recognized professional qualifications and to develop as individuals. Professional training is provided in two ways: through enrolment in full-time courses of study at recognized institutions either in-country or across border and by participation in short courses, seminars and workshops organized by various bodies.

Over the five-year project period it is anticipated that eight middle managers with first degrees will be assisted to gain professional qualifications or higher degrees. As the core activity of NWSC is technical the majority of higher degrees will be in engineering with a management component. Other degrees will include such topics as human resources and business administration while accountants will be enrolled in courses leading to chartered status.

Short-term professional training relies heavily on courses offered by the Eastern and Southern Africa Management Institute (ESAMI) who offer two-to five-week courses either at their base in Arusha or in other countries in the region. ESAMI offers a wide range of courses designed to assist executives to innovate and manage change. Other institutions offering courses identified in the short term professional programme include Crown Agents, WEDC at Loughborough University, Ghana Institute of Public Administration and Harvard University. In the first year of the programme 19 senior and middle managers participated in short-term professional training at these institutions.

Management training

Previous training programmes carried out within NWSC had concentrated on technical skills and little attention had been paid to management training. As a result, managers were technically competent in their chosen field but were poorly equipped for the role of manager. As the performance of NWSC is dependent on the individual and collective performance of its managers a management development programme focusing on understanding and applying modern management techniques was developed.

For management training to be successful and sustainable those in the management team have to be committed to self development. The success of the management development programme is, therefore, largely dependent on the commitment and action of the managers themselves. The programme focuses on self development and, through a series of twice-yearly seminars, aims to enhance the knowledge, skills and attitudes of the management teams. Participants are encouraged to make use of self learning facilities in the resource centre to reinforce their knowledge in the periods between seminars.

Two series of seminars are provided — one for senior managers and another for middle managers. The seminars for senior managers include such topics as:
- institutional development;
- corporate planning;
- commercial orientation;
- management information systems;
- leadership;
- organization behaviour;
- customer orientation.

The same topics are included in the seminars for middle managers but are covered in less detail. In addition the seminars for middle managers include:
- role of a manager;
- organizational goals;
- finance and budgeting;
- communications skills;
- staff development.

The techniques used in the seminars include formal teaching, brain storming, video presentations and case studies. With the commissioning of the computer network at the training centre practical sessions using spreadsheets to analyze and manage data and word processing to present management information have been added to the methods employed. To encourage interaction and to foster a common culture, joint sessions are held regularly with senior and middle managers.

The response to the seminars conducted so far has been good. Initially, the reaction of nearly all middle managers to most problems was that 'management should do something'. A change of attitude is noticeable as middle managers have become more aware of possible solutions and of techniques that they themselves can utilize towards problem solving.

Results

The results achieved by training activities are often difficult to evaluate. Hamblin has suggested that there are five levels at which evaluation can take place:
- reactions;
- learning;
- job behaviour;
- organization;
- ultimate value.

Evaluation becomes progressively more difficult at each level as factors other than training contribute to any change. At NWSC we routinely measure reaction at the end of every in-house course and, where appropriate, measure learning through informal test papers. An attempt is being made to link measurement of changes in job behaviour to the newly revised performance appraisal system in use at NWSC. Measures of organization and ultimate value are carried out in the management seminars by developing and monitoring financial and other performance indicators.

Conflicts between management and culture

Most modern management techniques have been developed in the western industrialized nations. They, therefore, reflect the culture and practices of a group that has little in common with those in less industrialized nations. It is tempting to attempt to transfer these techniques and force them to fit into an environment for which they were not intended. This undoubtedly leads to discord when these techniques run counter to cultural practices. An obvious example is the principle of appointing and promoting personnel solely on the basis of qualifications and experience where in other cultures patronage is the accepted means of advancement. These conflicts should be respected and acknowledged. If we were to travel back to the Europe of last century we would find similar practices in force.

The aim of the NWSC training programmes is to provide the management team and the labour force with the knowledge and skills they need to run an efficient and effective public utility. They themselves are free to choose which techniques are acceptable and applicable to their culture and employ them accordingly.

References

Carefoot, N and Gibson, H. *Human Resources Development Handbook,* WHO, Geneva 1984

Hamblin, A. C. *Evaluation and Control of Training*, McGraw-Hill, 1974

Parastatal development — institutional strengthening

J.G.B. Mitchell, T. Borotho, D.S. Barraclough, Lesotho

WHEN THE WORLD Bank-financed BKS technical assistance team arrived at the Water and Sewerage Authority of Lesotho (WASA) in 1994 it was evident that the organization was facing three main obstacles to its sustainability:

- absence of a proper planning function;
- financial frailty; and
- limited institutional capacity.

This paper illustrates the problems, discusses how solutions have been approached and the extent to which strategies have been successful.

Lack of proper planning

The key task of the technical assistants is to develop a five-year capital programme for WASA from 1996/7 to 2000/01. This was problematic in WASA for several reasons; lack of corporate policies, poor base data and little information about beneficiaries.

First, it is clearly not possible to develop a plan for the future if the goals management are seeking to achieve are not explicit. In WASA there was no formal statement of policies. The technical assistants initiated the process of policy formulation by holding a series of seminars with senior management, with departmental heads contributing policy proposals.

The process of formulating a policy document adequate to submit to the Board of WASA took almost a year. This was because a number of the management team tended to view policy formulation as of secondary importance to day-to-day operational management. There is a real danger in this situation that technical assistants write the policy document themselves and then submit it to management for approval.

This leaves management with little 'ownership' of the process.

Our experience has shown that the single most important factor in developing a useful policy document is the support of the managing director of the implementing agency. Without this it is very difficult to involve staff at all levels in the process of policy formulation.

A second problem faced in the investment planning exercise was the very poor quality of base data. In WASA the quality of financial data is good, but the most basic operational data such as customer numbers and the capacity of existing infrastructure was often only accurate to within 50 per cent. A great deal of time was spent collecting accurate base data for the investment planning exercise and, whilst laborious, the creation of accurate base data has proved to be one of the most valuable spin-offs from the investment planning exercise.

The third, related problem was that WASA had no information about either their existing, or potential, customers. As both these groups of people will be the beneficiaries of any capital investment programme, it was important to understand who they are and their aspirations.

Building up a data base on existing customers proved relatively straightforward and inexpensive. A questionnaire seeking information on socio-economic variables, perceptions of service quality and price was included with the monthly bills, resulting in a response rate of about 10 per cent. This has generated invaluable planning data such as unit service demands for different categories of customer, willingness and ability to pay, and areas where WASA performance is poor. This exercise also has useful spin-offs.

For instance, by far the most common complaint from customers was also the cheapest to remedy, namely being informed in advance of interruptions in water supply.

Data on potential future customers was collected by hiring a local consultant to undertake a beneficiary assessment in a sample of peri-urban locations. This exercise cost some M100 000 (US$3.67 = 1 Maloti as at June 1995).

Whilst very large sums have been spent on four master planning exercises at WASA over the past five years, full account has never been taken of the needs and aspirations of beneficiaries. Master plans undertaken by European consultancies have tended to perpetuate the conventional approach of planning a very high level of service (direct house water connections, often with reticulated sewerage) for a small minority of consumers and no service for the majority.

The beneficiary assessment illustrated that this approach was not appropriate in Lesotho. What most people want in the peri-urban area is a clean, inexpensive and accessible water source and a ventilated improved pit latrine (VIP). Direct water and sewerage house connections cannot be afforded by most households, and in some cases, are not even desired (households living in a single room will not generally want internal sanitation).

This led to a radical shift in the philosophy underlying the capital programme away from 'everything for a few' towards 'something for everyone'. The coverage rate targets, outlined in Graph 1, drive the capital programme.

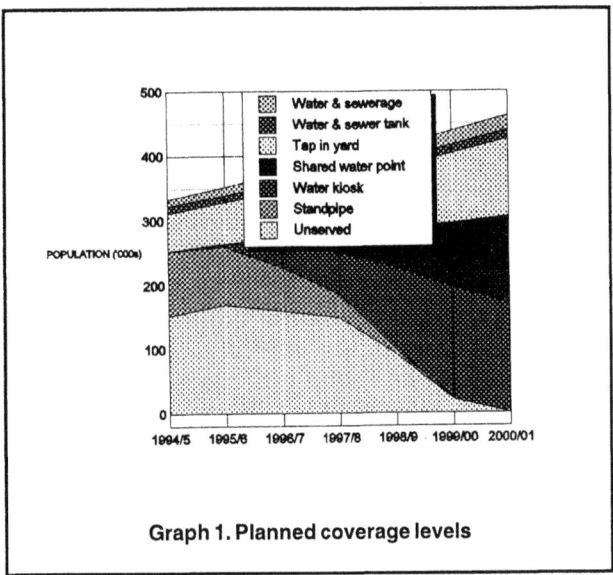

Graph 1. Planned coverage levels

Note that even with an acceleration in the rate of new connections, the 'conventional' water delivery mechanism of direct house connections scarcely keep pace with population growth. The number of people served by public standpipes also declines as these are closed, in response to government late payment.

The need to develop a universal, affordable and socially acceptable alternative delivery mechanism took WASA staff and technical assistants on a study tour in Swaziland to see some pilot schemes in operation. The pilot schemes involved two methods of community-driven water delivery.

The **water kiosk**: a lockable structure with a community-nominated attendant. Five taps which, controlled from inside the kiosk, deliver water to the public. The sale price of M0.10 per 20-litre container is split between the attendant, the community council and the water authority (with the latter receiving the equivalent of the 'basic needs' tariff).

Shared water points (SWP): these are essentially a lockable standpipe. Up to 20 households in an area get together and share the capital cost of extending the reticulation and building the SWP. After paying a deposit each household receives a key to the tap and pays a flat charge of M5 per month, provided water consumption is not excessive.

A very basic reticulated system with kiosks, and the capacity to be upgraded to SWPs or house connections, has a capital cost of about M0.6 million per km^2 (or M120 per capita). This will give everyone access to a water kiosk as a minimum. Individuals and groups can then upgrade to a shared water point and subsequently a direct house connection in accordance with their own means and aspirations. By way of contrast, a conventional water reticulation system would have a capital cost of about 70 per cent more (M200 per capita) than WASA's chosen option, and only serve the more affluent minority.

Full sewerage reticulation would cost about M2000 per head, and attract few customers.

WASA is only at the point of piloting these solutions in the peri-urban areas. However, the principles of community consultation, affordability and flexibility to upgrade appear to contribute to a truly sustainable capital programme.

Financial frailty

WASA's financial performance has deteriorated each year the organization has been in existence. This is despite the clear financial requirements of the Order establishing WASA, that revenues must fully recover all costs.

In its first year the Authority returned a small gross profit of M0.2 million. However, in 1993/4 the Authority made a loss of M0.8 million and in 1994/5 a loss of M2.1 million was reported on a turnover of M21 million. The 1995/6 budget anticipates an even bleaker future with a projected deficit of some M3.5 million. The reasons for this poor financial performance are both external and internal.

Externally, government has shown a reluctance to approve tariff increases proposed by the Board of WASA. Since the creation of WASA inflation has increased by about 39 per cent, yet tariffs have only been allowed to increase by four per cent, implying a real reduction in the value of the tariff of about a third. Government has justified its refusal to increase tariffs by highlighting the inefficiencies within WASA.

The deteriorating political situation facing the government was also a factor in reducing the enthusiasm for raising prices for water supply and sanitation services.

Internally, there have been very limited attempts to improve operational efficiency in WASA. Within the organization the civil service culture persists with management seemingly unwilling to implement reforms to raise productivity even when inefficiencies are obvious.

A tariff study was undertaken by the technical assistants and it was found that the current average tariff of M2.8 per m^3 would have to be raised to about M4.2 per m^3 in the short term to ensure financial viability.

The average tariff will have to be increased to about M5 (in 1995/6 prices) in the medium term to finance the capital programme to the year 2000. At the same time as the tariff study a series of workshops were held with senior WASA management to identify and quantify potential efficiency improvements within the Authority. These efficiency findings have been taken account of in the tariff analysis.

The technical assistants have sought to deal with the issue of requiring significant tariff increases in two ways. One has been to propose a three-band tariff structure to protect the poor with all 'basic needs' consumption charged at the O and M tariff, all 'normal' domestic and all non-domestic consumption charged at full cost recovery, and 'excessive' domestic water use charged at a level sufficient to cross-subsidize the cost of 'basic needs' water use.

Second, the related issues of the need for a significant tariff increase and efficiency improvements have been brought together in the form of a performance contract being developed between WASA and government. Essentially this specifies in detail the regulatory framework within which WASA will operate over a five-year period. The basis for annual tariff reviews is being negotiated as is the achievement of quantified corporate performance indicators required by government.

It is hoped that this will allow WASA to achieve financial viability but also put pressure on management to improve efficiency as the *quid pro quo* of tariff increases. The fundamental challenge remains that ultimately tariff and productivity reforms are decided by politicians, not technocrats.

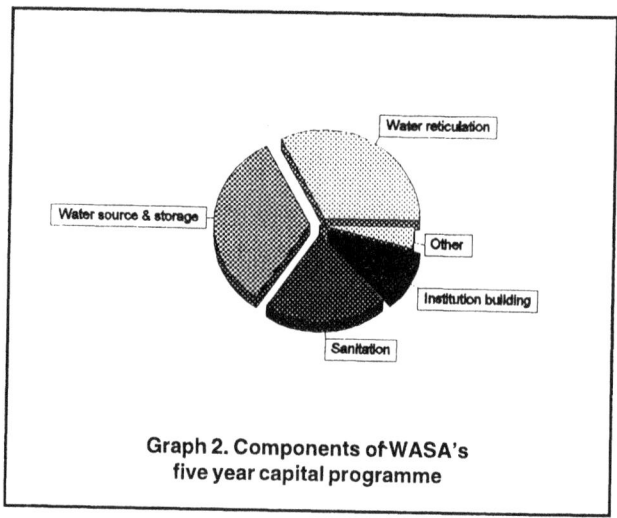

Graph 2. Components of WASA's five year capital programme

Institutional capacity

Whilst it has been relatively unproblematic to develop with WASA an appropriate capital programme, the extent to which the technical assistants have contributed to the capacity of the institution to be self-sustainable is much more limited.

This is implicity recognized in the capital programme planned for WASA from 1996/7 to 2000/01.

It has been estimated that, in order to implement the M¼ billion programme, some M24 million will be required in institution building projects (see Graph 2).

The central institutional problem at WASA is one of significant overstaffing in the Authority as a whole, but a very low proportion of professional staff. The total staff complement of 585, implies a staff per 1000 connections of about 29.

Notwithstanding the general overstaffing, only 19 staff on WASA's payroll (some three per cent) have a degree-level qualification, and only a further six per cent have diplomas. This means that the qualified and competent staff are often overstretched. The response to this has been for donors to finance, usually on a grant basis, technical assistants. This has real short-term advantages both for donors and the implementing agencies. Donors can be more assured that specific pieces of work, such as investment plans, policy documents, etc. will be produced to a satisfactory standard in a timely manner. Technical assistant projects also have the advantage to a bilateral donor that much of the budget is likely to be spent in the country of origin rather than destination.

The implementing agency also benefits to the extent that technical assistants essentially subsidize the payroll.

However, it could be argued that not only are technical assistants without proper counterpart not a long-term solution to the capacity building of institutions, but also that they are part of the problem.

The Basotho people are amongst the best educated in Africa and have a long history of seeking employment in South Africa, which surrounds Lesotho. Wage levels in South Africa are about 40 per cent higher than those in Lesotho. The reason that WASA requires technical assistants is probably more a reflection of the uncompetitive remuneration for senior management in the Authority rather than the absence of suitably qualified and experienced Basotho professionals. There is a danger that technical assistants may be an obstacle to developing the salary structure which would facilitate the smaller, more highly qualified and productive workforce required at WASA.

Lessons to be learned

1. A useful planning process requires the careful formulation of goals and collection of reliable technical and socio-economic data as a pre-condition. This may result in very different conclusions about the best use of scarce investment funds.

2. Given the current structure of the industry in Lesotho it is not clear what are the appropriate boundaries to government intervention in WASA. The performance contract may provide a useful formalization of this relationship, particularly if this places the annual tariff review process in the hands of an independent regulator and away from central government control. This may obviate the need for a more fundamental restructuring of the sector.

3. Technical assistants are not a long-term substitute for qualified, motivated and competent local professional management staff.

The authors wish to stress that this paper expresses their personal views only and does not reflect the views of BKS Incorporated Consulting Engineers, the World Bank, the Water and Sewerage Authority or the Government of Lesotho.

An approach for community-based sustainability

Patrick A. Okuni and John P. Rockhold, Uganda

DEVELOPMENT OF PROTECTED water sources in Uganda has traditionally been undertaken by government through the Directorate of Water Development (DWD) [formerly Water Development Department]. Development of water sources was generally treated as technical, with little community involvement in decision-making or actual construction. In addition some religious and charity organizations have provided some point water sources. Maintenance of rural water sources (especially handpumps) was conducted exclusively by the Borehole Maintenance Units (BMU) of DWD. These were regionally based and centrally funded, and covered about four districts each. They were equipped with service rigs and the necessary consumables. They received reports of breakdowns and travelled to carry out the necessary repairs. However the breakdown in government systems during the 1970s and early 1980s and the subsequent reduction in funding greatly affected the operations of the BMUs. Currently most BMUs are almost non-functional.

The water decade drew a lot of attention and resources into the rural water supply sector in many third world countries. Uganda is one of the countries that has received a lot of attention. On realization of the serious problems faced with breakdowns in water supply systems, government and the various donor-funded projects focussed a lot of attention on developing communities to take up the ownership and maintenance of their water sources, hence the development of the Community Based Maintenance System (CBMS). This forms the basic guiding framework, but is implemented slightly differently by different donors/projects operating in the country.

Background

The DANIDA-assisted Rural Water and Sanitation Project (RUWASA) covers eight districts in eastern Uganda, serving about four million people. RUWASA is due to complete 1049 springs, 184 dug wells, 343 augered wells and 1417 boreholes (294 rehabilitated) by the end of 1995. It has worked closely with DWD in developing and promoting CBMS for rural water supplies. The second phase of the Project will run from 1996 to 2000.

In Luwero district 90 boreholes are being constructed with assistance from Plan International. Implementation of the programme largely follows procedures similar to those of RUWASA.

Both programmes in addition to CBMS promote hygienic practices, with emphasis on proper water handling, safe excreta disposal and general hygiene.

Community-based maintenance system

The main philosophy behind this strategy is community self reliance, which ensures ownership, responsible use and sustainability. The approach is geared towards an effective community capability independently and willingly to manage facilities provided to them, so as to enhance long-term utilization for their good health and well-being. Preventive maintenance is emphasized as contrasted to repair after break down.

Some experiences from RUWASA, current approaches and planned future approaches for the two programmes are discussed below.

Community participation and ownership

Beneficiary communities have been involved in the siting and construction of water sources from the start of the RUWASA project. However the procedures were unclear, with communities being asked initially to suggest sites, resulting in unfavourable locations (elevated or pollution-prone areas). This resulted in community dissatisfaction with final source locations and types selected after hydrogeological considerations, and unsatisfactory success rates.

Presently beneficiaries are actively involved from the inventory and baseline survey stages of implementation. The current siting procedures link sociological and technical aspects, with a view to clarity and coherence, minimal time wastage by following primary hydrogeological investigation recommendations, and more demand-driven approaches. Participatory methodologies are used to ensure that the beneficiaries are (and actually feel) fully involved in the whole process, and any disagreements are solved at site.

Beneficiary communities contribute locally available materials and labour towards their water source. Hence construction work is done jointly by the beneficiaries and Project technicians. This strengthens their sense of ownership and responsibility. Subcounty water and sanitation committees (SWSC) and village water and sanitation committees (VWSC) were introduced by RUWASA to organize communities for latrine construction and hygiene promotion as well as water source allocation, construction and management. RC3 councils and SWSCs participate in water source allocation, and VWSCs organize the communities during the siting and construction stages. The Luwero Programme currently utilizes existing RC3, 2 and 1 development and health committees in implementation.

Water user committees (WUC) were later adopted from 1994 to manage water sources after construction instead of the original VWSCs. While the latter are based on administrative village boundaries, WUCs are drawn from actual beneficiaries. The confusion in villages with more than one source has also been cleared. This, coupled with the participatory methods of training, has significantly improved the management of water sources through more decision-making and confidence-building at community level.

Role of women

At an early stage the important position of women in water and sanitation-related issues was realized. Emphasis is therefore laid on their involvement at all levels. Presently it is required that at least 50 per cent of members on all committees are women, with some holding key management positions. While initially this was followed just because of the project guidelines, the participatory methods have helped involve women more into participation, hence giving them more confidence. Currently women constitute about five per cent and 10 per cent of chairmen and treasurers of WUCs respectively, in the RUWASA Project area.

Various training and communication materials (charts, booklets, plays, etc.) have been modified or developed to reverse the stereotype roles of men and women.

In order to involve women in the technical aspects of O and M, in mid 1994 RUWASA devised a system whereby training of female HPMs is fully funded, whereas subcounties that select male candidates meet 25 per cent of the cost at present. However this has not yielded much success, and so far only one female HPM has been trained out of 33 trained since then. But with continued support, promotion and positive discrimination more success is achievable.

Technologies used

Technologies used for both water supply and excreta disposal are simple and relatively cheap ones, based on both the capital and maintenance costs. However emphasis has been laid on use of proven technologies in order to ensure quality is not compromised resulting in high O&M costs to the beneficiaries. Generally the order of preference of water source technologies is spring protection, borehole rehabilitation, augered wells, boreholes and gravity schemes. Problems initially arose with communities prefering boreholes to other technologies. However, the approaches used during siting help explain the reasons for variations. Work and material quality is now being stressed more at all stages of construction to avoid problems of leakage and diversion of springs.

The Uganda Government has standardized the use of the U3 (India Mark III) handpump for deep well settings, and with the Uganda National Bureau of Standards (UNBS) developed standards. Presently most rural water projects use this handpump. This has helped to harmonize training approaches and skills development, and will assist in ensuring ready availability of necessary spare parts and other inputs. Studies are still underway on the performance of shallow well handpumps, with a view to standardization.

Initially RUWASA installed U3 with GI riser pipes and rods. However corrosion was identified as a major problem in the Project area. As a result all old handpumps are now being reinstalled with stainless steel components. Presently all new installations have stainless steel components. This will help significantly reduce O&M costs related to replacement of pipes and rods.

Hygiene and sanitation

In order to ensure sustainability of facilities developed, much attention has been paid to hygienic practices. Emphasis is laid on water hygiene, to ensure the water does not get contaminated from source to use. Hygiene education helps communities appreciate the importance of facilities developed.

While latrine construction has been encouraged as a precondition for water provision, hygiene education is also provided to ensure use, cleanliness, handwashing after use and replicability. Experience has shown that with intensive hygiene education, latrine construction and sanplat purchases increased significantly in areas where the 'latrines before water' precondition was not applied.

Monitoring and evaluation

Information on water source performance and maintenance is currently gathered by government extension workers. Some information is directly obtained from HPMs and spare part dealers for a small fee. This information is then analyzed at district and central level to track progress and identify areas that need improvement or additional support.

Currently attention is being paid to developing a community self-monitoring system. This would reduce the reliance on information from extension staff and HPMs, which in some cases is corrupted or inaccurate. The districts' capacity to collect, analyze and use data is also being strengthened.

Private sector involvement

RUWASA initially adopted a partially community-based operation and maintenance (O&M) system. The Project trained water source caretakers and handpump mechanics (HPM), and provided tool kits and starter sets of spare parts free of charge. Each district and subcounty were required to open bank accounts and stores for handpump spare parts distribution. The funds were then to be used on a revolving basis to replenish stocks as communities purchased spare parts. Implementation of the system started; however problems arose with the management of the stores and funds.

In early 1993 RUWASA developed a system of distribution of spare parts through existing private dealers right from the manufacturer/suppliers to beneficiaries. This, however, has been effective where the number of handpumps is large enough for profitable operations. To date (June 1995) US$ 1750 worth of spare parts have been reported sold, mainly comprising fast wearing rubber parts. This is about 70 per cent of the total sales. With the progress in construction and formation and training of WUCs, establishment of the network is improving. In addition, trained HPMs are provided with tools on loan. They pay for these from their earnings.

Construction work in RUWASA is at present largely done by Project internal staff. However privatization has gradually started with spring protection. The aim is gradually to privatize all construction work. In Luwero currently all construction is carried out by the private sector.

In order to bring privatization benefits closer to the beneficiaries, teams of local HPMs were organized to carry out reinstallation of handpumps with stainless steel equipment. The exercise started in April 1994, and will help demystify construction tasks, provide experience and allow the teams acquire the necessary tools. So far it has been very successful and cheaper, and is likely to be adopted for new constructions in future.

Training of HPMs is also being privatized, with local technical schools being brought up to take over fully.

Preventive maintenance

The original maintenance system has been repaired after maintenance. However currently regular preventive maintenance of handpumps is being promoted as a more viable approach. WUCs are encouraged to buy the requirements for source caretakers to open the pump head and carry out simple maintenance. HPMs then carry out the other tasks.

As an initial step WUCs are required to enter into a two-year agreement with their local HPMs to carry out quarterly preventive maintenance (one major and three minor services). During maintenance the caretakers informally learn to undertake the simpler tasks. Eventually from experience it can then be agreed how often a HPM should visit. To date 203 preventive maintenance contracts have been reported signed; however preventive maintenance has been carried out on 1108 handpumps, catering for 74 per cent of the handpump equipped sources at about US$3350.

Communication

Various media have been used to disseminate information and educate beneficiaries. Print media like booklets, flyers, calendars and posters, as well as caps, T-shirts, drama and radio have been used to depict themes promoting sustainability.

Conclusion

The CBMS has registered some success in establishing a sustainable system. Already the private sector has taken interest and got involved in the various activities. Local government structures are also more integrated now than at the start.

However a lot of emphasis should still be laid on hygiene education and the private spare parts distribution and handpump maintenance systems to ensure their continuity. The latter will be better achieved with higher coverage of water sources. Backup support and continued follow-up through extension staff will be needed for some years to ensure complete sustainability.

References

1. Guidelines to Community Based Operation and Maintenance of Handpump Equipped Water Sources, RUWASA, April 1994.
2. Semi-Annual Progress Report, RUWASA, Jul. to Dec. 1994.
3. Luwero Plan of Action, Carl Bro Uganda, May 1995.

Role of industries in sustaining water quality

Dr F.A.O. Otieno, South Africa

NAIROBI, THE CAPITAL of Kenya and a major industrial town in the region, has an estimated population of 2 000 000 people. This population far outstrips the available facilities to the extent that a large percentage of the populace remain without adequate and satisfactory services, e.g. water, sanitation and garbage collection.

There are several rivers draining through the city of Nairobi; the bigger ones include Ngong, Nairobi, Mathare, Ruaraka, Kasarani. All these rivers eventually drain into Nairobi river which in turn empties into the Athi river.

Most people in rural areas of Kenya use untreated water from rivers and streams for drinking and other domestic activities. Where water treatment is provided in piped water supplies, treatment failures are known to occur frequently due to mechanical problems, lack of chemicals and other reasons. It is therefore important that pollution of streams and rivers is reduced to a minimum.

From existing reports on the status of the Nairobi rivers (Nyikuri, 1994; Otieno 1991a, 1991b) it emerges that there is a general awareness of the pollution problem, its levels and trends. It is also evident that the existing legislation, while requiring some amendment and review is adequate but that there is not enough enforcement. These findings also indicate that there is little commitment by industrialists to play the role they should play in order to protect and indeed improve the quality of the environment.

Sources of pollution

There are several categories of pollution entering Nairobi river. These include, but are not limited to:

- Industrial effluent emanating from factories, godowns, business premises especially from the industrial area. There is no justification for this state of affairs as Nairobi City Council (NCC) by law allows industries within 200 feet of a sewer to connect to it. Even when this is not the case, industries can easily obtain permission from NCC to install a form of treatment that will enhance environmental conditions.
- Raw sewage from blocked, broken or overloaded sewers.
- Sewage and other polluting agents from the informal sector such as slums, markets, jua kali premises.
- Effluent from public and private sewage treatment works. This happens when sewage is not properly treated as it passes through the treatment works. Industries could also indirectly pollute the rivers by discharging wastes that are not compatible with other sewage and thereby interfering or inhibiting the biological processes responsible for sewage treatment.
- Effluents from petrol stations and other garages.
- Surface runoff.
- Solid wastes/garbage dumped in rivers and their surroundings.

Pollution profiles

From the pollution profile of Nairobi river, it is evident that it becomes increasingly polluted from the point it enters the city. The pollution levels reach their peak as the river passes through heavy industrial and commercial areas and reduces again when the river goes through less polluted areas and recover quite rapidly once the river leaves the city. (Note the improved dissolved oxygen levels in Table 1). This is attributed mainly to self-purification due to oxidation, especially where the gradient is steep or at falls, and is aided by the favourable temperatures and light conditions commonly experienced in Nairobi.

It is possible to tell by looking at the profiles at what point a dose of pollutant has been injected into the river and hence easier to establish the culprit. Unfortunately, the enforcement mechanism of the law is quite poor and so culprits get away with such acts. The ongoing National Environmental Action Plan (NEAP) process is aimed at

Table 1. Oxygen levels along Nairobi River

Station	Distance downstream (Kms)	Oxygen level (mg/1)
Nyongera Up	0.0	2.60
Nyongera Down	3.5	7.00
Muthuri Road	5.0	6.40
Loreto Convent	10.0	6.60
Chiromo	13.5	6.76
Kerichwa	14.0	6.60
Museum	15.0	7.40
Kijabe Street	15.5	7.24
Roundabout	16.0	2.60
Racecourse B	17.0	1.90
Shauri Moyo	20.0	0.27
Outer Ring Road	24.0	1.15
Kariobangi Up	26.0	2.60
Kariobangi Down	26.5	3.20
Mathare	30.0	0.16
Njiru	36.0	0.30
Nairobi Falls	51.0	3.36
Athi at Munyu	75.5	5.80
14 Falls	86.0	6.80

redressing this shortfall and one hopes that once this is implemented, industrialists can see their role in preventing further pollution of existing water resources in Nairobi and in Kenya in general.

Trend of pollution

Data gathered over the years (Otieno 1991a, 1991b; Office of the President 1991) regarding the pollution of Nairobi river indicates that the level of pollution has not changed much in the last ten years or so. This can be attributed to:

- The expansion of the sewage works to a large portion of the city; most industrialists not yet connected should take advantage of the works and connect.
- The flushing effects of the rains on the rivers.
- The favourable nature of the tropical climate which allows for a significant amount of self-purification.

All the above notwithstanding, the rivers are still heavily polluted beyond acceptable levels for domestic, industrial and agricultural origin.

The role of industries in water pollution control

The main culprits in the pollution of Nairobi river are industries. Given the level of environmental awareness and indeed the increase in the same, it is in the interest of these industries that they keep Nairobi river clean. However, since the benefits to such industries would be indirect and long-term, most of them do not see the need to be involved in such measures. For example, very few of the industries surveyed were willing to pay to install pollution abatement equipment despite the fact that many of them were not only aware that they were polluting but even knew that there was technology available to deal with this menace.

When one looks at this scenario in depth, it becomes imperative that certain incentives, e.g. tax rebates presumably paid by the government need to be put in place if industrialists are to spend money on pollution abatement. This approach has been tried with success in some countries (Otieno, 1991b).

The question of awareness on the part of the consumer could also force industrialists to start worrying about pollution abatement. For example, if consumers rejected products on grounds that they were environmentally unfriendly, industrialists would be forced to act responsibly. Another way of enforcing environmental responsibility is for companies that do not protect the environment to be denied access to the international market (it has been argued that such companies are actually spending less on production costs and are therefore enjoying an unfair advantage). A stringent approach to ensure that they do not continue to enjoy this benefit is to ensure that they play a positive role in environmental pollution control.

What about sustainability?

It is not just enough to insist that companies inject resources into environmental pollution control. The entire process has to be sustainable. And so how do we build sustainability into the pollution control of Nairobi river?

There are certain rules for ensuring sustainability. Goldsmith (1992) suggests the following for ensuring sustainability:

- Securing beneficial commitment to priorities, projects and interests, in this case, the process of pollution control of Nairobi river.
- Choosing an attainable organizational mission and allocating resources to these attainable goals.
- Having a strategy for sustainability early in the life of the project, in this case trying to impress on all players the need for keeping Nairobi river clean.
- Building a network of alliances among the beneficiaries of pollution control.
- Differentiating between perceived and actual payoffs.
- Providing avenues for continuous training of industrialists, enforcement officers and the public in general.
- Having a blend of both short- and long-term planning horizons.

Conclusions

Given the increased environmental awareness and existing technologies for pollution abatement, and the desire by consumers for products of a green nature (whose production processes have positive regard for the environment), it would seem naive for industrialists to try and save money today instead of putting it into pollution abatement strategies. It is therefore suggested that the government of the day, in an effort to try to ensure a market for the industries tomorrow, should provide certain incentives for industries to see the benefits of investing in environmental protection. Any forward-planning industrialists would not be waiting for the government to provide these incentives but should instead lead the way in environmental protection.

References

Goldsmith, A.A. (1992), 'Promoting the Sustainability of Development Institutions : A Framework for Strategy', *World Development*, Vol. 20 No. 3 pp 369-383.

Ndwaru, W.T (1994), A Report on Findings of the Nairobi Rivers : Pollution Survey and the Need for Pollution Control.

Nyikuri, R.N (1994), Reducing Pollution Along Nairobi River, Final Year Civil Engineering Project, Department of Civil Engineering, University of Nairobi, Kenya.

Office of the President (1991), Permanent Presidential Commission on Soil Conservation and Afforestation: A Report on Pollution Problems in the Rivers Passing Through Nairobi.

Otieno, F.A.O (1990)., Poison in the River System - How Safe are Our River Systems ? Proceedings of Environment 2000, Nairobi, Kenya.

Otieno, F.A.O. (1991a)., 'Assessment of Pollution Status of Nairobi River : An Overview'. Proceedings of Seminar on Water Health and the Environment, pp 169-174, Nairobi, Kenya.

Otieno, F.A.O. (1991b)., Chief Sources of Water Pollution in Kenya, *Journal of the Institute of Management*, p 42 - 46, Vol. 10, No. 3.

Participatory techniques and didactic methods

Dr J.V. Pinfold, Uganda

WATERAID IS A charity created to help people in Africa and Asia improve their water supply and sanitation. Here in Uganda WaterAid has been providing a variety of water systems to rural communities for over eight years. More recently there has been a greater emphasis on integrating sanitation activities with water projects. WaterAid has always been committed to community participation but has learnt that for true sustainability, participation means more than just contributing local materials and labour for constructing a water supply.

There has been a lot of talk about how 'empowerment' of communities is needed to achieve any real sustainability. In practical terms this means that communities must feel that they own the water system and are therefore responsible for its operation and maintenance (O and M). Furthermore, they need to be involved in selecting and promoting improvements in sanitation and hygiene practices, not just be told (read 'educated') what to do. This is easier said than done. Communities need external assistance but donors have to be careful in their approach to communities to make sure their participation in the project leads to sustainable systems.

This paper provides the experiences of Programme Support Unit (PSU) which was set up to help develop an approach which enhances the way communities participate in water supply and sanitation initiatives.

Participation techniques

One of the roles of PSU has been to introduce 'tools' that make community participation easier. These techniques have been adapted or subsequently developed from those employed in PRA, PROWWESS, RRA and some are described in the following (Chambers 1989; Srinivasan, 1990; Scrimshaw and Hurtado, 1987).

Community mapping

Community mapping involves participants in drawing a large map of the local area on the ground. A variety of information may be included such as homes, paths, boundaries, services (e.g. health centres, schools), traditional water sources, natural resources (e.g. sand, rock, gravel) and crops. Active participation and co-operation in drawing the map helps give participants confidence to discuss and analyze community needs. It has proved very valuable as an entry point for introducing water and sanitation activities to communities, particularly on first contact.

The responsibility chart
The responsibility chart divides roles and contributions between donor and beneficiaries, thus specifying exactly what is involved in constructing the water supply and clarifying any unclear issues (usually regarding who is responsible for repairs).

The seasonal calendar
The seasonal calendar helps the community and project staff to plan the actual construction of the water system together. First, busy months of the year for the community are marked on a large calendar drawn on the ground (e.g. harvest time). In the next step, pictures depicting the various construction activities and quantities of materials needed are placed on months of the year. Discussions then centre around which activities need completing before others can begin, the best time to attempt allotted tasks and an expected completion date.

Story with a gap
Story with a gap uses pictures to stimulate community discussion about what steps need to be taken to transform a broken water supply into a well-maintained system. It is very useful for raising awareness about the need for the community to contribute funds for O&M. It also helps them appreciate the role of the committees in O&M and can be useful in discussing any problems with the current water committees, especially management of funds collected.

The sanitation ladder
The sanitation ladder encourages all participants to contribute to discussions on latrine use and common types of latrine in their community. Pictures of different latrines are place in order from worst to best (sanitation ladder) with the advantages and disadvantages of each discussed. Participants then select the most suitable latrine type for their community after discussing the constraints to changing defecation practices and improving existing latrines.

Hygiene behaviour (three pile sorting)
Hygiene behaviour (three pile sorting) procedure takes participants through a process of arranging pictures of (un)hygienic behaviours into piles of common or uncommon practices within their community. Pictures are then resorted according to what they feel are good or bad behaviours. Common good and uncommon bad behaviours are then eliminated from the pile and participants

discuss constraints to changing the remaining behaviours. An action plan is devised for promoting two or three priority behaviours with the least constraints.

Gender analysis
Gender analysis is very useful in demonstrating the importance of women in water and sanitation projects. Again participants divide pictures of everyday chores between women's work and men's work. Discussions then centre around how a better balance of duties could be achieved e.g. what activities could men and women share.

Schools
Children can play a very special and important role in promoting improvements in sanitation and hygiene behaviour both in their homes and at school. Materials developed specifically for schools include faecal-oral routes where pupils draw pictures of important factors in transmitting germs from faeces to mouth. These are then placed on the ground and lines are drawn between them to show the direction of transmission routes. Pupils then discuss ways of breaking these routes emphasizing, activities that can be managed by children. Versions of sanitation ladder and hygiene behaviour (three pile sorting) described above have also been specifically adapted for school children. After each exercise two action plans are made, one for childrens' homes and the other for the school itself.

Feedback from the field
Training on participatory techniques has been conducted through specially designed workshops and by on-the-job training. Those trained have, in the past, been used to a more didactic approach in dealing with communities and include both technical and nontechnical workers from WaterAid, partner organizations and community members.

The response from fieldworkers using these techniques has been very positive. Generally, in comparison to traditional didactic methods there has been better attendance at meetings (with, tellingly, a vast reduction in the number walking out before the end because sessions are more interesting), an enormous improvement in active participation and a more equitable contribution by those attending (particularly from women). Just as important, especially where voluntary trainers are utilized, there has been a marked improvement in the confidence of trainers because they now receive requests from the community for the illustrated materials used during the sessions and to come back again.

In more formal meetings, information tends to be provided in one direction, from the speaker to audience. Although questioned may be raised and answered in this forum, participants may not always understand what is being discussed and may not be confident to speak out.

Water supply
Discussing the community map always leads to a greater number of participants voicing opinions or providing information. For instance fieldworkers may want to know about traditional water sources, whether this is available the whole year round and what the water is used for. This sort of information is automatically cross-checked because everyone understands what is being talked about and can come to a consensus about any particular subject. People who want to manipulate matters by giving false information are quickly exposed. Moreover, this technique automatically provides accurate baseline information.

The amount of community participation in planning the construction of water systems has improved dramatically. One thing the water engineer quickly learns is that these techniques allow for better communication between himself and communities. Technical maps of gravity systems mean little to the average community member but once this information is transferred onto the community map then it is readily understood. Such issues as siting a well or locating positions for tap stands have a chance for debate and communal agreement so that potential conflict can be resolved before it is too late.

Engineers often complain about the difficulty in managing construction of a water system when the communities have to provide local materials and labour. This leads to uncertainty in planning because communities may not be ready when the engineer wants them to be or vice versa. The seasonal calendar facilitates dialogue between the community and engineer so both sides can plan together. Usually communities are not used to planning this type of project and the engineer can use the calendar to explain what resources are necessary before certain activities can begin and communities can show when they are likely to be busy with other ventures. Thus the community and engineer can negotiate the timing of various activities. This has not only helped provide a realistic plan for the community but also leaves them something to use as a yardstick which can be constantly reviewed according to their progress.

In our experience communities usually try to get the most they can out of a project. Often opinion leaders or local politicians may start rumours such as the government provides water for free, with no contributions expected from the community. These issues need to be aired so everyone understands and agrees who is responsible for what. Story with a gap and the responsibility chart makes dialogue between beneficiaries and donors clear and open. These need to be introduced as early as possible to avoid any misconceptions about ownership of the water supply. Conditions can also be set before a project begins.

Sanitation
Perhaps the most enthusiastic response about the participatory techniques has come from fieldworkers involved

in promoting sanitation and hygiene activities. Communities are actually led into a process of analyzing their own situation and deciding what they want to do about it. This is a far cry from being told what to do by someone who often feels the community is ignorant.

Initially, health educators are often reluctant to accept ability of communities to select hygiene behaviours through this technique. In our experience, communities have been fairly consistent in their selection of hygiene behaviours and the most popular have been hand washing particularly before cooking and after latrine use or cleaning a baby's bottom; washing dishes immediately after eating; and disposing of childrens' faeces in the latrine regularly. On the other hand, boiling drinking water is the behaviour traditionally stressed by health educators. Although this behaviour is usually considered a good if not uncommon practice by the community, it is always near the bottom of their priorities because of the high constraints involved (e.g. time, fuel costs, effort and inconvenience). A certain amount of manipulation has been made in choosing the behaviours used in this procedure but interestingly research suggests that those behaviours selected by communities are more likely to be effective in reducing disease than advice traditionally given health educators (Esrey et al. 1985).

Thus, this procedure not only assists the community analyzing hygiene behaviour for themselves, but it also gives 'health educators' an important opportunity to listen and learn from the community about constraints on behaviour change with reasons why. A more positive role for health workers has been to arrange meetings for demonstrating facilities that assist the selected behaviours e.g. 'tippy-taps' for hand washing. This sort of approach is compatible with social marketing where projects, in collaboration with communities, can play an important role in helping to provide appropriate communication support.

Similarly the sanitation ladder leads communities to analyze their existing situation and discuss constraints on changing this. Consequently, improvements to facilities selected through this process are both appropriate and manageable. This contrasts with the previous procedure where the health officers imposed their selections that were often neither practical nor appropriate. Once this exercise has been completed the community is then in a position to produce an action plan for improving latrines and latrine usage. Gender analysis has also played an important role in encouraging men to take a more active role in supporting women by sharing some chores and helping with sanitation in the home.

Activities are likely to be more sustainable through participation as communities feel in control of their actions. Previously, some communities used to be told what to do by the health educator who assumed a position of being more knowledgable. Communities were then encouraged to follow this advice by using competitions and giving away prizes to the winners. What we have now found is that although there was some limited success with reward method, all sanitation activities ceased once the prizes stopped coming.

We have been very encouraged by the success of including school children in our programmes. They provide an eager and willing resource but it is important that any action plan focuses on activities that children are able to manage at home (e.g. washing dishes, bathing younger brothers and sisters, disposing faeces into latrine). Action plans for improving sanitation in schools are also discussed amongst teachers so that it can be combined with health clubs or other school lessons (e.g. poster competitions in art classes). Teachers have also been keen to promote various facilities in school and at home (e.g. tippy-taps). The school visits have proved very successful and they are arranged around the same time as village meetings so similar messages are reinforced from different sources.

Perhaps the best sign of 'empowerment' comes when the community is involved in monitoring its own efforts. For example, we have assisted in developing a community-based system for monitoring the number of tippy-taps owners as an indication of hand washing behaviour. Members were initially taught how to make these from plastic cooking oil containers after selecting hand washing during the hygiene behaviour exercise. The community then used the community map to indicate homes with tippy-taps and this in itself has led to a dramatic improvement in both behaviour and demand for facilities.

There is a lot more to making water supply and sanitation activities sustainable than just applying these participatory techniques. Nor can we say that these techniques have provided a magical solution for 'empowering' communities. However, what we have found is that the participatory techniques are a distinct improvement on the traditional methods previously employed. Furthermore, they give a practical focus for training which makes it much easier to train people to be more participatory in their approach to communities.

References

Chambers R. (1983) *Rural Development: Putting the last first*. Longman, Harlow.

Scrimshaw C.M. and Hurtado E. (1987) *Rapid Assessment Procedures for Nutrition and Primary Health Care. Anthropological Approaches to Improving Programme Effectiveness*. UCLA, University of California, LA.

Srinivasan L. (1990) *Tools for Community Participation - A Manual for Training Trainers in Participatory Techniques*. PROWWESS/UNDP, New York.

Esrey S.A., Feachem R.G. and Hughes J.M. Interventions for the control of diarrhoeal disease among young children: improving water supplies and excreta disposal facilities. *Bull WHO*; 63: 757-772.

Demand-driven approach for sustainability

Ms Anu Saxén-Rosendahl, Kenya

KENYA FINLAND WESTERN Water Supply Programme is co-financed by the Governments of Finland and Kenya. The programme operates under the auspices of the Ministry of Land Reclamation, Regional and Water Development, Kenya.

Kenya Finland Western Water Supply Programme started its operations in Western Province in Kenya in 1981. The programme has the overall objective of enabling the rural communities in Western Province to develop and manage sustainable water projects. During the two first implementation phases (1985 - 1993) more than 3300 water points and 50 piped water supplies were constructed or rehabilitated. All these were implemented using the Supply Driven Approach, which was found inappropriate. This approach laid more emphasis on meeting physical targets and giving less time to develop a sustainable water supply. Phase IV, started in May 1993, introduced the demand-driven approach, as an operational strategy in which the planned activities are determined by the people's demand, willingness and ability to participate in the implementation process and in operations and maintenance of water supplies.

Demand driven approach

The strategy empowers the beneficiaries to become controllers of their own development. The demand-driven approach refers to a development strategy where the people themselves are expected to take the initiative and the responsibility for improving their water supply situation rather than being passive recipients of the government services. In this approach support is given only to activities which are genuinely required and requested by the beneficiaries. The beneficiaries should be willing and prepared to take over responsibilities for managing the projects and paying for construction, operations and maintenance costs. This implies that the consumers are to be the controllers of their development process and the programme and the government are facilitators.

Under this new operational strategy the programme has prepared promotional materials in the form of modules to facilitate the communities toward water supply development and sustainability. The eight modules form a complete 'information package'. Each module carries specific information regarding water supply development and sustainability as summarized below.

Module I: **demand-driven approach in water development**

Covers policy issues governing water supply development and various development partners and how they relate to one another.

Module II: **General information and procedure for the development of community-managed water supplies**
Summarizes all the steps and stages of community preparations towards development of a water supply.

Module III: **Technological options**
Highlights on the technological options used within the programme area.

Module IV: **Community piped water supplies**
Provides guidelines on how to develop and run community-owned piped water supplies.

Module V: **Health education**
Discusses the importance of health education, water-related problems and diseases and possible solutions.

Module VI: **Self management support**
Presents back-up support systems for sustaining water projects on self-help basis.

Module VII: **Handpump maintenance and spare part distribution system**
Provides guidelines on operation and maintenance of handpumps used in the programme area. It also discusses spare parts procurement and distribution system.

Module VIII: **Training**
Summarizes the information on training of user groups and the authorities involved in operating and maintaining the developed water supplies.

Procedures for development of water supply

For actual work to start, the following should be accomplished:

- application for a water supply to the district water engineer (DWE) through the divisional water officer
- formation and registration of the management committee, opening of the bank account and proceed land easement
- site verification that includes preliminary surveys, socio-economic/technical assessment, feasibility studies. This is a joint venture carried out by the DWEs, programme, Ministry of Culture and Social Services (MoCSS) and any relevant NGO's staff
- provision of the agreed construction materials and labour

- cost estimates will be prepared and the beneficiaries will be invoiced before the commencement of construction works
- the selection of contractor(s) will be made at district level and beneficiaries are expected to send at least a representative to be present
- the beneficiaries will be required to sign the contract of agreement forms before construction is sanctioned
- once the construction starts, the beneficiaries are expected to co-operate and accomplish their agreed part. The works will be executed by the selected contractor(s) and supervised by the beneficiaries, DWEs, MoCSS and programme
- a certificate of completion will be prepared and awarded by the DWE once construction is completed. The community chairman will sign on behalf of the community
- the water facility will be given a one-year guarantee period.

Role and responsibilities of parties involved
The community
The role to be played by the communities will depend on the type of activities being carried out and the stage of implementation as follows:

Planning
- identify a site/intake
- provide land for the project development
- form a water committee to co-ordinate the activities.

Officials of the water committee will sign contract agreements on behalf of the community for water development and make necessary payments in accordance with the contract.

Implementation
- provide available labour and materials which will be quantified and reduced from their required monetary contributions
- supervise and report on the development of the works
- participate in inspection
- provide required local inputs and participate actively in all stages.

Operation and maintenance
- raise funds, open a bank/postal account and pay for repairs
- organize for security of the supply
- provide personnel to be trained and take responsibility for use and care of the water supplies.

The government
The role of the government will incorporate all the efforts and contributions of the government ministries supporting community development activities including water supply development. To facilitate the implementation of the water projects the government will:

- provide funds as local contribution according to what is agreed upon
- provide technical staff and advice
- promote, support and supervize the works during project implementation
- co-ordinate water activities at all levels of development (sub DDC, district development committee (DDC), national)
- ensure promotion of health education and sanitation by training the community and staff
- be responsible for community development activities
- mobilize and support the communities to strengthen institutional building
- promote intersectional linkages within its ministries and NGOs
- register and promote water committees
- ensure that land easements are registered for legal safeguard and to guarantee accessibility
- assist in certifying the information given by the applicants in liaison with the local development committees
- advise the communities on the means to conserve the water resource
- provide training opportunities on environmental hygiene to keep the water facilities clean.

Kenya Finland Western Water Supply Programme
The role of the programme will mainly be advisory and catalytic in the development process. The programme will provide limited support for the water development in Western Province and technical assistance. In addition the programme will:

- arrange and organize necessary training to facilitate transfer of technology and skills
- develop promotional material, create awareness on safe water in collaboration with the Ministry of Health (MoH)
- provide logistics and operational support, co-ordinate transfer of technology and skills, and develop local delivery and distribution of spare parts
- liaise with ministries and NGOs to promote intersectoral collaboration.

Note: The programme role will be limited to the above issues till the end of 1995.

Non-governmental organizations
These are both externally and locally funded voluntary organizations assisting the local communities in achieving certain goals. The NGOs will collaborate and co-ordinate with each other and relevant government departments to:

- mobilize the communities for the participatory planning

- give back-up support in terms of training opportunities and transport
- encourage income-generating activities
- give direct cash donations if possible
- find marketing channels for the products from the initiated income-generating activities.

Private sector

This comprises the profit-making organizations, businessmen, insurance companies, contractors etc.. They can be found both in and outside the community. Its roles will be to:

- sell materials to the communities
- sell services to the communities
- advance loans and credit to the communities in need of such services.

Cost sharing

The typical costs of the water points are as follows:

Protected spring	USD	700 - 900
Hand dug well	USD	1300 - 2500
Borehole	USD	9000 - 17 000

The community contributions for the implementation and training costs have been as follows:

Community water point	25 per cent
Community water point, potable water already closer than 500 m	50 per cent
Institutions (schools, health centres etc.)	75 per cent
Private	100 per cent

The minimum cash contribution is 2 per cent of the total implementation costs. The remaining share could be paid either by providing materials or labour. Approximately 37 per cent of the community contribution has been paid in cash, 44 per cent in materials and 19 per cent in labour.

In addition to the water points the programme has implemented four community piped water supplies where the communities have contributed 30 per cent of the implementation costs. (A separate presentation on community-managed water supplies is given during the conference).

Lessons learned and experience gained

The DDA strategy has been adopted to:

- ensure sustainability
- provide adequate time for beneficiaries to understand the relationship between water, health and standard of living
- help the communities to understand technical, financial, institutional and organizational implications of the water supply systems.

During the year 1994, 980 applications were received, 631 field investigations, cost estimates and pro forma invoices were completed and sent to the communities. Altogether 254 communities paid their invoices out of which 225 were community water points, 10 were institutions and 19 private.

The programme has successfully achieved its target and mainly with good experience and feedback. However, some problems have also been faced:

- it has been difficult to verify whether the application has been submitted by a community or a private person
- land easements for project sites have proved to be very difficult. The problem arises when the water point has been registered as a community one but has later proved to be private, and the land owner does not allow the community members to enter his yard to fetch water
- registration within the MoCSS is a very slow process; some of the communities existed only on paper
- communities have difficulties understanding the importance of collecting funds for future maintenance
- spare parts of the installed pumps are quite expensive and not easily available
- the number of applications decreased drastically when the programme stopped the subsidy.

The further development of DDA to promote sustainable water supply without any external subsidy seems to be difficult. The communities' real ability or willingness to pay remains to be seen.

The World-Wide Web and sustainable development

Rod Shaw, WEDC

SINCE WEDC WAS formed in 1971, it has been committed to keeping alumni, their sponsors and other supporters in touch with current activities and new initiatives; to disseminating the results of its research; and to sharing experiences gained from consultancy assignments undertaken in many low- and middle-income countries throughout the world.

As a means of extending this commitment, WEDC is developing a site on the World-Wide Web, one of the latest developments of the Internet — the global network of hundreds of thousands of personal computers. This paper examines the nature of the 'Web' and considers the extent to which it may be used as an effective communication tool for sustainable development. It introduces the WEDC site and those with which WEDC is closely linked.

The Internet

The Internet was originally conceived in the 1970s by the United States military as a global communication network to be used in the event of nuclear war. An important feature of the early network (known as ARPAnet) was the use it made of an electronic communications protocol called TCP/IP. This enabled a computer to send and receive data to and from another computer. Local computer networks evolved and were linked to others to form much larger networks comprising many organizations. The vision, at that time, was to provide the opportunity of maintaining communication with as much of the world as possible, should any region or countries be devastated by war. The advantage of an international network based on TCP/IP is that it is decentralized — many computer file servers across the world maintain the links between organizations and institutions.

With the threat of global nuclear war diminished since the end of the Cold War, the Internet is now widely used by academic institutions, businesses and other organizations. It provides services for millions of people — typically the sending and receiving of electronic mail (email), electronic conferencing and, with the development of the World-Wide Web, personal publishing and broadcasting (Figure 1).

The World-Wide Web

The World-Wide Web (WWW) is a means of providing and retrieving information across the Internet. It makes use of a programming language, developed by the then Conseil Européen pour la Recherche Nucléaire (CERN) in Switzerland in the early 1990s, which is now known as the European Laboratory of Particle Physics (Segal, 1995). This language is known as the *hypertext mark-up language* or *html*. Related html files can be linked directly to one another using the *hypertext transfer protocol (http)*. This is the case whether the files reside on the same computer or on other computers situated in different parts of the world. A passage of text is highlighted in the source file and contains a reference to a related file (Figure 2). The selected text is usually underlined and displayed in mid-grey, on black and white monitors, or in blue on colour

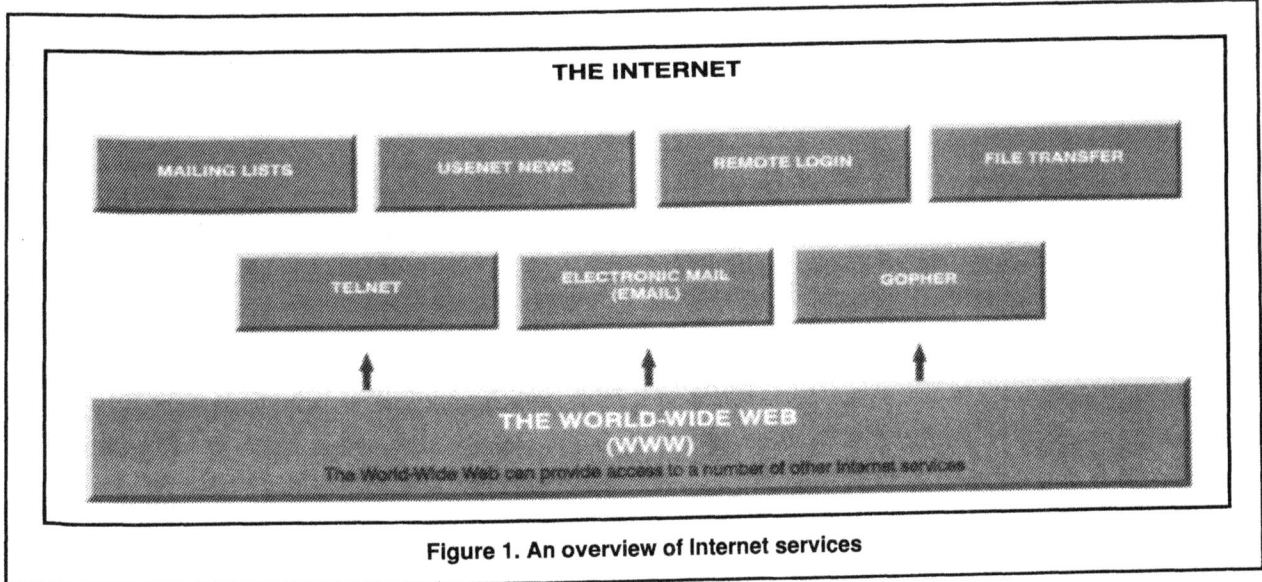

Figure 1. An overview of Internet services

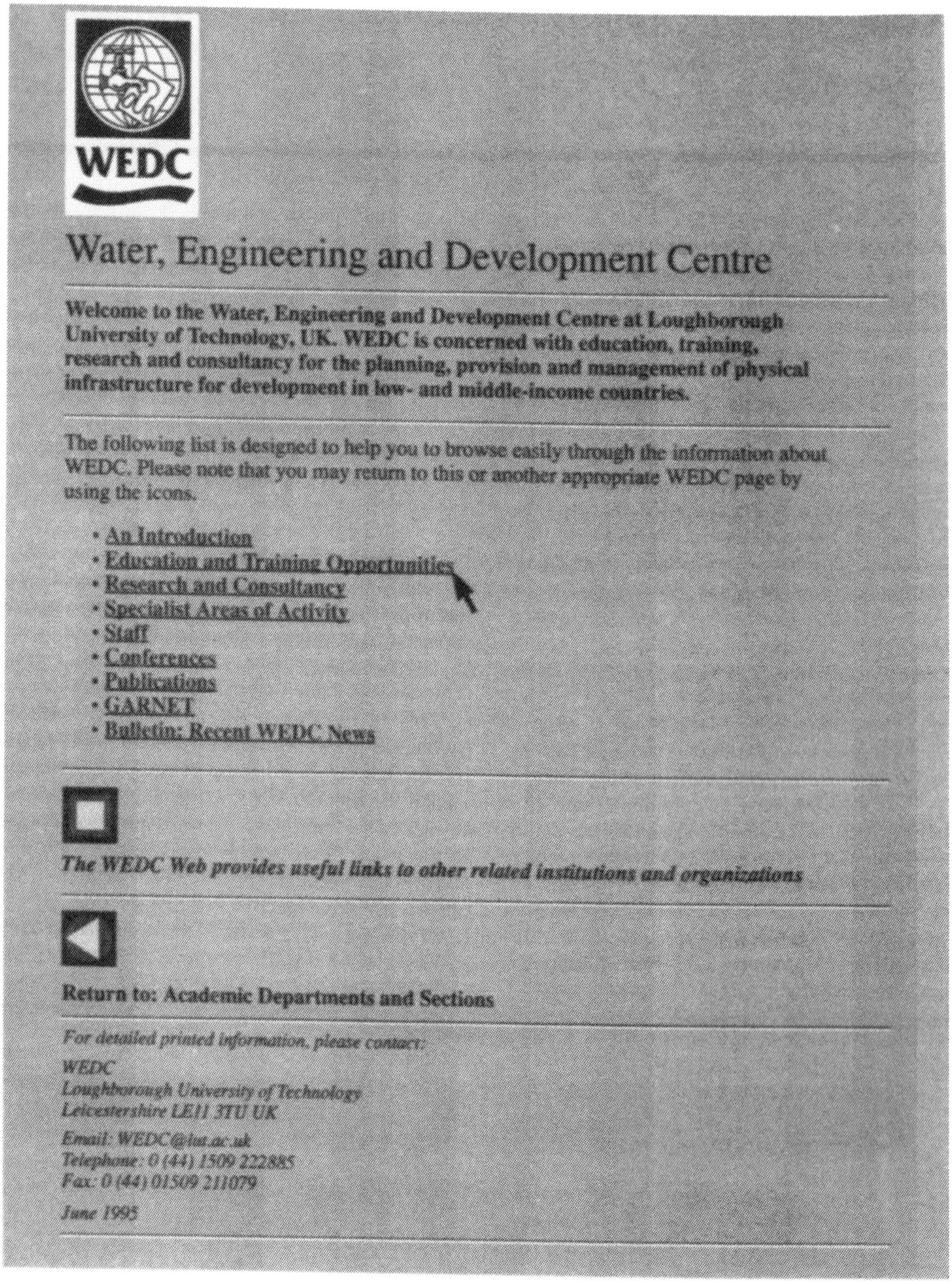

Water, Engineering and Development Centre

Welcome to the Water, Engineering and Development Centre at Loughborough University of Technology, UK. WEDC is concerned with education, training, research and consultancy for the planning, provision and management of physical infrastructure for development in low- and middle-income countries.

The following list is designed to help you to browse easily through the information about WEDC. Please note that you may return to this or another appropriate WEDC page by using the icons.

- An Introduction
- Education and Training Opportunities
- Research and Consultancy
- Specialist Areas of Activity
- Staff
- Conferences
- Publications
- GARNET
- Bulletin: Recent WEDC News

The WEDC Web provides useful links to other related institutions and organizations

Return to: Academic Departments and Sections

For detailed printed information, please contact:
WEDC
Loughborough University of Technology
Leicestershire LE11 3TU UK

Email: WEDC@lut.ac.uk
Telephone: 0 (44) 1509 222885
Fax: 0 (44) 01509 211079

June 1995

Figure 2. The WEDC 'home page' on the World-Wide Web

Note: The linked page will appear by selecting one of the underlined options

monitors. The reference itself is not displayed but is hidden within the hypertext document. Such documents are viewed by using one of several programs known as 'browsers'. Connections to the Internet, and hence the World-Wide Web, are usually made via modems. These are small, and relatively inexpensive, units which make use of telephone infrastructure.

The World-Wide Web has developed into a huge electronic library of information (of both text and images) which is growing by an estimated ten per cent per month. Because its growth is so explosive, no-one can be sure exactly how many people are now using it. During May 1995, estimates ranged from between 10 and 50 million people. Web sites hold information on many subjects — some very specialized — from architecture to zoology, and from the study of bats to the study of human behaviour (Yates and Leavy, 1995).

Benefits of the World-Wide Web

The World-Wide Web offers millions of people the opportunity of rapidly sharing their ideas, information and experiences. In this respect it is similar to email or electronic conferencing. Unlike email, however, it is not interpersonal. Instead, it enables contributors instantly to 'publish' or 'broadcast' literature globally for any other user of the Web to view — and it does not require the intervention of an external publisher or broadcaster.

After the initial investment in equipment, the use of the Web is charged at the price of a local telephone call. Publishers are attracted to the Web as there are no printing, paper or postage costs incurred. The main attraction for development professionals is the access the Web provides to remote (and hitherto inaccessible) information. The World-Wide Web is also rapidly becoming an international standard for access to databases of many types (Segal, 1995).

Reardon (1994) describes the ways in which the UNDP has facilitated the global exchange of information by establishing national computer networks in many developing countries. He notes that *sustainable development networks (SDNs)* are now operating in Angola, Bolivia, China, Honduras, Indonesia, Nicaragua, Pakistan, the Philippines, Poland, the Republic of Korea and Tunisia, as well as 22 island countries in the South Pacific. He maintains that 'SDNs provide a timely and cost-efficient medium for individuals, organizations and governments to communicate ideas, share information and relate experiences that bear on the environment and development.' He goes on to suggest that, in some instances, they can even help to 'break down antagonisms among users and help overcome the tendency in many countries to deny access to information'.

Limitations of the Web

Clearly, the Web has limitations. Most of the material is published in English and access demands a significant level of computer literacy, appropriate hardware and software, and a link to a participating file server. As a result, most sites are currently found in the North. 'Downloading' files between countries can be slow. Cabling is expensive too, and beyond the reach of the economies of many southern countries.

Not least of the Web's limitations is the present difficulty of easily locating relevant and useful material. Literature available on the 'information superhighway' is seemingly without limit, and much of it seems trivial. It is possible to search the Web using keywords, but the facilities available to do this can be unreliable. Furthermore, because the World-Wide Web is constantly changing, an index will soon be out of date. The response of many users to this problem is to create attractive sites which provide a focus for a particular area of interest and encourage new links. The World-Wide Web 'address' (known as the *Uniform Resource Locator* or *URL*) is then advertised in other, more traditional, ways.

The Internet seems likely to overcome some of these limitations in the near future. Satellite technology promises access to the Web from anywhere in the world without the need for a cable link. Already, email, faxes, data and telex messages can be sent and received in this way following the launch of GemSat for Windows. Developments in technology should also increase the speed at which information is sought and transferred.

Information or communication?

The real concern among some observers is that an increasing dependence on information technology, not only diverts economic and human resources away from core development activities, but also contributes to the 'process of detachment' of the North from the South. Zadek (1992) argues that an interest in communicating with one social group directly affects the ability of an individual or organization to communicate with other social groups. He refers to examples of some NGOs who, by developing an international, if influential, role in development affairs (aimed at bringing about political change) diminished their ability to communicate with the very people they had first set out to help.

Another fear is of the effect that electronic-based media may have in undermining other patterns of indigenous communication which may already be fragile because of weak domestic and regional support. Certainly, the World-Wide Web has produced a surfing subculture comprising an international population far removed from real life in the South. It is also apparent that innovations in information technology can lead to an excess of information or 'information overload', if improperly managed. It is clearly important to remember that information about something we already know is worthless as information, and that information about something we do not already know is equally worthless unless we have a need to know about it. A further criticism of information technology *per se* is that it has blurred the boundary between information and communication. Fuglesang (1982) reminds us that 'we do not communicate by cramming an enormous quantity of information bits together in a monologue, but by being socially intelligent and capable of listening to what others have in mind before we respond'.

The WEDC site
The WEDC site is being developed with sensitivity to the benefits and problems the World-Wide Web presents and with the acknowledgement that the information superhighway is only one of many communication tools. The site focuses on water, sanitation and other infrastructure, management and environmental issues. Information available about WEDC currently includes:

- details of education and training opportunities;
- an overview of specialist areas of WEDC activity;
- profiles of WEDC staff;
- monthly bulletin updates; and
- WEDC publications.

Future developments will include:

- further reports of research and consultancy projects;
- free access to selected papers from over 20 years of annual WEDC conferences; and
- regular additions to 'The WEDC Web' — a database of other useful World-Wide Web sites with common interests such as United Nations' agencies, the World Health Organization, and non-governmental organizations.

GARNET
In line with plans to promote the network as widely as possible, the Global Applied Research Network (GARNET) has also established a home page on the World-Wide Web. This is designed to compliment normal, traditional networking methods. Users are able to obtain a range of information about GARNET including:

- background information to the initiative — purpose, history, structure;
- profiles of individual topic networks — aims, activities, recent output;
- recent publications from GARNET;
- previous WSS applied research output, organized by keywords; and
- pointers to other Internet sites with specific interest for WSS researchers (Saywell, 1995).

One World On-line
One of the most significant sites concerning development in the South so far is *One World On-Line*, an initiative of the One World Broadcasting Trust. One World On-line provides access to the World-Wide Web for over 80 non-governmental organizations and a number of other institutions. Oxfam, for example, is sending out press releases and first-hand reports from potential disaster 'hot-spots'. The WEDC site is also linked to this experimental venture.

Conclusions
Despite the limitations of electronic-based media, and the additional fear that the Internet may be dominated in the future by multinational corporations demanding payment for access to their data, the World-Wide Web presents a growing percentage of those who have a genuine desire to build a better world with a new and exciting means of co-operation and collaboration. Within its own context, the Web is truly democratic. It has no hierarchy, and there is, as yet, no censorship. Of course, there is the potential to misinform, to bias and to corrupt, but this has always been the case with mass-communication media. In 1932, Berthold Brecht lamented the limitations of broadcasting:

'What a wonderful apparatus broadcasting could be if it would only receive as well as transmit, make the recipient speak instead of just listen, relate him to others, instead of isolating him from them'.

The Web experiment is a step towards the realization of Brecht's dream. One World On-Line hopes to take a further step forward at the end of this year by offering NGOs the opportunity of introducing audio and video clips to their sites. Video conferencing is on the agenda for the next millennium when people in different parts of the world will be able to participate in live visual discussions.

The long-term success of the World-Wide Web as a serious communication tool for sustainable development, however, will ultimately depend on the widespread introduction of low-cost connections in the South, and on the generous and regular provision of appropriate and accessible information.

References
Brecht, Berthold (1932), *Der Rundfunk als Kommunikationsapparat* in: Oepen, Manfred (1992), 'Community Communication', *Development Communication Report*, No. 73, US Agency for International Development, Arlington.

Fuglesang, Andreas (1982), *About Understanding: Ideas and observations on cross-cultural communication*, Dag Hammarskjold Foundation, Upsalla.

Reardon, Christopher (1994), 'Getting On-Line for Sustainable Development', *Choices*, Vol.3, No.2, UNDP, New York.

Saywell, D.L. (1995), Personal communication.

Segal, Ben M. (1995), *A Short History of the Internet* at: http://www.cern.ch/

Yates, John, and Leavy, Alan (1995), *Making Connections*, Loughborough College of Art and Design, Loughborough.

Zadek, Simon (1992), 'Why communicate, anyway? Why not?', *Appropriate Technology*, Vol.19, No.2, IT Publications, London.

World-Wide Web addresses:
WEDC and GARNET:
http://info.lut.ac.uk/departments/cv/wedc/index.html
One World On-Line:
http://www.bbcnc.org.uk/online/oneworld/top.html

Buying into rural water systems

Michael Wood and Negash Dinna, Ethiopia

ETHIOPIA HAS BEEN called 'The Water Tower of Africa'. No fewer than 14 major river systems flow out of the country into neighbouring countries like Sudan, Somalia and Kenya. Each year, following the main *'Krempt'* rains in July and August 91.5 million cubic metres of water leave the Ethiopian highlands.(1)

Despite this endowment, only an estimated 19 per cent of the total population of 55 million (1984 census projection) has access to a safe water supply (2). Of this 19 per cent, about 12 per cent of the population has been provided with water by the government while the remaining seven per cent has been provided by non-government organizations. Of the 12 per cent of the population served by the government, about 90 per cent live in urban centres including the estimated three million who reside in Addis Ababa. Taking this into account it can be seen that the small percentage of the rural population of Ethiopia (estimated at 48 million) who have been provided with safe domestic water supplies, have been provided by NGOs. According to UNICEF, 37 NGOs were active in the rural water sector in 1992 (2). Since then about 20 more NGOs have become active in this field (3). As in other countries in Africa, NGOs are major players when it comes to provision of rural water supply.

Sustainability

Sustainability in this context may be defined as an intervention which the community can maintain and manage for more than ten years with the minimum of outside assistance. In this context, the rural water systems installed by the government in Ethiopia do not have a very good record. For example, in the former southern provinces of Bale, Borana, Sidamo, and Gamo Goffa, it was reported in 1992 that 40 per cent of the systems installed by the government were not functioning for a variety of reasons (4). One of the main reasons was that the beneficiaries were not involved in the system until it was handed over to them upon completion. The users were not properly trained in how to maintain or manage the system. Maintenance was seen and is still seen in many communities, as being a government responsibility.

However, systems installed by NGOs tend to have a far better, although by no means perfect, record of sustainability. The principal reasons for this are:

- NGOs work in smaller areas, therefore they are closer to the communities.
- Rural people tend to trust NGOs more than they do government organizations who have ripped them off in the past, particularly under the authoritative Derg regime which was in power from 1974 to 1991.
- NGOs have involved beneficiaries to a greater extent at all stages of the project cycle.
- NGOs tend to respond to requests from communities to intervene, therefore initiatives are demand-driven, not driven from the Central Planning Office in Addis Ababa.
- NGOs tend to have better human and material resources than GOs and NGO staff tend to be more motivated.
- NGOs are usually able to respond quicker and in more appropriate ways than GOs, to the needs of communities.

The example of one international NGO operating in Ethiopia will be cited as an example.

CARE in Ethiopia

CARE, arguably one of the largest non-government, non-sectarian organizations in the world, has been operating in Ethiopia since 1984 when it was involved in famine relief. Since then, CARE has diversified into more long-term development activities in Oromia, the largest of Ethiopia's 12 regions. Since 1989 CARE has been involved in a natural resource development project in Western Hararghe zone, about 400km east of Addis Ababa. Funded by the Overseas Development Administration of the UK, the project is working with about 13 000 rural families in two woredas (districts) ranging from the arid lowland of the rift valley, to the highland area forming the Western part of the Hararghe mountain range.

The CARE Habro Community Based Development (CBD) Project is mostly concerned with increasing crop yields and helping farmers to reduce soil erosion. A participatory extension approach is used to introduce sustainable interventions with particular attention being given to the needs of women.

One of their needs is improved water supplies. Communities are assisted in the construction of shallow wells equipped with handpumps, and in protecting springs.

Community awareness

The first stage of CARE Habro's approach was to create an awareness in the communities of the benefits and advantages of improved water supply. This was done through meetings convened by project extension agents, many of whom are women, and by showing videos of water schemes in other villages and by cross-visits. This process helped create the demand.

Community involvement

The farmers and their families actively participate in water development activities. The project works with communities through democratically elected community development committees (CDCs), which include respected elders and traditional leaders. People articulate their needs to the CDCs which get in touch with the project through the extension agents. The projects' water engineer then visits the community and conducts a technical feasibility study with members of the CDC to determine the type and cost of the system.

The CDC is then told how much the system will cost, and how much the community will be expected to pay.

In the CARE Habro project area, communities normally contribute between 60 to 70 per cent of the total construction cost. This includes a cash contribution of between 30 to 80 birr (US$ 5 to 13) per household plus contributions in kind like labour and providing project technicians with board and lodging during construction. Before work starts, the beneficiaries have to deposit at least half of their cash contribution with the project and make an access road to the site. The cash contribution depends on the communities' ability to pay. This is assessed by a socio-economic survey carried out by the project sociologist. This community input instills the all-important sense of ownership of the completed system and has been found to be one of the major factors contributing toward the sustainability of the systems. This approach is diametrically opposed to that taken by the government.

The government approach

Normally the government requires no cash contribution and only minimal in kind inputs from beneficiaries when constructing a rural water system. This approach guarantees dependency on outsiders and more or less ensures that the system will not be sustainable. For example, there is a water system installed by the government in a village adjacent to the project area which has been broken down for more than 12 months.

Let us now see, as an illustration, two specific examples of two communities which have contributed surprising financial commitments in order to get potable water through the technical assistance of CARE Habro.

Hidha Medar

There is one spring in this community which is the only source of drinking water, not only for human beings but also for the large livestock population in the area. It was really amazing to see the struggle between people and their livestock to get water from this source.

To alleviate these problems, the community started mobilizing themselves and contributed the required amount of money to have their spring protected. With the assistance of the people of Hidha Medar, CARE Habro protected the source of the spring and built a simple distribution point. Besides this, other facilities were also built, like a cattle trough, clothes washing facility and even a shower with two bathrooms.

The actual cost of this project is calculated as follows in Ethiopian birr.

Cost of Hidha Medar Spring

Item	Unit	Quality	Cost
Cement	qtl	25	1000
Sand	cu.m	12	240
GI pipe	pcs	30	1500
Ring	pc	1	354
Ring	pc	1	177
Nipples	pc	4	60
Reducers	pc	10	100
Tee	pc	10	20
Total material cost			3451

Unskilled labour cost		2000
Total community contribution		5451
CARE contribution (Transport, skilled manpower)		3400
Total cost		8851
Community cash contribution		2224
Community labour contribution		2000
Total community contribution		4224

Thus, the community input was birr 4224 (US$681) which is 47 per cent of the total project cost. The CARE input was birr 4627 (US$746) which is 52 per cent of the total project cost. The protected spring serves 80 families so the community input per family is birr 52.8 (US$8.50) and hence the project input per family was birr 57.83 (US$9.32).

The per capita cost works out at birr 18.43 or US$3.00.

Gorometa community

Another of the communities in which CARE has assisted is Gorometa, 2800 metres up in the highlands of Gubakoricha woreda. There was an acute drinking water problem as there are no rivers, streams or springs in the vicinity. So the community agreed to dig a well and, assisted by technical input from CARE, fortunately found ground water at a depth of four metres. They requested CARE to install a handpump, so an Indian Mark Two was installed for the community and they are now enjoying a safe and reliable drinking water supply. The total cost, in birr, of constructing the well and installing the handpump is as follows;

Cost of Gorometa handdug well

Item	Unit	Quality	Cost
Ring	pc	4	448
Handpump	pc	1	2400
Cement	qtl	5	200
Rebar	pc	8	376
Sand	cu.m.	8	160
Total materials			3584

Masons per diem	7	168
Unskilled labour cost		1950
CARE skilled labour and transport		4000
Total cost		9702
Community cash contribution		2104
Community labour contribution		1950
Total community contribution		4054
CARE contribution		5648

Thus, the community input amounted to birr 4054 (US$653) which is 41 per cent of total cost.

The CARE input was birr 5648 ($911) or 58 per cent of total cost. The handpump serves 60 families. Therefore the cost per family is birr 161.7 ($26). The project input per family is birr 94 ($15). The total cost per capita works out at birr 26.95 ($4.34).

NGO — Government co-operation

One of the criticisms of NGO interventions in developing countries like Ethiopia is that they are not sustainable.

- What happens when the NGO leaves the area?
- Does the NGO have a proper counterpart relationship with government organizations who are there for the long term?
- Has the NGO made an effort to involve GOs so that a smooth handing over process is in place?

These are some of the questions that both indigenous and international NGOs will have to address.

Governments too, have an obligation to provide NGOs with guidelines so that water systems are built to the required standard. Poor quality systems are being constructed by well-meaning but sometimes technically deficient NGOs.

Governments must also be able to inspect systems built by NGOs and have the authority to reject systems that do not come up to established standards.

Agreements

It is in the interests of both parties to have a tripartite agreement to include the beneficiary community in each and every system built so as to ensure that the community has some outside source of assistance should they encounter technical problems which are beyond their capacity to solve.

In the case of Ethiopia, guidelines for NGOs were drafted by the government agency responsible for rural water supply, but due to the turmoil surrounding the change of the government in 1991, these guidelines were never finalized, so NGOs are still working on their own. Therefore, NGOs are building systems the designs for which have not been approved by the concerned government organization.

So there is a risk that some poor quality systems are being built as they are outside the remit of any control body.

Most NGOs in Ethiopia regard GOs with apprehension and tend to steer clear of government bureaucracy in order to get the job done on time.

However, this does not augur well for the future sustainability of water supply systems. The question of who is to take over the maintenance of rural water systems when NGOs leave has not been adequately dealt with.

NGOs must make it their business to keep government organizations informed at each stage of constructing and maintaining water systems. They must strive to train government staff in the management and maintenance of the systems and hand over resources such as vehicles and spare parts to government agencies in a timely fashion.

Governments, for their part, need to come up with practical guidelines for NGOs to follow, so as to ensure quality is built in to rural water systems.

Both sides have room for improvement if the goal of providing safe water for all by the year 2000, only five years away, is to be achieved.

References

1. RRC News, February 1995, Addis Ababa.
2. UNICEF/Water Resources Commission Report, 1992; UNICEF, Addis Ababa.
3. CDRA Report, Addis Ababa, 1994.
4. Evaluation of Southern Regional Rural Water Supply and Sanitation Project, CIDA, 1992.

SECTION B

WATER AND THE ENVIRONMENT

Community-oriented hygiene and sanitation

Moses Bagbiele, Oduro Sarpong, Elizabeth Kidd, Ghana

In this latter part of the 20th century, hygiene and sanitation (H&S) activities have featured prominently in water supply projects. This paper supplies a brief background of H&S activities in the Upper Regions (UR) of Ghana, describes the current strategies being tried with illustrations through case studies, looks at sustainability and raises some concerns around the approach.

From 1986 to 1991 the Water Education For Health Programme (WEFH) under the Water Utilization Project (WUP) focused on H&S issues around water in rural pump communities in the Upper Regions (UR) of Ghana. Diarrhoeal diseases were the major cause of infant mortality. Malaria was the most common clinically identified disease. Guinea worm was a major cause of debilitation and deformity. Environmental sanitation and personal and food hygiene among rural children and mothers poor. Clean water from boreholes was contaminated by the leaves used to prevent the water from splashing from the vessels.

The WEFH programme trained one man and one woman from each village pump community to take up some health education duties at the community level to encourage knowledge transfer and some community-based action towards improved H&S. These community water organizers (CWOs) were mostly illiterate members of the community. The education process was reinforced through radio programming including locally produced drama and songs. There were different topics for each year's campaign depending on the most prevalent water related diseases recorded by the UR health institutions and from interviews with community people.

Although the delivery of the education was interactive and participatory, the messages were designed and delivered through a centrally planned mass campaign, unintentionally negating many of the participatory benefits.

Statement of the problem

In 1990, a survey conducted by the programme indicated there had been significant knowledge transfer with little or no attitudinal change and no statistically significant change in the incidence of disease (Wardrop 1990). In effect, community members had knowledge of problems but were not acting on that knowledge. Why?

Current objective

The current objective is to focus on behavioural change, community management and sustainability of community hygiene and sanitation programmes.

Since 1994, the Community Water Project (COWAP), funded by The Canadian International Development Agency (CIDA), has built on this basic work of WUP. COWAP aims at supporting rural communities in identifying and solving their own H&S problems, putting decision-making in the hands of community people to encourage sustainability.

Part of changing behaviour is understanding traditional values. Along with these traditional values come constraints that challenge change. Mark Twain said, 'Habit is habit and not to be flung out of the window but coaxed down stairs a step at a time.' (Participatory Evaluation)

In the UR, diseases are believed to be caused by angry ancestors, gods and inadequate sacrifices, not environmental conditions. Examples include:

- diarrhoea is caused by drinking dirty water, but it is angry ancestors that make one drink this contaminated water. Western medicine can stop the diarrhoea but it will recur without sacrifices.
- It is a taboo to bury the faeces of a child if one has never lost a child. Burying the faeces is equated with burying the child.
- Mosquitoes breed in herbalists' pots containing water and herbs, but it is a taboo to use a lid because the presence of the larvae indicates the potency of the herbs.

Non-traditional constraints include women's workload. The women state it is often impossible when returning from the farm in the late evening for them to fetch water, wash bowls, bath children and still cook early enough for the family before children fall asleep.

Here are four strategies COWAP is using to support communities in their decisions around changing behaviours.

Strategies

Interactive Drama (ID)

ID is Community Animation Theatre, 'in the round', where problems and solutions are acted out by community members. The drama starts and stops with different members' ideas acted out and accepted or rejected as the reality acceptable to those present. Communities now own the initiative in problem identification and problem solving. Using ID as a situational drama, drawing on peoples' personal experiences and using the community members as characters is a new technique for us. ID usually ends with community members coming out with practical solutions to their own problems. ID appears to be effective because it provides an indirect approach to discussing community issues. This indirect approach is consistent with traditional problem-solving styles.

When a priority issue is identified critical questions such as; How is this a problem here? Is this a real situation? Why is this a problem? are asked and actors are invited from the audience to act out their perceptions of the problem. When consensus on the problem is reached, possible solutions are acted out until a decision for action is arrived at.

Case study
In one community, an expensive, government-built and funded septic tank latrine attached to the Health Centre, was losing its roofing and clogged. Since the government had built the latrine, the community simply looked on, expecting the district assembly to bring about a solution. About 12 kilometres away in a community in which we used ID, the villagers identified the lack of latrines as a problem. They contributed 128 000 cedis (USD 128) and undertook the construction of six 'Mozambique latrines'. It should be noted these communities have a similar resource base, but the chief of the first community is a well educated teacher and an old politician, while the chief of the second community is an illiterate farmer.

A second pilot program for H&S is working with the UR School Health Programme in both urban and rural sectors. The children range in age from 10 to 15 years. Latrine building meets some of their curriculum demands in a practical way.

Case study
In one school, children have built two 'Mozambique latrines' and two urinals. Before undertaking the building, we spent time discussing and demonstrating principles of siting, latrine design and options. The students shared this information with their rural counterparts in two rural pilot schools and members of their parent teacher association. Using the skills gained, and with good support from their head master, the students are beginning to build the latrines for community members and interested schools.

Self-monitoring
Self-monitoring of the activities agreed upon is at the local level and by the community members, however COWAP does its own cross monitoring. Indicators are chosen after using questions like; How do you want to do this? How can you know you are making progress? Who shall be responsible for what?

Case study
Two communities, one in the Upper East Region (UER) and one in the Upper West Region (UWR) have set their own indicators for H&S. In the UER one community declared all members as health inspectors. They divided the community into three sections and agreed to monitor compound cleanliness inside and outside, as well as the disposal of the refuse. This community identified behaviours of men in the compound that were unhygienic; spitting, bringing manure to the compound etc.. The men agreed they did this and would try to change. On the last visit the community was very proud of their clean compounds and the women said the men were trying to change. They felt their monitoring of each other was very effective. We will return in the rainy season to check this community and perhaps help with drainage issues that will be relevant at that time.

Schools identified the programmes they would undertake and came up with their own indicators. Some of those identified include:

- unkempt hair/hair lice
- personal hygiene
- compound littering

Teachers noted the incidence when students were sent home for hair or personal hygiene problems had dropped by at least 30 per cent. Another school achieved compound cleanliness by dividing the compound into four sections and having a weekly competition.

A rural school has extended its H&S program to the community where clean-up campaigns are now organized and monitored by the students before each market day and women are encouraged to wash their calabashes between customers. It is too early to come out with quality indicators except to say there is a growing community spirit. One community chief said, 'This COWAP, it has shown us we have to take charge and try to make change in our community, not just wait for others to show us how.'

Participatory rural appraisal (PRA)
Communities have their own system of keeping records of factors important to them. COWAP has re-emphasized this by assisting the communities to draw maps of their communities indicating houses, water points, schools and other important features.

Gathering base line data by the community has been possible through PRA. Base line data can then be related to health, hygiene and sanitation issues and increase awareness of population pressure as against sanitary facilities available in the community. The community utilizes and expands their system of keeping records, not an imposed system and the information kept is seen as meaningful to the community, not something COWAP wants kept.

Case study
Seeds, local and readily available in a community, are used to record and monitor population in two communities. Different types of seed represent men, women and

children of different ages. Additionally, the number of marriages and divorces could be recorded in the same fashion.

Radio programming

Interviews, music and songs from the community are recorded in the community and used in the daily half-hour time slot provided by Ghana Broadcasting Corporation (GBC). After one such broadcast one older gentleman who heard his neighbour being interviewed said, 'This is interesting. I'm going to buy myself a new radio.' No longer is the information only from outsiders. Local peoples' opinions and ideas are being heard. Often the musicians are young people and they are very pleased to hear their music on the radio. Feedback through the interviewers leads to more interviews and a sharing of ideas and opinions. This participatory approach is new in radio and we are still learning.

Indicators of sustainability

These four strategies lend themselves to sustainability of community-initiated programmes because communities are able to:
- recognize and define the problem
- discuss the problem
- decide to act on the problem
- know what action they will take to monitor their own compliance.

Communities soon realize they are in charge of change.

Issues of concern
- How do we ensure strong ID skills in our practitioners. ID is a very powerful tool. Used inappropriately, 'top down' rather than 'bottom up' it could reinforce dependency rather than develop community capacity to make decisions.
- How can we support the development of qualitative indicators at the community level?
- How do we manipulate traditional barriers that affect H&S issues?
- How do you give away this pilot project? To whom and with what training?

Conclusion

Our participatory approach in H&S is new in the region and growing in popularity as we share our ideas with collaborating agencies. We have much to learn and we feel sure the communities will continue to help us grow as they take charge of change.

References

1. A Review of WUP Hygiene and Sanitation Campaign: Wardrop Field Paper, 1990.
2. 'Drama For Community Management'. COWAP Field Paper, Ross Kidd 1994.
3. Participatory Approaches in Community Development

The early recognition of environmental impacts

C. Binder, R. Schertenleib, J. Diaz, P. Baccini, Switzerland

IN DEVELOPING COUNTRIES problems concerning water quality have increased during the last decade. While in industrialized countries the traditional and modern types of water pollution (e.g. domestic, industrial, nutrients) occurred over a 100-year period, in developing countries however they have occurred within one generation [WHO, 1989].

Short-term technical measures have important immediate effects, but for achieving sustainability it is critical to develop tools for long-term planning which allow a better understanding of how different strategies affect outcomes and how strategies are sensitive to different levels and types of financing [Bower, 1989].

In industrialized countries the method of material flux analysis (MFA), has been shown to be a suitable instrument for early recognition of environmental problems and evaluation of environmental measures [Baccini and Brunner, 1991]. It has been shown that it is possible to combine data from market research on one hand with data from urban waste management on the other hand to observe the metabolic dynamics of a region [Baccini et al., 1993]. However, this method has not been applied yet in developing countries due to the low data availability and the poor data quality.

The aim of this paper is to show how the method of MFA was applied to a region in a developing country with regard to water resource management.

Methods
Characterization of the research region
Tunja is the capital of the county of Boyaca. It is located in the eastern chain of the Andes at an altitude of 2800 m above sea level and has an area of 117km2. Tunja has 114 000 inhabitants, with 95 per cent living in the urban area. The population growth from 1985 to 1993 was 2.7 per cent/year [DANE, 1994]. The project was carried out together with the local university, UNIBOYACA.

System analysis for water
The system for the waterbalance (74km^2) is defined by the catchment area in the south, east and west and by the political border on the northern part of the municipality. The following processes were chosen to define the water balance in the region:

Water supply
Supplies *households*, *industry* and *institutions* of the municipality with water. The water is imported from an external reservoir and extracted from the *lower aquifer*. The losses in the supply are about 40 per cent, whereas the illegal consumption is assumed to be 15 per cent [EAAT, 1993].

Soil/upper aquifer:
Includes 1m of *soil* (pedosphere) where evapotranspiration, interception, CO_2 fixation take place and 9m corresponding to the *upper aquifer*. The area is divided into sealed, agricultural and unproductive soil.

Household/industry
In this process the water is consumed. The consumption of *households* is 84 per cent, of *institutions and commerce* 13 per cent of the total consumption. In this region *industry* (three per cent of total consumption) does not play an important role.

Groundwater, lower aquifer
The *lower aquifer* is divided into two main aquifers, which have together a magnitude of 70 to 200m. In the valley they are located at about 200 to 400m below the surface.

Surface water
The internal surface water is the Rio Chulo. In Fig. 1 the system analysis for the water balance is shown.

Parameter or element choice
The parameters were chosen taking into account three aspects. First, they had to be measurable with the infrastructure available at the UNIBOYACA in Tunja, so that monitoring could be carried out. Second, they had to reflect the human activities taking place in the region. Third, they had to be representative for pollution and nutrients. As only three per cent of the water is consumed by *industry*, it was assumed that the sewage quality was dominated by *household* sewage. In studies of urban regions in industrialized countries it was shown that the phosphorous (P) content in sewage is generated by faeces and washing water, and thus the P-flux can be correlated to the amount of food and detergents consumed [Baccini et al., 1993]. Carbon (C) is a good indicator for organic pollution and can also be correlated with the human activities 'to nourish' and 'to clean'.

Data sources
The data sources can be divided into measured data and calculated or estimated data. The measured data are marked in Fig. 1 with (*). On one hand they were taken from regional or national statistics. On the other hand during two months (one month dry and one month wet

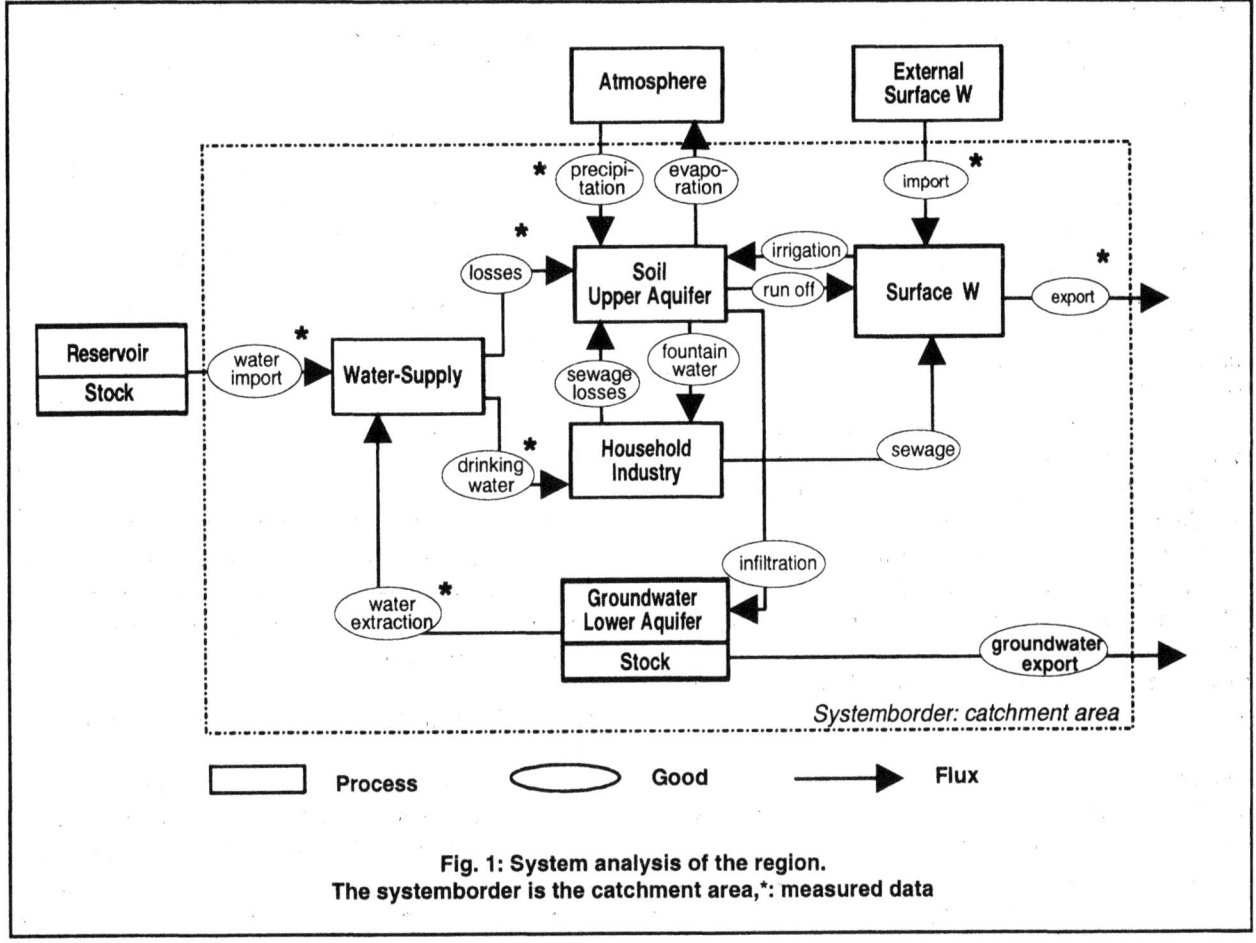

**Fig. 1: System analysis of the region.
The systemborder is the catchment area, *: measured data**

season) measurements of the water flux were carried out at the surface water before entering and before leaving the system and at the external surface water.

The dilution capacity of the surface water for sewage (carrying capacity) can be determined in two ways. First it is given as the rate of sewage to exported surface water. Second it is the rate of the concentration of the indicator element in the sewage and the concentration of the indicator element in the surface water leaving the region. P as dissolved orthophosphate (40 per cent of the total P, [Boller, 1994]) and C as Chemical Oxygen Demand (conversion factor COD to TOC of 3:1 [Boller, 1994]) were measured at the marked points including spot checks of sewage and water used for irrigation.

A plausibility control of the element fluxes (water flux * concentration) was made calculating the fluxes from the input side into *household*. With a survey the amount of food and detergents consumed were measured. The element fluxes were calculated as good amount *concentration. Both element fluxes were compared.

Results

Figure 2 shows the water balance for the study area for the year 1993. The error margin of the fluxes is about 20 per cent.

The largest fluxes in the system are precipitation (*atmosphere* to *soil/upper aquifer*) and evapotranspiration (*soil/upper aquifer* to *atmosphere*) consisting of the evaporation from the precipitation and the evapotranspiration from irrigation of plants. The total evapotranspiration is more than 90 per cent of the precipitation. Thus the net input from *atmosphere* is 2 mio m3/year.

The second important input flux is the import of drinking water from an external reservoir to *water supply*. It makes 85 per cent of the total flux into *water supply*. The other 15 per cent of the water are extracted from *lower aquifer*. The total amount of water entering *water supply* is about 70 per cent of the water amount leaving the region in form of surface water. Only a small proportion of 15 per cent of the *surface water* leaving the region originates from surface water entering the region (*external surface water*).

The infiltration rate into *lower aquifer* is about 2 mio m^3/year and lies in the same order of magnitude as the extraction rate. A doubling of the amount of water extracted could already lead to an overexploitation of the groundwater. Due to the geological conditions of the region no significant sewage infiltration due to leaking sewage sytems into *lower aquifer* is expected [Alarcon, Suarez, 1991].

In the urban area about 6 mio m^3/year are consumed, which correponds to 160 l/cap.year. The supply losses are 4 mio m^3/year. Eighty seven per cent of the consumed water is transported to *surface water* without any treatment and makes up about 30 per cent of the total output flux. That means that the carrying capacity of the region is about three. The measured P and COD concentrations in sewage were 15 ± 4 mgP/l and 420 ± 60 mg COD/l. The concentrations found in the surface water were 6.5 ± 0.5 mgP/l and 230 ± 30 mgCOD/l, thus leading to a dilution factor of two to three [Calixto, Valcarcel, 1994], [Rios, Tovar, 1994]. The high variation of more than 20 per cent for the sewage data is due to the high daily fluctuations in concentration and the low amount of samples taken. Nevertheless the dilution factors calculated out of both data series are in good agreement. The concentrations of P and C in the surface water before leaving the urban area are 100-and 40-fold respectively higher than the concentration in the surface water before entering the region.

In Table 1 the element fluxes calculated from the measured data in the environment and the element fluxes calculated from the measured data are shown. The results are in good agreement. This finding verifies that even with poor data availability and quality it is possible to establish an element flux, knowing the main sources of origin of this element and crosschecking it with spot measurements [see also Baccini et al., 1993].

Discussion

The MFA is used to analyze two possible scenarios in water resource management. The first scenario is an installation of a complete sewer system according to Swiss standards, the second an on-site sewage treatment, for example the installation of septic tanks. The changes in the system are shown in Figure 2.

Scenario 1: Installation of a complete sewer system

The installation of a complete sewer system would lead to fewer losses of sewage and to an increase in the flux sewage to surface water. Therefore, the water flux of the

Table 1: Comparison calculated P and C fluxes from measurements in surface water and measured inputs.

	P- Flux	C-Flux (TOC)
Calculated fluxes from measured values (concentration and water flux)	88 ± 18	1100 ± 300
Calculated fluxes from inputs	81 ± 17	1300 ± 490
"To nourish" (excreta)	60 ± 5	550 ± 46
"To clean" (washing water)	54 ± 15	970 ± 270
Irrigation (losses)	19 ± 2	390 ± 40
Sewage leakages	28 ± 5	400 ± 70
Erosion [Baccini, von Steiger, 1993]	14 ± 1	600 ± 400

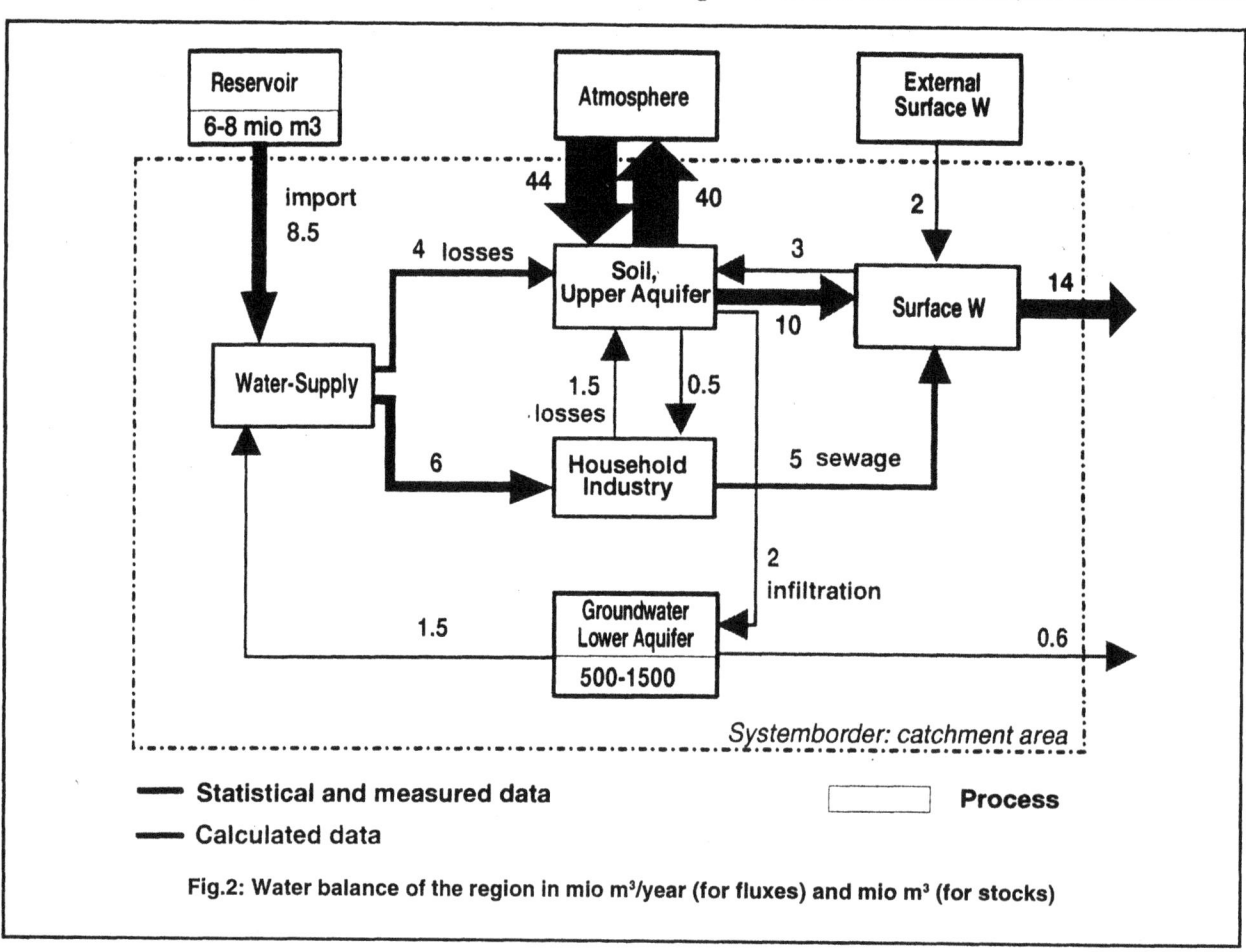

Fig.2: Water balance of the region in mio m³/year (for fluxes) and mio m³ (for stocks)

surface water will increase with growing population and water consumption per capita, thus doubling onto the year 2020 assuming a population growth rate of 2.7 per cent and no augmentation in water consumption per capita. This means that the dilution capacity of the region will be reduced to 1.5. The installation of a sewage treatment plant would reduce the P and C-flux to the surface water at about 80-95 per cent [Boller, 1994]. The concentrations of P and C in the surface water would be reduced compared to the situation today but will still be about 20 times higher (P) and 3 times higher (C) than the concentrations in the surface water before entering the region.

Scenario 2: On site treatment of sewage and disposal (septic tanks)

In this scenario the direct sewage flux to surface water will be zero. The water will infiltrate into *soil/upper aquifer* from where it later evapotranspirates to *atmosphere*, is exported by the *upper aquifer*, infiltrates to *lower aquifer* or exfiltrates to *surface water*. The amount of evapotranspiration is dependent especially on the vegetation around the soaking pits. It is assumed, that it is about 25 per cent of the infiltrating water. The amount of water exported by the *upper aquifer* or infiltrating to the *lower aquifer* is estimated to be 25 per cent. This, however has to be verified. Thus, the amount of exfiltrating water will be about 50 per cent of the sewage water. The quality of the water in the *upper aquifer* will decrease and not be suitable for drinking water. The quality of surface water will be determined by the quality of the exfiltrating water which depends on the water quality infiltrating from the septic tank and the capacity of the soil to adsorb (P) or degrade (C) pollutants. If it is assumed that 30-40 per cent of the pollutants are degraded in the septic tank, 90 per cent of the rest is adsorbed in the soil, and a part is exported by the *upper aquifer*, the proportion of pollutants exfiltrating to *surface wate*r will be about five per cent of the original load. Thus, the concentrations of P and C in the surface water leaving the region will be 10 times higher (P) and about double (C) the concentrations in the surface water before entering the region, being in the same order of magnitude as the concentrations found in scenario 1.

Conclusions

Even with low data availability and poor data quality the MFA can be applied as an instrument for early recognition of environmental problems. Thus future environmental consequences of planned activities can be recognized early, affording the possibility of avoiding resource depletion and evaluating environmental measures for improvement of water quality.

References

Alarcon M., Suarez L. M. (1991), 'Investigación de Aguas Subterráneas para Abastecimiento Urbano en la Ciudad de Tunja', Diploma Thesis, Universidad Pedagógica y Technológica de Colombia, Sogamoso.

Baccini P., Brunner P. (1991), *Metabolism of the Anthroposphere*, Springer Verlag, New York, Berlin, Heidelberg.

Baccini P., Daxbeck H., Glenck E., Henseler G., (1993), METAPOLIS: Güter-und Stoffumsätze in der Privathaushalten einer Stadt, Nat. Forschungsprogramm 25 'Stadt und Verkehr', 34 A + 34B.

Baccini P. von Steiger B., (1993), Die Stoffbilanzierung landwirtschaftlicher Böden- Eine Methode zur Früherkennung von Bodenveränderungen, Z. Pflanzenernähr. Bodenk. 156, 45-54.

Boller M. (1994), Vorlesungsskript Verfahrenstechnik I, Swiss Federal Institute of Technology, Zurich.

Bower B., Hyman E., White R. (1989), *Urbanization and Environmental Quality in Urbanization and Environment in Developing Countries*, US Agency for International Development, Washington D.C. 20523.

Calixto R., Valcarcel V., (1994), 'Caracterización Cualitativa y Cuantitativa del Abastecimiento de Agua para el Municipio de Tunja', Diploma Thesis, UNIBOYACA, Tunja.

DANE, (1994), Censo 1993, 1994.

EAAT, Empresa de Acueducto y Alcantarillado Tunja, (1993), Statistics and personal communications Javier Rodriguez.

Rios O., Tovar D., (1994), 'Analisis de Fuentes Receptoras y Vertimientos de Agua Residual en el Municipio de Tunja', Diploma Thesis, UNIBOYACA, Tunja.

WHO (1989), *Global Environmental Monitoring System, Global Freshwater Quality*, Basil Blackwell, Inc. p. 293ff.

Sustainability in guinea worm eradication programme

E.I. Braide and O.M. Obono, Nigeria

FOLLOWING AN AGREEMENT between Global 2000 of the Carter Foundation and the Nigerian Ministry of Health, the Nigeria Guinea Worm Eradication Programme (NIGEP) was inaugurated in 1988 with the objective of eradicating guinea worm disease from Nigeria by 31 December, 1995.

This paper examines strategies and structures established by NIGEP to ensure sustainability of eradication in the post-intervention period. It maintains that without maximum participation and empowerment of endemic communities towards guinea worm eradication, the sustainability of programme objectives in the post-intervention period may be jeopardized. South East Zone is the focus for discussion this paper.

Status of programme

At the apex of the organizational framework of the programme is the national steering committee (NSC), a body which co-ordinates eradication activities nationwide and provides linkage between NIGEP and agencies participating in the programme. Four zonal task forces (ZTFs) replicate the functions of the NSC at the Zonal level, each overseen by a zonal facilitator. State task forces (STFs) liaise with the zonal office and state governments. Within the state, local government task forces and village-based health workers (VBHWs) are the pivot of the eradication programme, reporting and managing cases and providing continuous health education in endemic communities. Their role has been enhanced by the establishment of village guinea worm eradication task forces (VTFs). By providing VBHWs with the support of local authorities, VTFs have integrated programme objectives with traditional and local patterns of governance (Figure 1).

Thus far, NIGEP has recorded an 88 per cent reduction in number of cases nationwide from 1988 to 1993 (Figure 2). NIGEP South East Zone has recorded a reduction of 93.6 per cent in cases from 278 635 cases in 1988 to 17,685 in December, 1994 (Figures 3 and 4) (NIGEP 1991, 1992, 1993, 1994).

This reduction has been achieved through health education, filter distribution/use, case management and water source protection. Chemical treatment of ponds with abate and provision of new water sources have only begun to feature significantly in eradication activities during the past year (Figure 5).

Strategy for sustainability

Health education is already being provided continuously by VBHWs and teachers but it is crucial that it be intensified at this time. The communities are being encouraged to take up surveillance of guinea worm-related activities for themselves beyond 1995. The rehabilitation of broken wells and provision of hand-dug wells, sand filtration and rain harvestation systems have commenced in the South East Zone both as a final onslaught against the guinea worm disease and as a basis for its sustainable eradication. In view of the high level of awareness of the aetiology of the disease, the production and distribution of cloth filters will become unnecessary once safe water sources are available to vulnerable communities. The

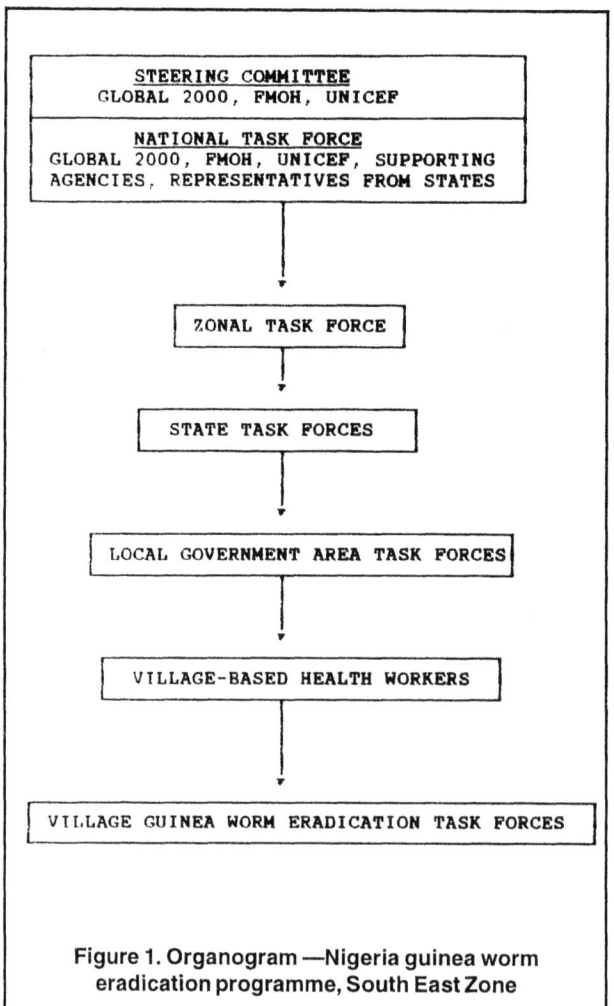

Figure 1. Organogram —Nigeria guinea worm eradication programme, South East Zone

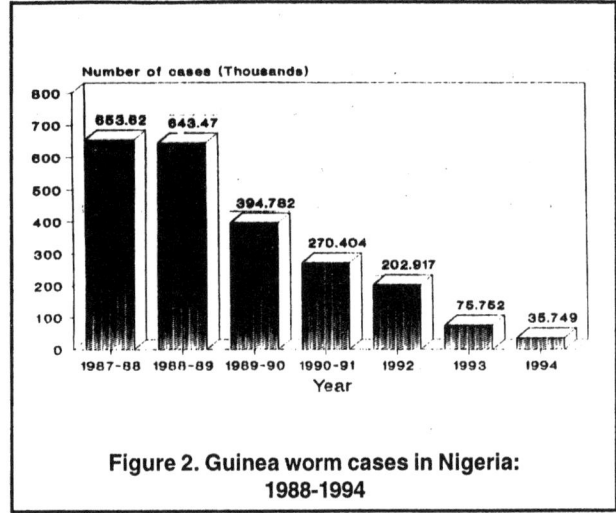

Figure 2. Guinea worm cases in Nigeria: 1988-1994

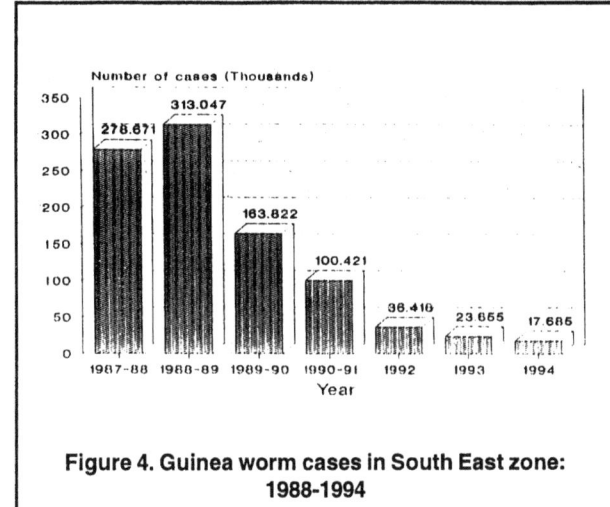

Figure 4. Guinea worm cases in South East zone: 1988-1994

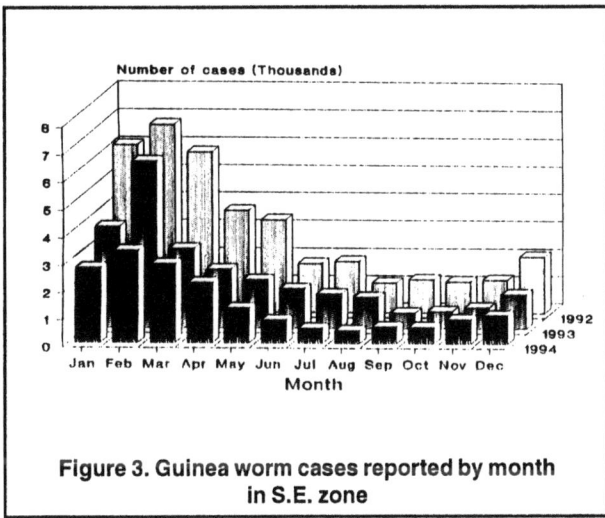

Figure 3. Guinea worm cases reported by month in S.E. zone

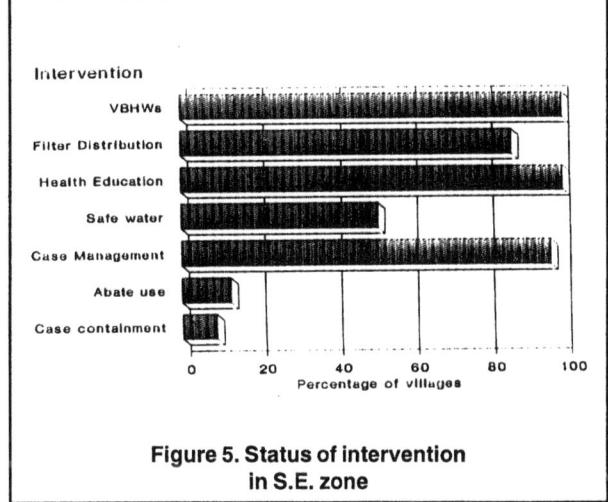

Figure 5. Status of intervention in S.E. zone

de-emphasis of NIGEP's focal strategy thus becomes a signal for community empowerment, with a view to stopping further transmission of the disease and contamination of water sources.

The eradication of guinea worm is demonstrably sustainable where the following conditions exist:

- A high level of awareness of the aetiology of the disease which has been achieved through NIGEP's South East Zone intensive and continuous health education especially in schools.
- Active surveillance to detect and manage new cases in order to prevent contamination of water sources which is already in place.
- The provision of adequate safe water supply which is the thrust of intervention in the last transmission season.
- A community-based initiative which will monitor, supervise and ensure compliance in the post-intervention period. This has been initiated in the formation of village task forces.

Obviously, the sustainability of guinea worm eradication hinge on a community-based initiative. In NIGEP South East Zone, village guinea worm eradication task forces (VTFs) have been inaugurated in 1239 (89 per cent) of the 1396 vulnerable villages.

VTFs are composed of religious leaders, teachers, representatives of womens' groups, age grade leaders, health club leaders, village development officers, leaders of village development committees, etc.. Each VTF has the village head as its chairman and the VBHW as secretary and is charged with protection of existing water sources, pond treatment with abate as well as provision of a safe alternative water source (preferably hand-dug wells).

Central to the use of the VTF as a community-based initiative is the fact that it makes guinea worm eradication sustainable while at the same time empowering the community to achieve this.

References

Adeniyi, J.B., Braide, E., Brieger W., Edet, E., Nwobi, B., Diaz A.L. 1992. Health Education and community mobilization strategy in NIGEP - Guidelines for Local Programme managers. 47pp.

NIGEP 1991. Third National Case Search Statistical Summary: July 1, 1989 - June 30, 1990. 48pp.

NIGEP 1992. Fourth National Case Search Statistical Summary: July 1, 1990 - June 30, 1991. 129pp.

NIGEP 1993. Monthly surveillance report January - December, 1992. 130pp.

NIGEP 1994. Monthly surveillance report January - December, 1994. 126pp

NIGEP S.E. Zone/Unicef/CUSO 1993. Manual for training of primary school teachers for school based health education. 36pp.

NIGEP S.E. Zone 1994. Inventory of water sources in guinea worm endemic villages of South East Nigeria. 26pp.

Sustaining health from water and sanitation systems

Steven A. Esrey, New York

HEALTH IMPROVEMENTS ARE often cited as a rationale for investing in water and sanitation. Many donors justify investments in water and sanitation from health budgets. Health benefits are also cited as a measure of success or outcome of water and sanitation improvements. Many projects are evaluated by health indicators. These differences, rationale and outcome, are not trivial differences. For example, people demand water for convenience, which improvements provide by bringing piped supplies closer to people and offering more water for a variety of uses. Donors provide funds for water to improve health. Is convenience achieved or health improved and are both sustained? If both the rationale and the outcome are not considered, it is unlikely that both objectives can be achieved much less sustained.

Why provide water and sanitation? There are many reasons for investing in water and sanitation besides the obvious linkages with health. They are basic human needs and rights; economic benefits, including re-use of waste, increasing tourism through a hygienic environment, and overall savings to society from reduced disease care; and increased dignity, convenience and quality of life. Nevertheless, the same question should be asked if sustainability is important. For example, is human dignity the reason for investing in water and sanitation or is human dignity the expected outcome of investing in water and sanitation?

Three types of information indicate that there are substantial health benefits from improvements in water and sanitation. These include theoretical, historical and epidemiological. Theory, backed up by empirical evidence, suggests that as pathogen exposure is reduced so is disease (Esrey et al., 1995). A healthy person or child may become exposed to pathogens, and if the load is sufficient, become diseased. If the disease is severe enough, (s)he will die. This progression of events (Figure 1) also highlights three points of intervention, primary, secondary and tertiary. For the example of diarrhoea, a tertiary intervention would be oral rehydration (ORS). ORS prevents death, once a child has diarrhoea. ORS also treats diarrhoea. Tertiary interventions are not intended to reduce exposure to pathogens and do not impact on the subsequent severity of disease except that early diagnosis can help make a tertiary intervention effective in preventing death. In a similar vein, secondary interventions are not concerned with the amount of exposure, but try to prevent or reduce disease severity. Immunization (e.g. measles) prevents disease and consequently death, while effectively treating exposure. Primary interventions work in much the same way with the exception that they are intended to prevent people from being exposed to pathogens in the first place. Sanitation, hygiene and water prevent exposure to pathogens, thereby preventing disease and death. As such, a primary intervention treats health. Thus, water and sanitation are health care, while immunization and ORS are disease care interventions.

In a similar fashion, sanitation, hygiene and safe water can be considered as primary, secondary and tertiary barriers between health and exposure to disease (Figure 2). Sanitation is the primary barrier to vent pathogens gaining access to the environment. Said in another way, without sanitation, the environment is exposed to pathogens. Hands, food, objects, soil and water become contaminated. Effective secondary barriers are needed to prevent continued transmission of pathogens. Thus, hygiene practices such as hand washing, better food handling, cleaning the living and cooking areas, personal and domestic hygiene and making water safe can be effective interventions to prevent humans from ingesting pathogens. As shown in Figure 2, attempts to improve one hygiene area (e.g. safe water) does not reduce transmission through food, soil, objects and hands. Thus, a multiplicity of efforts are required to reduce transmission of pathogens. Single hygiene effects are unlikely to reduce disease unless the pathogens are transmitted through only one route.

Historical evidence indicates that preventive measures effectively reduced disease and death due to a number of killing diseases (McKeown et al., 1975). These preventive measures include better water and sanitation conditions, better and more varied diets, increased education and understanding of the germ theory of disease. The improvements in water and sanitation included better sewage disposal, higher quality water, and more water for keeping people and their environments clean. Thus, the improvements in water and sanitation could not be ascribed to any one component of the improvements. This raises the question, if only one condition was improved, would the improvements in health or life expectancy have occurred?

Recent epidemiological studies have helped in separating out the external influences (e.g. education) from water and sanitation improvements, as well as the influence of one component of better water and sanitation (e.g. safe water) from another (e.g. more water). Two types of analyses have been completed. The first was a review of all epidemiological studies (Esrey et al., 1991). Based on this review the relative reduction in diarrhoea was estimated from improvements in safe water, increases in water quantity, better hygiene practices, and improved sanitation (Figure 3). The largest improvements were found for sanitation and hygiene improvements, about a 35 per cent reduction in diarrhoea. Increases in water quantity were associated with a reduction in diarrhoea of about 20 per cent percent, while safe water was associated with only a 15 per cent reduction in diarrhoea. This suggests that sanitation acts as a successful primary barrier to reduce environmental exposure of pathogens and better hygiene acts as secondary barrier further to reduce transmission of pathogens.

The question of why safe water has less of an effect, or even a marginal effect, on diarrhoea than improved sanitation or better hygiene goes against traditional thinking. A recent review of waterborne outbreaks (Ewald, 1991) indicates that many outbreaks of pathogens associated with diarrhoea are in fact not waterborne. While cholera was reported to be predominantly waterborne, a recent analysis of cholera outbreaks suggests that for every waterborne outbreak there are two non-waterborne outbreaks. Less than 50 per cent of outbreaks from common diarrhoeal pathogens (e.g. shigella, coli, and campylobacter) are food borne.

A recent study examined the joint effect of water and sanitation on diarrhoea and nutritional status of children 3-36 months of age (Esrey, 1995). Three types of water and three types of sanitation systems were examined, unimproved, intermediate and optimum. Unimproved systems included ponds, lakes and traditional water sources and fields for sanitation. Intermediate water usually indicated a communal tap while intermediate sanitation was predominantly a pit latrine. Optimum water was a supply on the premises or in the dwelling, while optimum sanitation included pour flush toilets or sewage connections. The analysis included nearly 17000 children, two-thirds of whom lived in rural areas, from eight countries in three continents. The results on diarrhoea among urban children for the nine different water and sanitation options are shown in Figure 4. The highest rates of diarrhoea were found among children without improved sanitation, regardless of the type of water supply found. The effect of sanitation was largest when improved water was absent, an 11 per cent difference in the prevalence of diarrhoea between unimproved and intermediate sanitation in the absence of improved water. This was equivalent to a 44 per cent reduction in diarrhoea prevalence. The difference in diarrhoea prevalence for intermediate water compared to unimproved water in the absence of improved sanitation was two per cent, or the equivalent of an eight per cent reduction in diarrhoea. Similar findings were found when nutritional status was examined. Water had a small effect, while improved sanitation had a substantial effect on nutritional status, both height and weight.

The effects of improved water and sanitation were greatest when improvements occurred together. The complementarity of effects has also been reported in other studies (Burger and Esrey, 1994). As a general rule the effect of improvements in sanitation are greatest when improved water is available and vice versa. In addition, the effect of WES interventions may be enhanced when other external factors are present, including higher education and higher income. Thus, efforts to reduce disease and improve health can be maximized by seeking linkages with other programmes.

Besides reductions in diarrhoea, improvements in water and sanitation also reduce the prevalence and severity of other diseases, such as guinea worm, intestinal parasites and skin diseases (Esrey et al., 1991). Improvements in nutritional status, including a reduction in the prevalence of stunting and wasting of children (Esrey, 1995) as well as savings in energy expended (Diaz et al., 1995) have also been reported.

These impacts helped form the basis for the conceptual framework for UNICEF's Water and Environmental Sanitation (WES) Programme (Figure 5). Briefly, the objectives of UNICEF programmes are child survival, protection and development. The WES contributions to this are safe environmental sanitation, better hygiene practices and maternal care, and household water security. These programme interventions, which should be integrated to maximize impact, are mediated through less disease, better nutrition, less time and energy spent in collecting water, better education of children and greater income potential from water and sanitation improvements. All of the mediating factors are well documented.

The lower half of Figure 5 indicates the conditions necessary to secure household water security, better hygiene and maternal care and safer environmental sanitation at the community level. These are primarily greater equity in the access to and control of available resources. Yet access to and control of resources will not provide sustainable resources unless people are empowered to act for themselves, including their participation in the design, implementation and evaluation of WES interventions.

References

Burger SE, Esrey SA. 'Water and sanitation: health and nutrition benefits to children'. *Child Growth and Nutrition in Developing Countries: Priorities for Action*, Ed. by Pinstrup Andersen P et al. Cornell University Press, Ithaca NY, 1995; Chapter 9:153-175.

Diaz E, Esrey SA, Hurtado E. Social and biological impact of piped water in rural Guatemala. Report prepared for CIDA, 1995.

Esrey SA, Feachem RG, Hughes J. 'Interventions for the control of diarrhoeas diseases among young children: improving water supplies and exoreta disposal facilities'. Bulletin of the World Health Organization, 1985; 63:757-772.

Esrey SA, Potash JB, Roberts L, Shiff C. 'Effects of improved water supply and sanitation on ascariasis, diarrhoea, dracunculiasis, hookworm infection, schistosomiasis, and trachoma'. Bulletin of the World Health Organization, 1991; 69(5):609-621.

Esrey SA. 'Incremental improvements in water and sanitation and incremental improvements in health'. *American Journal of Epidemiology*, 1995 (Accepted).

Ewald PW. 'Waterborne transmission and the evolution of virulence among gastrointestinal bacteria'. *Epidemiology and Infection*, 1991; 106:83-119.

McKeown T. Record RG, and Turner RD. 'An interpretation of the decline of mortality in England and Wales during the twentieth century'. Population studies, 1975; 29:391-422.

Sack D, Shamsul Hoque ATM, Huq A, Etheridge M. 'Is protection against shigellosis induced by natural infection with Plesiomonas shigelloides?' *Lancet*, 1994; 343: 1413-15.

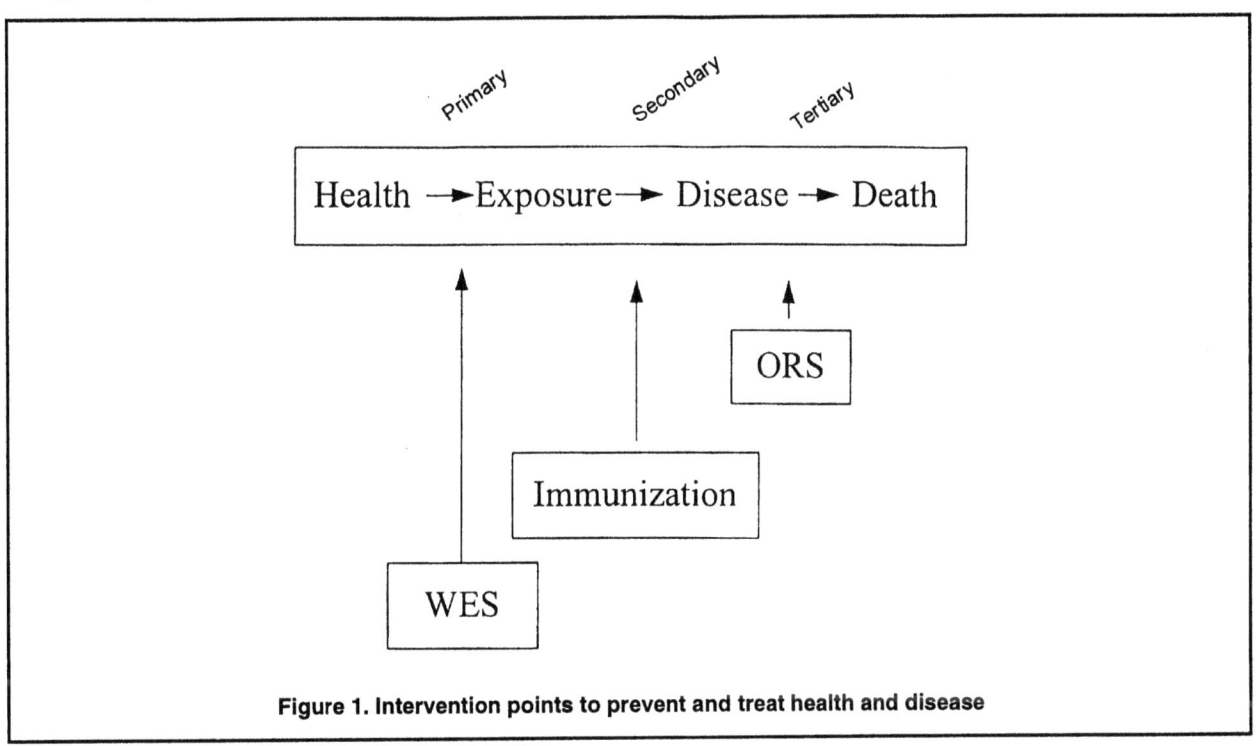

Figure 1. Intervention points to prevent and treat health and disease

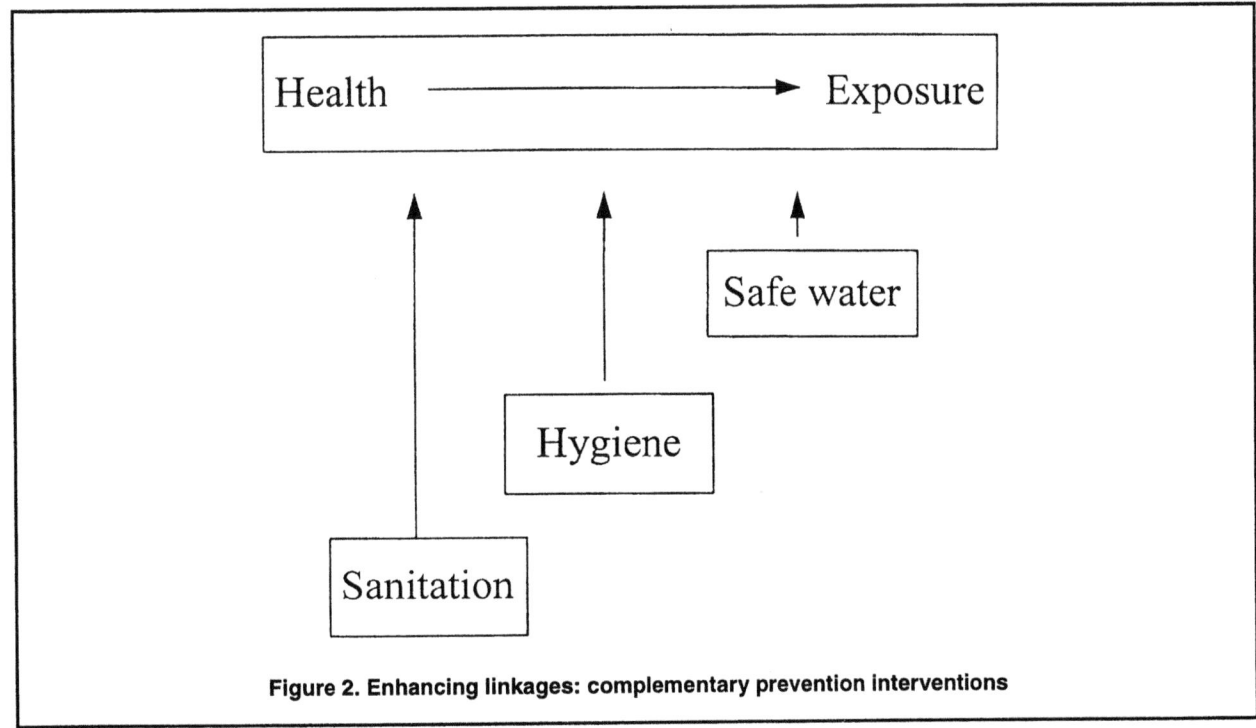

Figure 2. Enhancing linkages: complementary prevention interventions

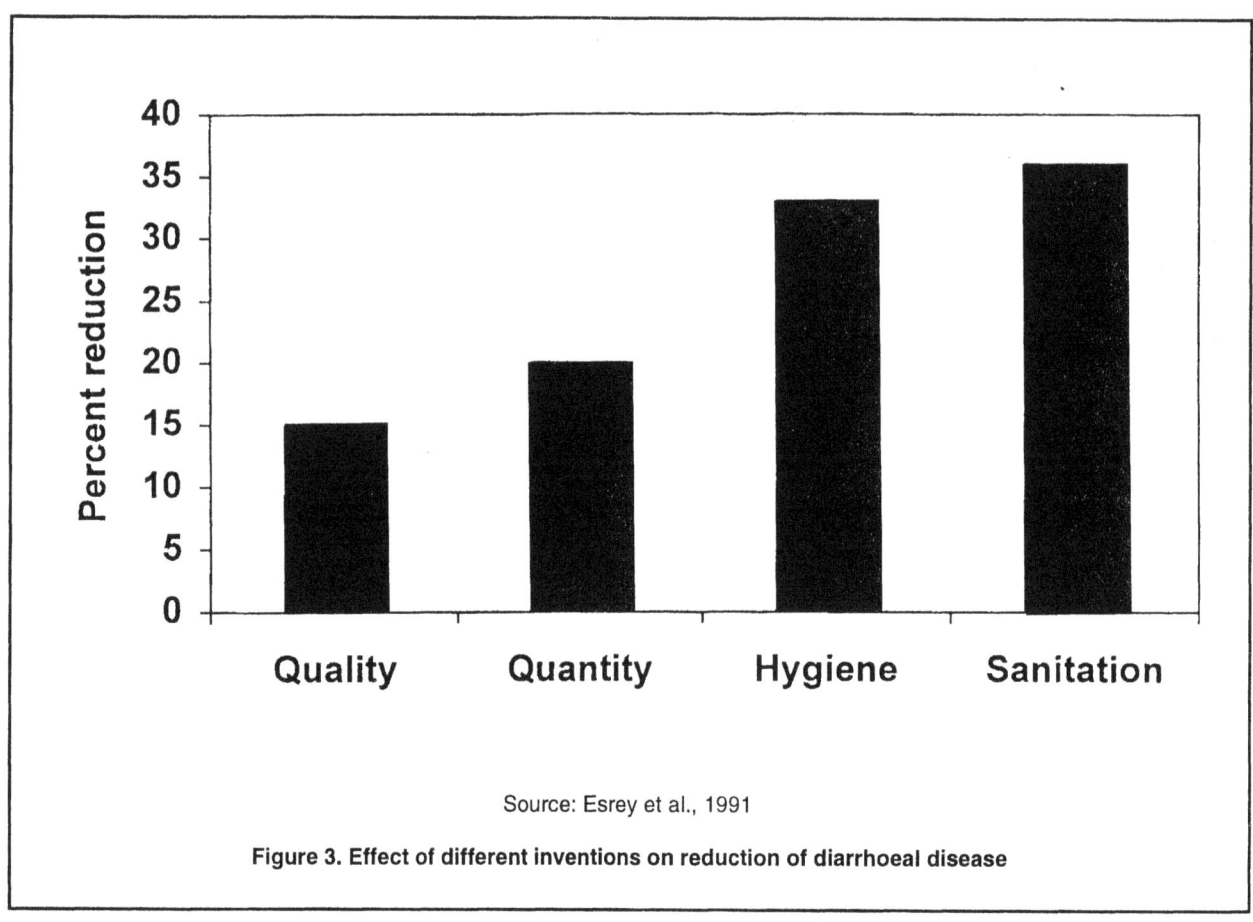

Source: Esrey et al., 1991

Figure 3. Effect of different inventions on reduction of diarrhoeal disease

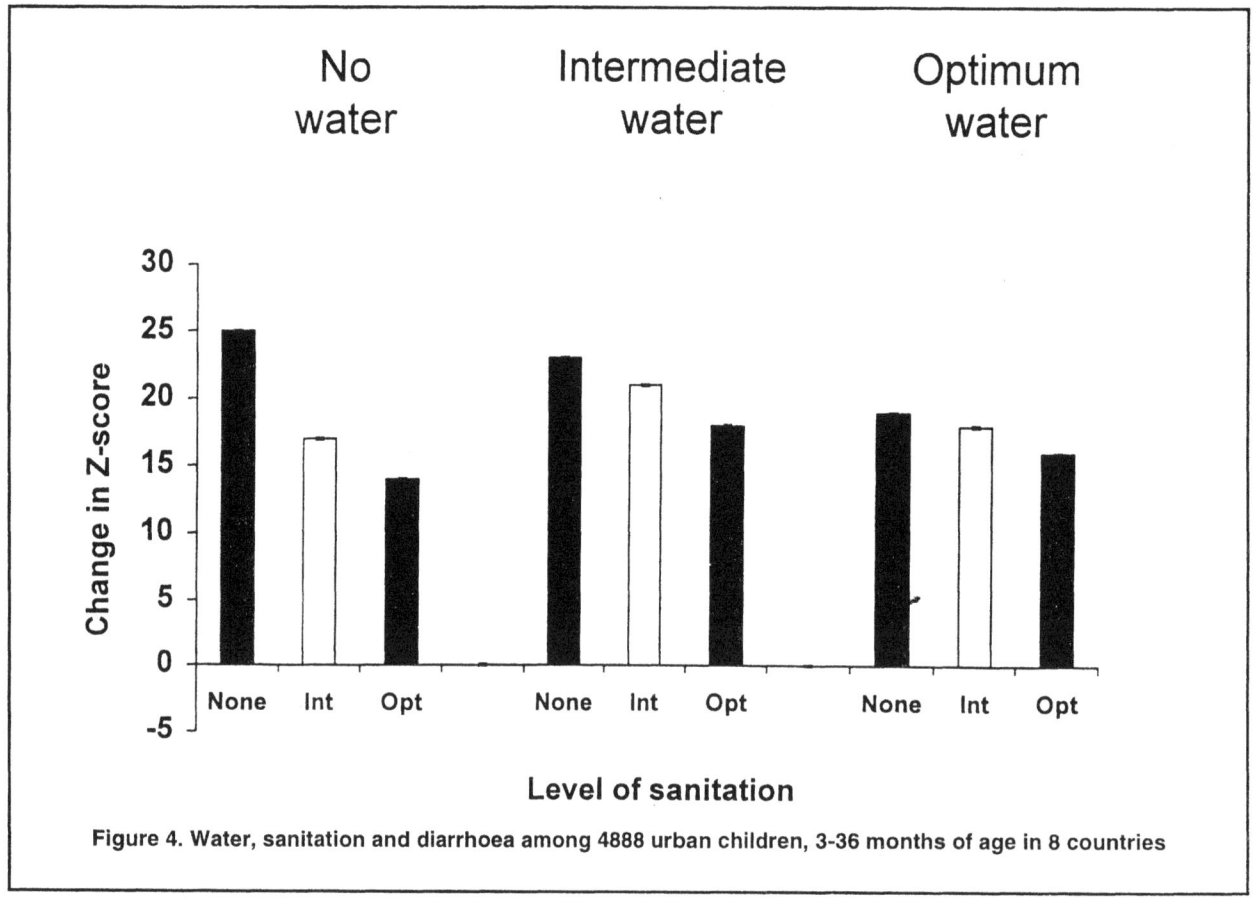

Figure 4. Water, sanitation and diarrhoea among 4888 urban children, 3-36 months of age in 8 countries

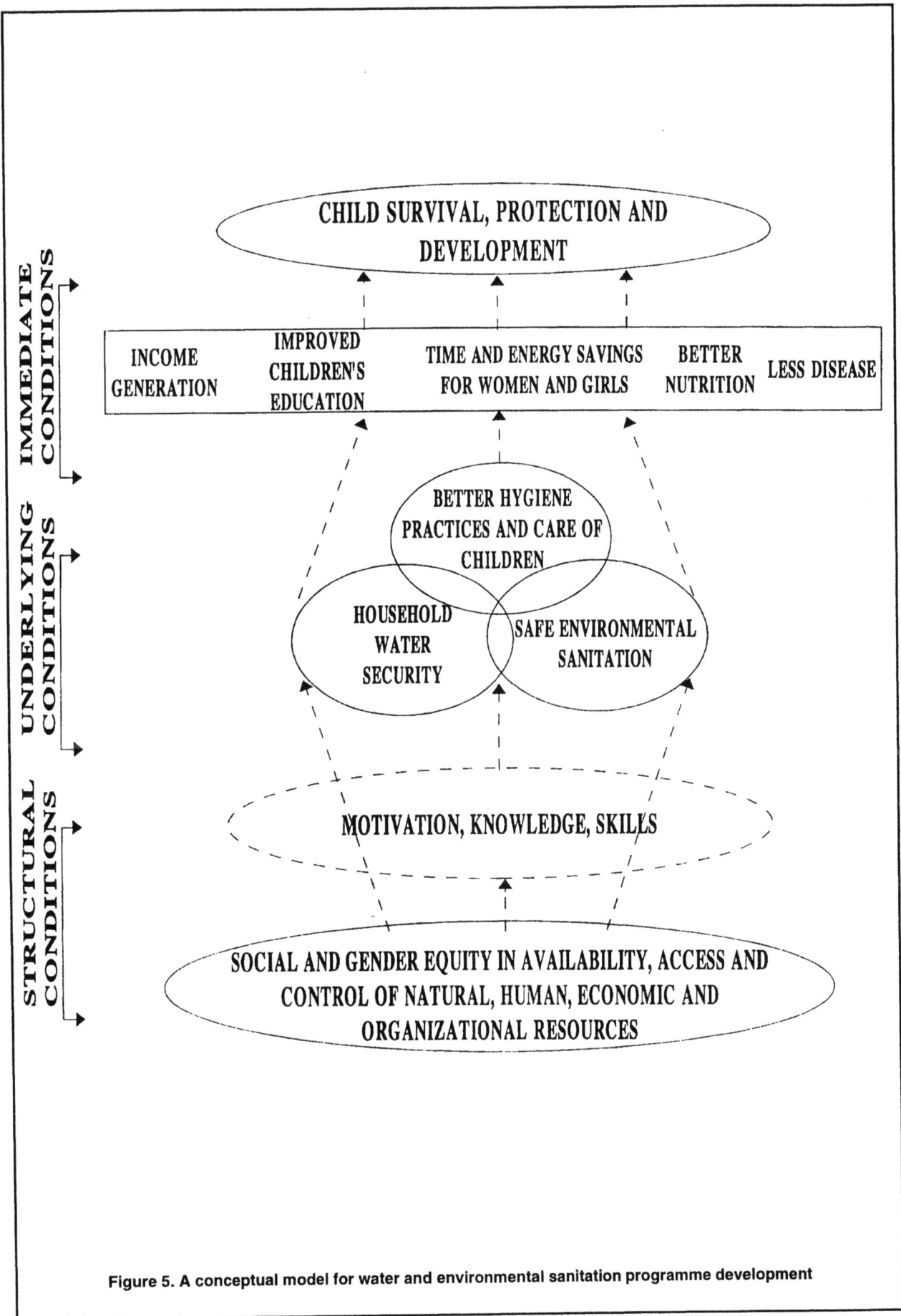

Figure 5. A conceptual model for water and environmental sanitation programme development

Reducing water losses in Vietnam

Malcolm Farley, UK

THE VIETNAMESE WATER industry is entering a period of change, acknowledging water losses of 45-70 per cent of production, and striving to reduce them. The recent 'open door' policy has increased the pace of change by exposing companies to new markets, improved material standards and quality, and the transfer of technology. In 1994, the Ministry of Urban Construction issued an order to water companies to reduce water loss by 50 per cent over the next ten years, and issued guidelines on how this should be achieved. The steps are; to review losses and identify the components, to calculate the cost of control, to eliminate flat rate tariffs, and to improve public awareness. The initiative was supported by the World Bank, who appointed the author as a training consultant to work with water company directors and senior engineers to help them develop short-term action plans and longer-term programmes which are appropriate to the Vietnamese culture, and sustainable within their social and political structure. To this end, training workshops, in Hanoi and Ho Chi Minh City, were organized throughout 1994.

The workshops

The workshops were attended by 70 delegates representing almost all of the water supply companies in Vietnam. The majority of delegates were directors, vice directors, and heads of technical, financial, and planning departments. The primary objective of the workshops was to enable each delegate to design both short-term and long-term programmes to reduce water loss in his or her particular company. This would be achieved by bringing together delegates from different water companies, but with common problems, so that ideas could be developed from discussion groups and by example (some delegates had achieved success in 'model' or pilot areas of their company). The training consultant's task was one of facilitator — the aim was not to compare Vietnamese practice with other countries, nor to dwell too much on the technology of leakage monitoring and detection. The aim was to encourage delegates to develop their own sustainable solutions, to build on what they have rather than devise solutions which are unworkable or unaffordable. This philosophy was implemented during the workshops by encouraging delegates to:

- examine the scale of water loss
- identify the causal factors
- assess the relative significance of non-physical and physical losses
- review appropriate tools, methodologies and equipment to support programmes to reduce water loss
- design programmes which were feasible and sustainable for the Vietnamese economy, culture and institutional organization.

Delegates were therefore encouraged to discuss openly the constraints and weaknesses (and also the strengths) of their system characteristics and their existing procedures, and to propose only those solutions or actions which could be realistically implemented. The workshop style of training course was unfamiliar to the delegates, but one which they welcomed. Previous training had consisted of formal lectures with few opportunities for discussion and no participation by the delegates.

Components of water loss

Delegates were appraised of water loss figures for countries worldwide, noting comparisons between developed and developing countries, the varying significance of the ratios of physical losses to non-physical losses, and their components. Delegates were then divided into two discussion groups and asked to consider which of the components were most significant in the Vietnamese water industry. From the presentations which followed this exercise, several important points arose, which influenced the priority tasks for the action plans.

Non-physical losses

These are generally higher than the physical leakage from the distribution system. The main components of the non-physical losses are;

- meter under-registration caused by oversized meters and inaccurate recording at low flows
- meters not working (poor quality, worn out, broken or deliberately damaged)
- theft and waste of water from illegal connections or from by-passed meters
- waste of water from consumers on flat rate tariff.

In addition, there is widespread loss of revenue, influenced by the dubious practice of meter reading, billing and revenue collection all being performed by the same employee. This leads to misreading, mis-billing or non-billing, and withholding of collected revenue. Some companies are trying to overcome this factor by imposing stricter controls and supervision on the meter readers.

Physical losses and detection techniques
Discussions with the delegates established that physical losses are of secondary importance to non-physical losses. In common with distribution systems worldwide physical losses in Vietnam are from leakage in the distribution system, from joints, flanges, gaskets, valve spindles, and ferrule connections on service pipes. Leakage in Vietnam is particularly influenced by:

- poor quality materials and fittings (one company used thin walled steel pipe previously used as an oil pipeline)
- poor main-laying practice
- shallow cover and damage from traffic vibration
- damage caused during road-building, from subsidence, and from bombing during the war.

Leakage control policy in all companies is passive, i.e. only visible leaks are repaired. However, one company, Haiphong, has introduced pilot areas to demonstrate district metering, a methodology for monitoring night flows into a discrete area. Delegates were shown alternative control methodologies, emphasizing the benefit of monitoring flows into small districts to detect invisible leakage and using simple sounding sticks to locate individual leaks. However, delegates felt that most leaks appeared at the surface and regular sounding is unnecessary. Flow metering principles, particularly the benefits of temporary insertion turbine meters for checking production and bulk meters, were also illustrated and discussed. Most companies had no means of accurately measuring production or consumption due to lack of production meters to measure flows into the distribution system, and inadequate or inaccurate consumer meters.

Immediate action plans

It was accepted by all delegates that the main source of water loss is from illegal connections or illegal use, and from consumer meter under-registration. The points to address in an immediate action plan are therefore:

- to ensure that all consumers are metered, removing the flat rate tariff, which does not encourage wise use of water
- to stop illegal use by introducing more rigorous investigation of illegal connections, damaged and by-passed meters, and by ensuring fines are imposed (sometimes by public 'shaming' through the media).

Secondary actions would include the replacement of non-working meters, and a meter purchasing policy which ensures that only meters which can accurately measure low flows are used — the Chinese meters used by most companies are grossly inaccurate.

One company is entering a joint venture with a French meter manufacturer to produce a low-cost locally made meter, other companies are using meters imported from Thailand. Checking or installing production meters to enable more accurate water loss figures to be calculated was also a priority.

Some companies are also introducing organizational changes to improve the accountability of the meter readers. It was agreed, however, that most institutional and organizational changes would be part of a longer-term strategy.

Case studies

Water loss reduction programmes are being carried out in Hanoi and Haiphong, and these were used to give delegates guidelines for formulating their own programmes. Of particular significance in the Hanoi programme is a public awareness campaign, which has heightened the perception of the community to the value of clean water and the damage caused by waste. The problem of non-physical losses has been recognized by the authorities, and taken up by the community, represented by the Hanoi Peoples' Committee. In Hanoi, water loss is increasing (currently 160 000 cubic metres/day) while the source is being depleted — the groundwater level is dropping by 1.0m/year. Only 32 per cent of total production is billed. The 68 per cent of water lost comprises 43 per cent non-billed, 20 per cent leakage, and five per cent for the water company's own use. The volume of billed water is decreasing (28 per cent at the end of May 1994), despite the repair of 1000 leaks/year and disconnection of 2000 illegal connections/year. It is therefore assumed that the rate of increase of illegal connections is greater than the rate of leak repair. Consumer studies are seen as an immediate requirement to identify or address consumer waste, illegal connections, tariff charges and consumer contracts (only 50 per cent of Hanoi's 200 000 consumers have contracts for revenue payment). Solutions are linked to:

- improvements to the billing system, and meter reading/collection procedures
- changes to metering policy (one tap dripping at 0.4 l/minute wastes 600 l/day) to install better meters
- payment for the meters. If the company pays for the meter the payback on savings per consumer of 18 cubic metres/month would be less than four months.

Physical losses are also being addressed in Hanoi. One person has been nominated to lead a leak detection team. Sounding sticks have been issued, and staff are being trained in their use, and in the use of other leak detection equipment. An estimated 10-20 per cent water saving was made during a 'Water Week', a cost saving of US$50 000. However, people are slow to change their habits, and campaigns should continue, supported by changes to the tariff and billing systems, which at present give no incentive to save water. To support the programme further, and to emphasize the importance of institutional and organizational changes, the Hanoi water sector was reorganized in early 1994 into a new company — Hanoi Water

Business Company, whose business aims are to have 100 per cent of consumers registered, 100 per cent meter installation, not less than 85 per cent of production collected as revenue, tariff fully enforced, and a 24 hour service level.

At Haiphong Water Company, pilot studies are being carried out in three sub-districts. The studies have demonstrated the importance of institutional support — the company receives a government subsidy, but has also changed its management structure — it now has a supportive and enthusiastic director, whose philosophy is to reduce water loss, increase capacity, and improve management. Whilst recognizing that the company must continue to supply its consumers the only way to reduce losses is progressively to install new consumer meters and to monitor and control the flow into and out of the network via small 'management zones'. Increased level of service and increased revenue would follow.

Like the Hanoi study, the Haiphong study also emphasizes the importance of raising public awareness, with strong institutional support from the local authorities, the peoples' committees, and the police. Losses in the pilot area, after pipework rehabilitation, have been reduced to 20 per cent. Payment is now collected from 99 per cent of consumers, who pay their bills at a central office 5-10 days after being billed.

Conclusions

During the workshops delegates gave the impression that now that the government had initiated a 'wind of change' they wished to be empowered to activate action plans. The workshops concentrated on the programmes to reduce non-physical losses, because in most companies this is where the majority of losses occur. However, although the time for the introduction of advanced technology is still some years away, there are a number of techniques, like district metering, and some technologies, like flowmeters, insertion meters, and equipment for listening for leak noise, which were of interest to the delegates, and which are wholly appropriate to the Vietnam water industry.

The workshops highlighted the key steps for action to advance sustainable solutions. The use of local peoples' committees to lead public awareness campaigns and to enforce new practices is one of the strengths which can be developed.

Natural coagulants — a sustainable approach

Geoff Folkard, John Sutherland and Reya Al-Khalili, UK

THE *M. OLEIFERA* TREE is a native of Northern India which now grows widely throughout the tropics. English vernacular names include 'drumstick' (shape of the pods) and 'horseradish' (taste of the roots). It may be propagated from seeds or cuttings, even in poor soils, requiring minimal horticultural attention and is able to survive long periods of drought. It grows rapidly: growth of up to four metres in height, flowering and fruiting were all observed within one year during trials near Nsanje, Southern Malawi. Extended and multiple harvests in a single year are evident in many parts of the world. The many products and numerous uses of the tree are given:

Vegetable
- Green pods, leaves, flowers and roasted seeds are highly nutritious.

Oil
- Seeds contain 40 per cent vegetable oil by weight and may be used for cooking, soap manufacture, cosmetics base and as a lamp fuel.

Coagulant
- Seeds used traditionally for 'household treatment' in the Sudan and Kenya.
- Successfully used at pilot and full scale water treatment works in Malawi.
- Presscake remaining after oil extraction effective as a coagulant — bench scale testing.
- Potential for use as an aid to primary sedimentation in wastewater treatment — bench scale testing.

Other uses
- All parts of the plant are used in a variety of traditional medicines.
- Presscake as a soil conditioner/fertilizer and potentially as an animal/poultry feed supplement.
- Green leaves as a fertilizer — mulch.
- Powdered seed used in ointment to treat common bacterial skin infections.
- Grown as live fences and windbreaks.
- Fuelwood source following coppicing.
- Agroforestry within an intercropping system, also providing semi-shade.
- Wood pulp for papermaking industry.
- Planted for specific protective and soil melioration functions.
- Planted as an attractive ornamental tree.

M. oleifera is a multipurpose tree of enormous potential. Multipurpose trees are cultivated and managed in such a way that they foster sustainable land use with more than one product and/or function. They are particularly significant in agroforestry systems, performing specific, protective and stabilizing functions.

Water treatment

River water drawn for human consumption and general household use can be highly turbid particularly in the rainy season. River silt is churned into suspension and runoff from fields and other surfaces carries solid material, bacteria and other micro-organisms into the river. It is of paramount importance to remove as much of this suspended matter as possible prior to a disinfection stage and subsequent consumption. This can generally only be achieved by the addition of coagulants to the raw water within a controlled treatment sequence. In many developing countries proprietary chemical coagulants, such as alum and synthetic polyelectrolytes are either not available locally or are imported using foreign exchange.

A viable alternative is the use of crushed seed of *M. oleifera* as a natural coagulant. The seed pods are allowed to dry naturally on the tree prior to harvesting. The seeds are easily shelled, crushed and sieved using traditional techniques employed for the production of maize flour. The crushed seed powder, when mixed with water, yields water soluble proteins that possess a net positive charge. Dosing solutions are generally prepared as 1-3 per cent solutions. The solution acts as a natural cationic polyelectrolyte during treatment. (Sutherland et al., 1990)

River water treatment at pilot scale

It is now regarded as axiomatic that both water and wastewater technology for developing countries must be no more complex than strictly necessary, be robust and cheap to install and maintain. A prototype treatment works was designed founded on this philosophy. The pilot plant was constructed within the grounds of the Thyolo Water Treatment Works, the works being controlled by the Ministry of Works and Supplies Water Department of the Malawi Government. The system was successfully commissioned during the 1992 rainy season with the source river exhibiting turbidity levels in excess of 400 NTU throughout the study period. Solids removal within the plant was consistently above 90 per cent following a gravel bed flocculation stage and plain horizontal flow sedimentation. Subsequent rapid gravity sand filtration gave a final, treated water turbidity generally well below 5 NTU. *M. oleifera* seed dose ranged from 75-250mg/1 depending on the initial raw water turbidity. (Folkard et al., 1993)

River water treatment at full scale
In February 1994, the main Thyolo works was operated using *M. oleifera* solution as coagulant. The works comprise upflow contact clarifiers followed by rapid gravity filters and chlorinator. The clarifiers are in a state of disrepair with the impeller drives and chemical feed pumps inoperative. Alum solution is introduced into the incoming flow of 60 cubic metres per hour by simple gravity feed. Comparable treatment performance with alum was achieved. Inlet turbidities of 270-380 NTU were consistently reduced to below 4 NTU. This was the first time that *M. oleifera* had been successfully used as a primary coagulant on such a scale with the treated water entering supply. (Sutherland et al., 1994)

M. oleifera seed for the full scale trials was purchased from enthusiastic villagers in the Nsanje region. The tree is widely cultivated in this area, being highly prized as a source of fresh, green vegetable.

Alum and soda ash (for final pH correction) for the Thyolo works were imported from South Africa at an annual imported equivalent cost of £26 000 (March 1993). It was estimated that if the water utility established and maintained a plantation of *M. oleifera* trees for oil production/presscake coagulant, a net operating profit would be achieved.

Treatment of eutrophic water
Treatment studies have recently been conducted at bench scale on a eutrophic lake water serving the main treatment works to Harare, Zimbabwe. (Sutherland et al., 1995) The impounded water contains much light organic matter in suspension due to high algal growth and exhibits relatively low turbidity throughout the year. It is problematic to treat consuming significant quantities of alum (as primary coagulant) and activated silica (as weighting agent). Alum floc carryover from the clarifiers causes 'filter blinding' and the sludge from the clarifiers is voluminous, difficult to dewater and presents pollution problems on discharge to the receiving water. *M. oleifera* in combination with sodium bentonite as weighting agent produced a final water quality equivalent to that produced using the conventional chemical coagulants. The sludge was significantly more compact and represents a potentially useful output as a soil conditioner/fertilizer.

M. oleifera as vegetable/oil source
M. oleifera pods are an important commercial vegetable crop throughout India. They are also exported fresh under refrigeration and in cans to countries with sizeable Indian communities.

The leaves have outstanding nutritional qualities — amongst the best of all the perennial tropical vegetables. The protein content is 27 per cent and significant quantities of calcium, iron, phosphorous and vitamins A and C are also present. A particular advantage to people nutritionally at risk is that leaves can be harvested during the dry season when no other fresh vegetables are available.

M. oleifera seed contains 40 per cent by weight of oil. The fatty acid profile shows oleic acid at 73 per cent confirming that the oil is similar to olive oil and thus of high quality and high market value. Laboratory tests at Leicester confirm that the presscake remaining after oil extraction still contains the active constituents effecting coagulation. Coagulant may be regarded as a by-product of viable oil extraction. (Sutherland, 1993)

Edible oils are an essential component of human nutritional requirements. In developing countries, the production and marketing of edible oils is usually dominated by a few large-scale urban-based companies. Rural supplies of the finished product are erratic with increased prices due to additional transport costs.

The Intermediate Technology Development Group (ITDG) in Zimbabwe have successfully introduced technology appropriate for small-scale decentralized rural processing of edible oils. A recent evaluation of the 17 oil mills established to constitute this ITDG project concluded (Sunga and Whitby, 1995):

- the oil mills are commercially viable returning an average of 51 per cent on investment with profits of 21 per cent on sales
- a typical mill employs 10 permanent and three temporary workers
- ready cash markets for oil seed crops had been created
- lower cost oil of significantly higher quality is now available in the rural areas
- alternative edible oil seeds such as soya, cotton seed and *moringa* should be investigated
- the market for and sales of presscake are important for the overall viability and profitability of the mills; new outlets are required.

Conclusions
The products of the *Moringa oleifera* tree are underexploited resources. Realization of their potential will contribute towards sustainability in the rural areas, addressing major issues of current concern:
- **water quality and health**
- **food and nutrition**
- **employment opportunities**
- **income generation**

References
Folkard, G. K. & Sutherland, J. P. 1994, *Moringa oleifera - a multipurpose tree*, Footsteps, No.20, Sept. 1994, pp 14-15.

Folkard, G.K., Sutherland, J.P. & Grant, W.D. 1993, Natural coagulants at pilot scale; Pickford, J. ed. Water,

Environment and Management; Proc. 18th WEDC Conference, Kathmandu, Nepal, 30 Aug-3 Sept 1992. Loughborough University Press, pp 51-54. .

Jahn, S.A.A. 1988, 'Using *Moringa* seeds as a coagulant in developing countries', Journ. *AWWA*, 80, (6) pp 43-50.

Morton, J.F. 1991, The horseradish tree, *Moringa pterygosperma* - a boon to arid lands? *Economic Botany*, 45, (3), pp 318-333.

Ram, J. 1994, 'Moringa - a highly nutritious vegetable source', TRIADES Technical Bulletin No.2, Box E, Hakalau, Hawaii.

Sunga, I. & Whitby, G. 1995, Decentralized edible oil milling; an evaluation report, May 1995, ITDG, Rugby, England.

Sutherland, J.P. 1993, Oil and coagulant extraction from *M. oleifera* seed, Draft Report to the ODA, London, USA.

Pump and engine maintenance scheme

Richard Mtonga and Theron Scott Robson, Tanzania

DODOMA REGION COMPRISES four districts, namely; Dodoma Municipality, Dodoma Rural, Mpwapwa and Kondoa. There are more than 200 deep boreholes in the region, served by various diesel engines and pumps.

In much of Dodoma region there is no alternative water resource to the deep water aquifer, and these boreholes are therefore the appropriate technology choice.

Since installation in the 1950s to 1970s many of them have fallen into disrepair. This is attributed partly to inadequate financial resources, old age, theft, vandalism, lack of responsibility by the consumers, and failure of some sources.

In the past O & M was provided for by the government and the villagers tended to assume that the government had unlimited resources. As the government failed to allocate adequate financial resources, many of the schemes broke down.

The Regional PEMS Scheme aims at promoting a sense of community-based self-management and self-financing of water supply schemes. The scheme has been made possible by the provision of logistical and financial support from the UK charity WaterAid.

PEMS in Kondoa district

Role of regional PEMS
At a regional level, a mechanical engineer and a training coordinator were responsible for providing training to the PEMS staff in the four districts, and are the backbone of follow-up support.

Training of the district PEMS trainers concentrated on participatory techniques, communication skills, community motivation and mobilization, teaching and training techniques and a technical refresher course.

Role of district water department
The department is responsible for:

- Selection of district trainers, based on technical competence, communication skills and decision-making ability.
- Regular supervision of PEMS activities.
- Preparation of cost estimates for any maintenance required.
- Providing a mobile maintenance service for substantial repairs which are beyond the capabilities of the villagers.
- Provision of spare parts, pumps and engines.
- It is projected that private contractors will undertake some maintenance activities in the future and it will be the role of the department to supervise this work.
- In the future periodic pump testing of boreholes and monitoring of water quality will be undertaken.

Role of villagers:
Under the borehole rehabilitation programme villagers have to provide all labour as well as financial contribution of not less than Tshs. 200 000/= (UK£ 222.2).

In addition villagers are also responsible for:

- Election of a water committee (WC) and opening a bank account for the water fund.
- Selection of two pump attendants.
- Purchase of service tool kit.
- 250 hour service for engine.
- Selection of watchmen and provision of watchmen house.
- Security around pump house.
- Payment of full costs for all operation and maintenance needs.

Role of PEMS technicians
The first role was to train village pump attendants on:

- General cleanliness of pump house, surroundings, pump and engine.
- General service of engine including changing filters, oil, etc..
- Carrying out minor repairs.
- Use of log books.
- Reporting procedure.

Six two-week seminars are provided for a total of 71 village pump attendants (VPA) from 37 villages.

Two PEMS trainers have been appointed to visit villages under PEMS programme, using two motorbikes provided by WaterAid and the Kondoa Integrated Rural Development Project (KIRDEP) which is a Dutch funded programme.

These technicians visit every month during dry season and every two months during wet season. During a visit they complete a checklist of activities which includes the following:

- Check performance/logging of village pump attendant.
- Advise village water committee on the service/maintenance requirement of their scheme.

- Inspect their water installation.
- Providing them with required spare parts as per price list the district water engineer has circulated to them.
- Advise on pricing-tariff structure, and accounting.

PEMS shop

To facilitate smooth running of the PEMS, a PEMS shop has been established at the water department's store with a view to stocking the required spare parts for the engines.

A buffer stock of spare parts for the shop were provided by WaterAid. The sale price has been set to allow for a net profit to compensate for inflation and if possible to increase the stock of spares available.

In the future the water department is intending to include other items like parts for handpumps and pipe fittings in the shop stock.

District bank account

Two bank accounts have been opened, one for the PEMS shop and the other for the villages' monthly contributions.

The PEMS shop account is a revolving fund, that is, the money that accrues from the sales is used to purchase replacement stock.

The second account of monthly village contributions caters for a payment of mileage and allowances for the PEMS motorbike technicians.

Problems and solutions

In carrying out PEMS, problems have been experienced. Below are the main problems experienced and attempts/ plans made to overcome them.

Ownership/duty of care

Ownership is not well defined in the water policy.

Poor care of the equipment by some villages has raised concern over the 'duty of care' required of the villagers.

To address this problem, a contract of agreement between the water department and the water committee, detailing the roles and responsibilities of each party is being prepared.

Failure by the village to fulfil the requirements of the agreement will result, as a last resort, in the nullification of the village ownership of the scheme, and the equipment will then be repossessed by the water department.

Misuse/theft of water fund

Money from the water fund has been misused and stolen on a number of occasions, with the result that there was no money available to service and run the water project.

This can be resolved by enacting already legislated by-laws, and the department is striving to ensure the enforcement of these by-laws by the authorities.

Retrenchment exercise

Recently the Government of Tanzania sacked around 50 000 civil servants. The Kondoa Water Department Staff was reduced from 120 to 40 in July 1993. Cuts included all the government village pump attendants (58), putting pressure on an acceleration of the PEMS training to fill the gap. This pressure to train led to reduced follow-up support during the training period.

In the PEMS team two technicians were sacked, leaving only two technicians. To fill the gap we recruited two craftsmen who were formerly pump attendants. Having been trained on the job coupled with seminars these craftsmen are now doing a good job.

PEMS spare parts more expensive

It has come to our notice that some of the spare parts are cheaper in the private shops than in the PEMS shop. This is due to the fact that following trade liberalization spare parts come from all corners of the globe, many of which are not genuine, and are poor quality.

The PEMS technicians inspect the quality of these parts, and if of poor quality, they try to teach the villagers that poor quality parts will damage their engine and shorten the life of the machine.

Worn out pumps and engines

Some of the engines and pumps are worn out due to age and obsolescence. Breakdowns are frequent and parts difficult to procure.

Under the WaterAid and KIRDEP programmes old engines and pumps will ultimately be phased out, and wherever possible the new equipment will be standardized.

Wet season sources

During the wet season many of the villages resort to their traditional sources (as they are free of charge). These sources are often highly polluted.

In an attempt to solve this problem we are planning to protect seasonal water sources, with ring wells, promote rainwater catchment, and build infiltration galleries in seasonal rivers.

Concluding remarks

There are now 22 boreholes with diesel engines and pumps operational in the district, with six more rehabilitations/ refurbishments scheduled this year.

With the promotion of PEMS and its financial independence, the sustainability of what in the past has been a 'difficult' village level technology has now been improved.

We believe that with the integrated approach being adopted in Kondoa, and the development of the PEMS, the goal of 'providing access to clean and potable water...by the year 2002 and that the services so provided are sustainable' (Kikwete, 1993) is for Kondoa District not beyond hope.

References

J.M.Kikwete, Minister for Water, Energy and Minerals, Tanzania, September 1993. Opening address at Workshop on Implementation of National Water Policy.

Dam maintenance

Fati Mumuni, Ghana

THE OPERATION AND Maintenance of a water supply facility is a component which is always emphasized to forestall its sustainability. In Village Water Reservoirs Project, where earth dams are constructed, the management realized that the dams would need maintenance as soon as they have been constructed.

Earth dams are constructed in the dry season, November to May, awaiting the wet season to be filled up. It was realized that with the rains, erosion of the dam wall occurs forming gullies. A continuous erosion could lead to a major crack on the dam wall and a subsequent collapse.

Preventive maintenance activities

To forestall the collapse of a dam, the animation section of the project mobilizes dam communities in the wet season to transplant vertiva grass on the dam wall.

Vertiva grass grows wild in swamps. It matures in August, the middle of the rainy season. It has broad-based roots which keep the dam wall firm. The grass is transplanted in such a way that erosion gullies cannot be formed easily. It is drought-resistant; dries up in the dry season but quickly sprouts as soon as it rains. It is spread by the wind.

The transplanting of vertica grass is the same as that of guinea-corn and millet, cereals which are widely cultivated in the Northern Region, Ghana; the top of the grass is cut before it is transplanted. The communities therefore easily pick this up and all the animators do is to encourage and monitor this activity.

Mending of erosion gullies

Since the transplanting of vertiva grass starts in the middle of the wet season, it is likely that erosion gullies would form. While the grass is being transplanted these erosion gullies are also mended by the communities with the help of the animators. The mending of erosion gullies is also likened to women's activity in the plastering the floors of rooms in the areas, thus making it easy for the women to participate in the maintenance of the dam.

The transplanting of vertiva grass and mending of erosion gullies are therefore activities in which all members of the community are involved.

Long-term maintenance policy

Two years after a dam has been constructed the project officially hands it over to the dam community to manage and maintain. However, the project instituted a long-term maintenance policy with three phases to help participating communities to sustain their facility.

Phase I
In the first phase of the policy, the community has to pay a fee to the project for the project maintenance team (PMT) constituting members of the technical and animation sections (three members to visit the dam). This is termed routine maintenance visit. It is a biannual activity; before and after the rain. The PMT visits the dam with a checklist. At the village level, the village maintenance team (VMT) is involved with these routine checks. The dam is assessed by both the PMTs and VMTs after which the community as a whole is briefed on the state of their dam. The PMTs together with the community determine the problems that can be solved by them and those which need project help. At the project level a report is written and given to the community.

If a dam community does not participate in Phase I, it cannot seek help from the project.

Phase II
After the routine visits, the community with technical dam problems will have to call on the project for help to repair the fault. This leads to the phase II of the maintenance policy. The community has to hire the services of the PMT and pays for transport, workmanship, night allowances of the visiting team and materials for the repairs. These costs are not subsidized.

So far only two communities have completed this phase and it is interesting to note that one community could not pay their bill because it was too high.

Phase III
Phase III of the policy foresees a situation of dam failure which may need the use of heavy machinery. With regard to this phase the project advises all communities to open an account to fund such eventualities.

The communities' reaction to the policy

In the first year of instituting this policy all six communities with dams participated in the programme. However, in the subsequent years, one community could not mobilize funds to pay their bill and so dropped out.

As already mentioned, two communities needed technical help from the project. However, one could not pay their bill.

Two communities out of sixteen 16 deposited money with the project as savings for the future maintenance of their dams. The animation team has tried to sell the idea of harvesting the fish from the dams and selling them for the future maintenance of their dams, and this has been well received. However, the proceeds from the sale of fish are used to pay for Phase I. The team also tried to encourage the communities to make dry season vegetable gardens. The vegetables can be sold and the proceeds saved for maintenance but villagers are not sufficiently motivated. Another way of getting money was to ask neighbouring communities who come to fetch the water in the dry season to pay some money but the communities say they cannot sell water to their neighbours.

The problem of persuading the communities to save money for the future maintenance of their dam still remains.

Comments on the maintenance programme

The long-term maintenance policy was instituted by the project and put in the care of the animation section (the software). The technical section felt that it was their responsibility and not that of the animation section. This was agreed by the animation section but the project manager felt it should be headed by the animation section because it is the section which shows interest in the activity. There was therefore no co-ordination between the technical section which has the technical knowledge and the animation section which can mobilize the community but cannot solve technical problems.

The biannual visits were said to be unnecessary by the project maintenance team but the communities still had to pay the same amount for the yearly visit. To pay for this one visit, the animation section has to plead with the technical section.

At the project level, the maintenance policy is unworkable, because of the attitude of the technical section. There is also the problem of the animation section's inability to persuade the communities to save money towards the future maintenance of the facilities.

Conclusion

The Village Water Reservoirs maintenance policy is moving in the right direction but it is experiencing teething problems which may be solved with time.

Water supply in Rwanda: from war to sustainability

Dr P.G. Nembrini, Kenya

ONLY A FEW hours after the death of Rwanda's Président on 6 April 1994 an orgy of killing swept the country, reaching even the most remote hills and valleys. Systematic massacres and mounting terrors forced an endless stream of men, women and children to seek refuge in other parts of the country or abroad as Rwanda slid into chaos. Foreigners including most of the soldiers serving the United Nations Assistance Mission in Rwanda (UNAMIR), were hurriedly evacuated, and the country was left to its tragic fate. The ICRC decided that it had no choice but to stay, to try and save those who could still be saved.

Tens of thousands of people, mainly Tutsis but also Hutus suspected of belonging to the opposition, attempted to escape the carnage by congregating in certain locations, both in Kigali and in the provinces.

First in the north, then elsewhere in the country, camps for displaced people started springing up, and aid agencies began to organize relief for them. Beside **food, water supply and sanitation** to maintain a minimum of hygiene, were a priority.

The outbreak of cholera in the overcrowded camps around Goma dealt another devastating blow to the refugees, already weak and weary, creating overnight a new tragedy of unprecedented proportions [1]. ICRC water and sanitation engineers have been working hard throughout the country to provide safe water in hospitals and in camps for displaced people.

The water supply systems in Rwanda's main cities have been disrupted as a result of the conflict. Starting in Kigali and then moving on to other cities like Ruhengeri and Gisenyi, the ICRC carried out a rapid assessement to identify the main problems within these water treatment plants and to implement an emergency programme to restore and maintain the facilities in a proper order. Water distributions for the displaced camps and for the resident populations would then be organized by trucking water from these facilities until the normal network distribution could be put into operation.

Humanitarian co-ordination began to take shape, many relief agencies arriving to provide emergency aid. Then, with Kigali no longer under siege, it became possible to reach all parts of the country. Considerable efforts were deployed to co-ordinate the work of the myriad relief agencies assisting refugees and displaced people, and working relations were established with Rwanda's new government.

This paper describes how ICRC tackled the water supply problems during the war, when it had to set up emergency programmes to restore the main supplies of the cities, up to its current task within the rural gravity water schemes, carried out with the help of the local population and the governemental bodies, to attain a sustainable rehabilitation.

Programmes during the war.

Displaced people

The battle for the control of Kigali and the immediate control of the north-west part of the country by the former FPR army, resulted in the establishment of several displaced people camps, mainly from inhabitants who managed to leave the city. Simple emergency water supplies systems were set up to cope with the needs of about 12 displaced people camps (Ngarama, Mugango, Gatete, Ndarama, Nyange, Bushara, Mukoma, Mukarange, Manyagiro and Tabagwe), with a total population of about 250 000. Plastic collapsible storage reservoirs connected to distribution standposts were used and water was either from improved spring catchments or brought to the different sites by tanker trucks equipped with diesel-powered pumping devices. These systems are widely used also by other NGOs like MSF (Médecins sans frontières) and their use has been successfully tested in several other emergencies.

These kits are essential in the very beginning of any emergency and can be set up in a few hours. Having secured a minimum water supply, the engineers could then look for others, and implement more permanent schemes, either by rehabilitating existing gravity or pumped schemes, or by creating new water supplies using simple technology.

Spring protection and hand-dug wells are the more **sustainable** options but even if the technology involved is simple, they do require a minimum time and amount of materials and equipment. Most of the a/m displaced people camps in north-west Rwanda could be supplied with minor repairs carried out on the gravity schemes or by catchment of new springs.

Treatment was in general **not necessary** but was carried out as a preventive measure, in case of poor maintenance of the facilities or if an epidemic (cholera) was feared.

The same approach was followed within the cities to supply facilities most in need of water, like hospitals, health centres and vulnerable groups' accommodation sites. Ten orphanages and health centres were supplied by tanker trucks. Drinking water was available from a few springs within the city of Kigali and was sufficient to cope with the needs of an almost completely abandoned city. The camp of Nyarushishi (Cyangugu), where about 15 000 Tutsi were gathering, seeking for protection, was supplied by completing a 4 km gravity-fed scheme. Constant surveillance had to be given to the whole pipeline which was frequently damaged by sabotage, with engineers constantly under threat from opposing factions.

Main water treatment plants (WTP) supplying the cities

The main problems the WTPs of the cities had to face are listed in Table I.

ICRC engineers were in a position to assess the conditions of these major WTPs (2) before they were hit by the front line, being deployed by both factions, sometimes under considerable danger during the crossline operations.

This previous knowledge of the infra-structures enabled the ICRC to foresee most of the urgent needs, and particularly those for treatment chemicals. Immediate purchase orders were launched in an aim to decrease delivery delays, bearing in mind that most of these commodities had to be found and transported by truck either from Mombasa of from Dar es Salaam.

Only extremely urgent amounts were shipped to Kigali by plane, using ICRC but also UNAMIR logistical means. Specific damages were assessed when the front line moved further south or north, putting most of the WTP under the control of the present governmental army.

From mid-May 1994 until the end of May 1995, the ICRC delivered to ELECTROGAZ a total amount of about 900 MT of $Al2(SO4)3$, 50 MT of calcium hypochlorite (HTH) and about 400 MT locally purchased lime (Ruhengeri), sufficient to cover the needs of all the WTP of the country for more than eight months, taking into account the initial limited production capacities.

Table I. Main problems within the major WTPs of the country

- personnel was absent
- transport facilities were lacking
- funds to pay salaries were not available
- HT electrical power lines were cut and emergency power generators were insufficient
- chemicals to carry out treatment were lacking (aluminum sulfate, chlorine HTH)
- most of the maintenance tools were looted
- fuel was not available

Only minor damages were inflicted on the stations and the major problems the engineeers had to solve was to rebuild the former operation and maintenance teams. Some of the previous managers were quickly on the spot and were of paramount importance in the setting up of new teams. Their role in the preparation of the lists of the essential spare parts needed to carry out minor repairs and their knowledge of the modifications carried out on the treament schemes, were essential to avoid mismanagement of some of these complex facilities.

Incentives for ELECTROGAZ workers were supported by ICRC for the Kigali and Gisenyi WTP (about 150 people) and steps were taken to determine how long the government would require assistance in this field.

Four electrical generators (total capacity 300 KVA) were flown in to operate the intermediary pumping stations of the city of Kigali, but the network distribution went back to normality only when the HV line supplying power from the Mukungwa hydroelectric power station, as well as several transformers, could be repaired by ELECTROGAZ, with the support of GTZ (German Technical Cooperation). By the end of October 1994 the water distribution could be considered normal in Kigali and efforts were directed to the other WTPs of the country, in co-ordination with other agencies.

At the end of the year most of the major WTPs were operational again. Reliability was subjected to power cuts, shortages of fuel, but water distribution in the cities could be considered satisfactory and similar to the pre-war conditions.

Rural water supplies

Most of the rural areas are supplied by gravity supply schemes. A total of about 1100 schemes are listed in the files of the Ministry of Public Works (MINITRAPE), 79 of which are supplying the rural communities in the préfecture of Ruhengeri, one-third are listed for Gisenyi, 48 for Kibuye etc. (3). As a rule of the thumb aproximately one third of these schemes were out of order, one third were in a need of major rehabilitation and the rest were almost in working condition (4). For the northern 'préfectures' the poor state of the gravity-fed rural water supplies was not only due to the recent war. Complete neglect of operation and maintenance started in 1990, when the first skirmishes began. In these areas the war has added to the degradation of the systems but even in other 'préfectures' the neglect was significant.

The system prevailing before the war, in which 'water taxes' paid by the inhabitants of a 'commune' would support the 'fontainier' (water guard) in charge to carry out maintenance and to buy spare parts, like taps and pipes, was not working satisfactorily.

Lack of understanding of the functioning of the systems and particularly downstream impacts of upstream damages, gender considerations around women and children fetching water, men in principle in charge of surveillance and operations and sometimes poor design of the systems, were the main reasons for the continuing degradation. To that we should add that there was genuine feeling of responsibility for the water supply systems, exacerbated by the lack of social stability, by uncertainty of the future caused by growing conflicts and the presence of "newcomers".

At the beginning of September the ICRC began to rehabilitate some of these gravity flow systems, in the region located between Ruhengeri and Ruhondo. Fifteen gravity flow systems were completely rehabilitated (5), with the objective of providing as much water as possible, as fast as possible, to as many people as possible. The need for a sustainable repair was stressed, and the programme was extended to the préfectures of Ruhengeri, Gisenyi and Kibuye. Three teams were set up from personnel recruited through the American, Swedish and Australian National Red Cross Societies.

A socio-economist was added to the engineer in charge of the technical problems, with the aim of establishing a dialogue with the users and with the newly appointed authorities, in order to raise awareness on the crucial issues of maintenance, water taxes and how to attain sustainability.

In the Ruhengeri prefecture the 45 km-long Mutobo system, supplying water to the communes of Mukindo, Kigombe, Kinigi, Nkumba and Kidaho and the 35 km-long Ruhondo system, supplying water to the commune of Ruhondo, have already been rehabilitated, with about 70 000 people depending on these two WSS for their needs of water.

In the préfecture of Gisenyi the WSS of the commune of Rwerere (6 km of new pipes), Mutura and Kanama (Bizizi sector) have been rehabilitated. The two WTP of Mizingo and Yungwe, supplying the primary distribution network, received technical and financial support.

In the Kibuye préfecture, on 14 targeted existing WSS, those supplying water to the communes of Biramba (12 000 p), Rubengera (10 000 p), Muhororo (5 000 p) and Kibuye town have also been completed.

Sustainability

At the beginning of 1995 the Rwandan administrative structure began to function again. The natural counterpart in the rehabilitation, operation and maintenance of the WSS is the Ministère des Travaux Publics et de l'Energie (MINITRAPE) and more specifically the "Direction Hydraulique" in Kigali. A working agreement was signed with the MINITRAPE and the ICRC, specifying the nature of their partnership in relation with the local relevant authorities, with the aim of combining the traditional **rapid intervention approach** and the corresponding **visible short-term progress** with a basic educational process seeking to strengthen local capacities to solve maintenance issues in the future.

Much time and effort has been spent with local bourgmestres, "conseillers", school authorities and plumbers (fontainiers). As a result we observed a quite significant commitment to voluntary communal work and provision of locally available materials, including pipes.

The final objective of this medium-term work is to re-establish a local management committee and a payment system, in agreement with MINITRAPE policies.

War has disrupted the normal organization of the country and emergency programmes have been launched to bring it back to previous standards.

ICRC and other NGOs have taken the burden of the necessary assistance to run the WTP and to repair the rural water supplies in order to give to the affected communities a potential chance to achieve quickly a sustainable water supply.

References

1 'Public health impact of Rwandan refugee crisis: what happened in Goma, Zaire, in July, 1994?' *The Lancet*, Vol. 345. February 11, 1995.

2 G.J. Allison. Status report on the water treatment plants of Rwanda. ICRC. May-October 1994.

3 Inventaire National des Adductions d'eau Potable. République Rwandaise. 1992

4 Coopération autrichienne. Evaluation et besoins d'urgence au secteur Eau Potable et Assainissement dans la zone démilitarisée et la zone FPR. République Rwandaise. PNUD, mars 1994.

5 Q. Roell .Rural water supply rehabilitation in the NW of Rwanda. ICRC-TWB Benelux Cons. Eng. December 1994.

Sustainable community water supply in Nigeria

Dr A.O. Odumosu, Nigeria

NIGERIA IS THE most populous country in Africa having a total land surface are of 9 941 714 sq.km, with a total population (1991 census) of 88.5m people made up of 26.55m urban and 17.7m semi -urban and 44.25m rural.

It has abundant surface and groundwater resources reservoirs, yet the rural population are still grossly lacking in safe water supply. 1991 figures after the IDWSS puts the rural water coverage at 30 per cent, projected to 35 per cent for 1995 and 22 per cent for the year 2000. This low level of rural water supplies results in poor health, especially the health of young children's life having an infant mortality rate of 170 per 1000 live births. Of deaths from infectious diseases, approximately 65 per cent are accounted for by diarrhoeal disease and dysentery, malaria and tetanus, and the majority of these are related to children under five years of age.

The organizational policy for water supply and sanitation in the country rests with the three-tiers of government and at the community level. The federal level is mainly responsible for policy, followed by state for urban water supply and local government for rural water supply. The local government is directly responsible for the provision of rural water supply.

At present, the Federal Ministry of Water Resources and Rural Development with the assistance of UNICEF is advocating that each state (there are 31 states) should have a functional rural water supply and sanitation agency in order to facilitate effective resource mobilization to the communities.

The status of rural water supply in Nigeria are characterized by:

- Low level of coverage, resulting from relatively weak political commitment.
- Difficult geological strata.
- Inappropriate technology.
- Lack of operation and maintenance of existing facilities.
- Poor workmanship by dubious contractors.
- Lack of sense of ownership by the communities.

Where there has been some community empowerment, communities are now resorting to self empowerment to solve their water supply problem. In some cases, there have been tremendous incentives from non-governmental organizations (NGOs). The overall scenario is that communities are more than willing to be involved in solving their own problem. They have realized that government cannot do it alone, and in fact in Nigeria, provision of water supply for rural communities is often used as a political ploy to get votes and these political promises are often not fulfilled when government gets into power.

The story that follows tells of the present water status in three communities in Nigeria, their pains, their struggles and their aspirations.

Chinene community

Chinene is a small community comprising a total population of between 6 - 10 000 inhabitants. It is situated in Gwoza Local Government Area of Borno State. It is about 30km from the headquarters (Gwoza LGA). Unlike most of the populace in Borno State, Chinene is basically a Christian community. It has a total of 80 per cent Christian and 20 per cent Muslims. In spite of this, the community exists peacefully, there is a lot of religious tolerance, and all efforts made by the association are joint ventures between Christians and Muslims. Most are peasant farmers in the Lake Chad Basin, growing cowpeas. A small percentage are cattle rearers. At the moment, there exist five functional open wells (out of 11) and two earthdams. The first earthdam is fully completed and another dam is under construction.

History of water supply

Before 1988, the whole community fetched their domestic water from a river called Bala Iwaza which is at a distance of 4km from the centre of the community. The river usually dried up during the dry season. Another source of water supply is from the hills. Chinene is surrounded by the beautiful undulating Gwoza hills. The scenery is beautiful and peaceful. About 30 per cent of the community live on the terraced hills and the water that flows from the hills usually feeds the community.

However, from 1988 onwards, the period of the dry season seems to have grown longer and the hills no longer produce sufficient water for them. There was a growing awareness in the community about the need to tackle the acute water shortage problem. There was very little outside help, thus awareness was raised about self help in the community. The community came together in 1990 and officially registered itself as a non-profitable organization.

The Chinene Community Association is made up of 15 members all male committee.

It is to be noted that due to a large Hausa cultural background there are no women on the development committee.

Any adult person (male/female) having attained the age of puberty is free to join, for a registration fee of ₦25. An identity card is usually issued to a villager upon registration. Membership of the association is open to non indigenes as well.

The water project

Having formed the association, the association (according to verbal information) wrote many letters to the LGA headquarters and paid many visits to the LGA to aid the community with potable water, but there was no response from the LGA.

The association decided to launch an appeal fund, and held a launching of the Chinene Development Community. The launching raised a total sum of ₦22 000 (US 1000 dollars). Eleven hand-dug wells were sunk and only five were found to yield any substantial amount of water. The wells were cement lined. The first earth dam was built by the community with the help of a Canadian engineer from the Mennonite Central Committee. The community declared three working days for the construction of the earth dam out of five working days, i.e. Monday, Tuesday and Wednesday. The first earth dam was completed in 17 working days. The entire male community came out to work, whilst the women provided food and water to the male labourers.

Money soon ran out and the committee resorted to the community for some money. An extra 8000 Naira was raised via levies and sale of produce.

Levies

Those who had money and could contribute cash were divided into income groups and were asked to pay according to what they could afford.

Sales of produce

Those who had no money, but had farm produce contributed what they had. This produce was later sold by the committee.

The quality of well water was far from adequate. It is brownish and muddy. The villagers drink the water raw without any filtration.

The community feels it needs more water, and it does envisage building more earth dams (only one has been built and this has yet to prove its point, i.e. it is not fully functional). It stills needs more money and technical expertise. The Canadian sanitary engineer has left. WHO is advocating some financial and technical assistance to the community.

Water supply status in Otan Ajegbaju Community

Otan Ajegbaju is a small village within Osun state. It is situated in Ila LGA. Many parts of the state are well served with potable water by the local government, but not Otan. Fortunately, the village has produced many highly educated men and have constituted themselves into a community development club, namely, The Pacesetters Club of Otan Ajegbaju (OAPCS). One of their priorities is to provide water for the whole village. WHO was approached for technical assistance and a site visit to the village provided the following information.

Geology

The state is underlain by metamorphic rocks of the basement complex with outcrop over many parts. Rocks of the basement complex found here are schists, associated with quartzite ridges of the types found in Ilesa area.

Population

It has a population of 88 853 inhabitants.

Water supply

The village has abundant water resources, both surface and groundwater, but they are not being adequately harvested for the villagers.

Rivers and streams

Two major rivers were observed to run through the village. The larger river, river Aleremu is voluminous and meanders over a wide area. It is however seasonal and often runs dry during the long dry season. The river is slightly turbid. River Oroki is said by the villagers NEVER to run dry during the dry season and never to overflow its boundary during the rainy season. Both rivers are presently used by the villagers for drinking and other domestic purposes.

Spring water from the hills

The village is surrounded by beautiful undulating hills and from one of these hills flows spring water that is harvestable. This water was first harvested in 1959 by the Catholic Father and it serves the convent and some part of the town. The pressure from the breakdown tank is sufficient to climb up a story building without pumping. The rest of the water is fed into a ground clear water tank that serves the village.

At the time of the investigation, the tank (about 5000 gallons) was found everywhere to be rusty with holes, implying a loss of pressure of the water. This loss in pressure has made it impossible to have an overflow into the ground clear water reservoir, meaning that the part of the village serviced by the underground tank is no longer served.

It was however observed that the water reservoir from the foothills has sufficient capacity to serve the whole village.

The water is of very high quality such that it is taken directly without any pre-treatment.

The state government via the Directorate for Food Roads, and Rural Infrastructure have sunk two or three boreholes, but none is functional. In addition, there was abundant evidence that the state government had proposed to service the town with treated water from another town. An incomplete storage reservoir with a half built pump house and generator house beautifies the centre of the town and pipes were found neatly stacked in one section of the town. The only functional water points are from the following sources:

- Privately dug hand-dug wells with and without pumps.
- Rainwater harvesting scheme.
- Natural springs.
- Tapping water from the Oke Oluwa hills for the Catholic convent.

In order for the Otan Ajagbaju Pacesetter Club (OAPSC) to be able to meet their terms of reference of provision of potable water to the whole town, the following line of action were recommended:

- Divide the town into two sections.
- Section A can be served with the ground water, utilizing the derelict borehole to the state hospital. Another borehole can be sunk in the vicinity (verify site through hydrogeological studies). The water from these two boreholes can be distributed on a short-term basis via water tanker to the rest of the city, i.e. directly to their houses or into built storage reservoir. Some kind of cost recovery scheme would have to be put in place.
- Section B can be provided with water from the Oke Oluwa foothills. A bigger tank should be installed to carry the water and replace with bigger diameter pipes that can service the convent and this part of the city. The necessary repairs works to the ground storage reservoir should be carried out.
- Contractors should be invited to quote for the jobs.
- There are natural springs in the state. These should be preserved.

The lesson to be learnt from this community is the determination of the people to help themselves. To date, not much infrastructure has been put in place, but there are fundraising activities seeking to redress this situation.

Agagbe community in Gwer West local government of Benue State

This community represents one of the poorest in the whole country. A notable feature of this community is its geological characteristics. The geology of the state may be grouped into two, namely:- Metasediments occurring in the Benue and Katsina Ala river valleys and basement complex rocks occurring in higher ground.

The sedimentary formations are rich in limestones, coal and mineral salt. The community has a low population density. Total population of the community is about 73 396 with a population density of 56 sq.km. It is one of the poorest. It was depleted of its population during the slave trade. The villagers live in tiny compounds whose population range from 6 - 30 people most of whom are illiterate farmers. The state water resources include numerous rivers, streams, lakes, ponds and underground reservoirs. There are many mineral resources in the state most of which are still unknown due to inadequate geological survey. However, from what is known, it is believed that it is impossible to tap groundwater via shallow hand-dug wells or boreholes, due to the underlying mineral salts. The wells in the community only hold water during the rainy season and run dry during the dry season from December - April. Any attempt to dig further results in salty water. The only alternative is to tap the big rivers. A tributary of river Benue runs through the village i.e. river Apkean. The river has sufficient capacity to be utilized as a water supply reservoir, but it however contains high suspended solids. The villagers normally drink the water from the river untreated. It becomes obvious that these people cannot provide potable water for themselves. WHO went to assist the community via a functional literacy programme for the women in 1994. The villagers only agreed to participate in the project when WHO agreed to supply them with potable water. Getting potable water from a river source is very expensive and funds had to be found from another source. After a long search, the European Union came up with the necessary fund of about five million Naira. The scheme consist of an intake - > water treatment plant (WTP) (WTP consisting of coagulation and flocculation) —> rapid sand filter —> storage reservoir. This is now distributed into four places in the village. The villagers can go to any of the four points to get water. The ground tanks are fitted with about two taps each.

The WTP runs on diesel and when there is a shortage of fuel, there is concurrently a storage of drinking water. Provision of raw water is being followed closely by health education through the female functional literacy campaign. The plant is still under the supervision of the contractors and after a year it will be handed over to the communities for operation and maintenance. Luckily within the community lives a Catholic Reverend Father (Father Hunter) who provides the initiative for community mobilization and also a tremendous amount of technical expertise.

Concluding remark

It will be observed that all these communities except for Agagbe still lack potable water, but they are on their way to achieving their goal. There is still a need for outside assistance in terms of both technical and financial assistance i.e. building earthdams, drilling boreholes and harvesting rainwater. The major consensus is that these communities need to mobilize themselves in order for them to have sustainable potable water. The dawn of community participation in projects has truly arrived, communities want to help themselves and they must be empowered both technically and financially to achieve their goal of potable water at the rural community level.

With water only metres away

C.H. Ratnam, South Africa

IN APARTHEID SOUTH Africa, the government created Bantustans and homelands. This was to segregate people and to perpetuate separate development for the different black groups and whites. In 1977 an area of approximately 9500 hectares called Winterveld in South Africa was incorporated into homeland Bophuthatswana. Winterveld was a typical informal settlement, very common in South Africa, situated close to a well developed 'white' town, depending on it for its survival. Winterveld has no basic amenities, even drinking water. In Winterveld's case the 'white' town is the capital of South Africa, Pretoria.

The Bophuthatswana Government did not interact with the Winterveld community or the owners of the plot when it decided to provide water. The provision of services was considered the prerogative of the government. This was a trait of the South African Government when providing services to the black people, blindly followed by Bophuthatswana.

Water reticulation was provided in 1981 to Klippan, a part of Winterveld that was urban in character. It was to cater for 280 plots but only 84 plot connections have been installed to date. The people were suffering the torments of Tantalus, WITH (drinking) WATER ONLY METRES AWAY, underground, in pipes.

To understand the situation in Winterveld it is necessary to know its history. All development in Winterveld, present and future, is linked strongly to its unique history. In 1940 a group of white business people from Pretoria sold freehold rights of the Winterveld Agricultural Holdings to black people. This area became one of the few areas in South Africa where land was purchased by black people before 1948. It was surveyed and legally registered in the names of the owners and remains so today unaffected by the apartheid period.

North Winterveld is rural in nature, with 8.4 hectare plots. The south is urban in character with 4.2 hectare plots. Fig 2. The water was provided to Klippan, an area in the south. The landlord of these agricultural 4.2 hectare plots are mostly absentee landlords. They carried out large-scale irregular subdivision and rented them, creating random housing development at a time when agriculture became less profitable and when there was pressure for housing.

What is the reason that plot water connections were not given or taken? Legally only one connection per plot could be given to the owner. Owners were unwilling to obtain a connection because they had to pay a connection fee of R 1800 that is only 38 per cent of recovery of source development cost the other 62 per cent being subsidised. Furthermore they would have to pay for the water used by the tenants and be unable to recover the expense from the tenants. Water from wells and boreholes provided in their plot is sold at a high price and the income from such sales is higher than the rent collected. For these reasons the need for a water connection was a low priority.

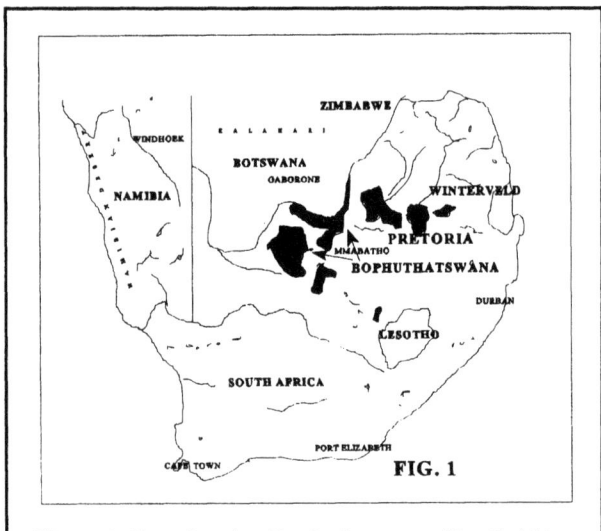

Figure 1. Map showing Bophuthatswana/South Africa

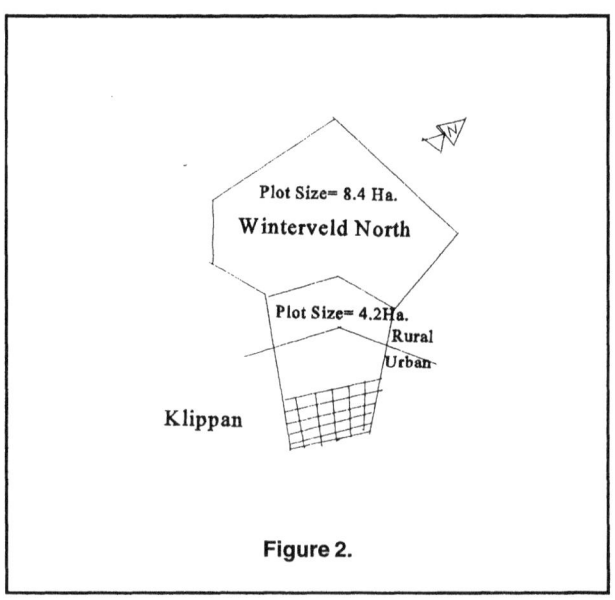

Figure 2.

The total number of dwellings in Klippan in 1990 was 20 244 in 520 formal plots averaging 38 dwellings/plot. Ninety-six per cent of the daily domestic water needs are obtained from informal sources, such as from wells, boreholes and the Toloane river. A survey showed the average household water consumption to be 120 litres/day or about 22 litres/person. This costs between R22 and R75 per month, that is 2.5 per cent of the income of a household.

Although the groundwater potential is not good, a high water table has ensured sufficient and reliable supply of water for primary and stock consumption. Most of the boreholes and wells are under the control of individuals thus creating a situation of dependency on the water sold by the landlords and other vendors. The price charged varies greatly throughout the area, depending on competition between vendors.

The people collect water mostly in plastic containers of 25 litres and pay 20-25 cents per container. Sometime they paid as much as 30 cents. Water is collected by women and children who walk between ½ to 1km to collect water. This pitiful situation is further aggravated by the water sold by the vendors being contaminated. In 1990 there was an outbreak of typhoid in the area. An investigation was carried out by the pollution section of the Department of Water Affairs. 34 wells and 25 boreholes were tested for faecal coliform bacteria. Tests showed that only 12 of the boreholes were free of the bacteria.

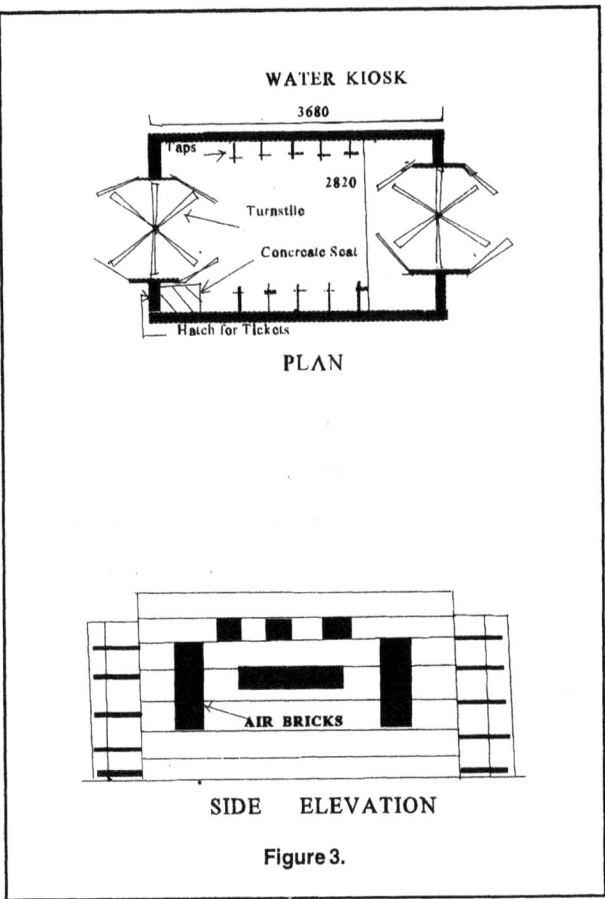

Figure 3.

Table 1. Water supply infrastructure

Type of infrastucture	1987	1995
Water mains	none	30km
Plots reticulated	none	280
Plots with yard taps or house connections	none	84

Table 2. Access to water infrastructure

Level of service	Population	%
House or yard connection	200	0.001
Borehole or well in yard	5600	3.1
Communal & vending taps	7800	4.3
Boreholes, wells, rivers	166000	92.25
TOTAL	180000	100

(See Figures 4 and 5). Test also showed salmonella, the cause of typhoid, in one borehole and in the Toloane river. These results are not surprising. This is due to the use of pit latrines close to the wells and boreholes and animals drinking water from the uncovered wells. Further the high water table and ground conditions are suitable for easy seepage from the pit latrines to the wells and boreholes.

The Department of Water Affairs was in a difficult situation as it could not provide water connections to the plots without the owner's request. The landlords were not interested in a connection, and all the land was thought to be privately owned. The Department of Local Government and Housing being responsible for administrating Winterveld investigated ways and means of providing water. The investigation showed that not all the land was privately owned. There were seven plots belonging to the government. It was then suggested to the community representatives that water could be provided on these plots and made available to the people to the people through water kiosks.

Community requested that water be provided free of charge. The government was not willing to provide water free, pointing out that the people were paying a high price for contaminated water from vendors, while the water provided at the kiosks would be safe drinking water at the same price. Costing allowed for capital expenditure, operating and maintenance. However the

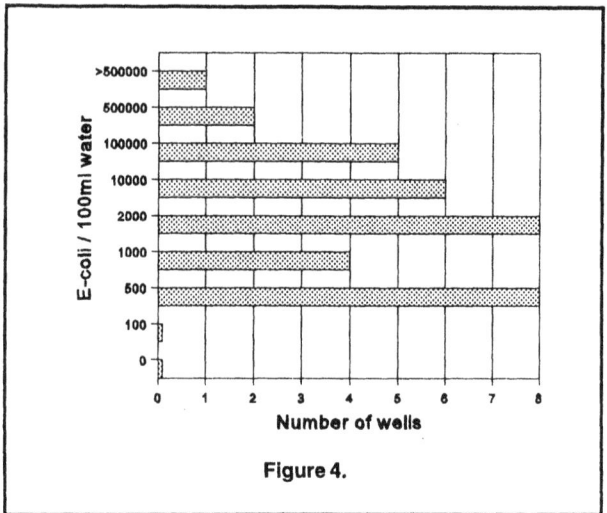

Figure 4.

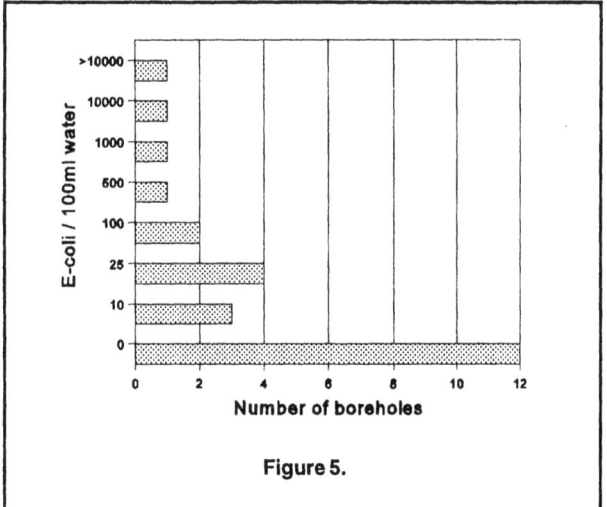

Figure 5.

community argued that the South African Government has given funds to the Bophuthatawana Government to provide services. This fund was given to entice the Bophuthatawana Government, who were reluctant to take over Winterveld, as the people in Winterveld were not of the same ethnic group as in Bophuthatawana. The department conceded to this and worked out the cost of water to cover only operation and maintenance. The cost was 8 cents/25 litres. The cost of water 22 per cent, operation 63 per cent and others 15 per cent. It was also pointed out that prices could come down if the consumption exceeded the estimated amount. This was because the operation cost would be constant irrespective of quantity of water used. This price 8 cents/25 litre being far below the price of the water vendors, the community accepted to pay this amount suggested by the government. The provision of water through these seven water kiosks was a short-term solution to redress the non-availability of affordable potable drinking water in the area. Although the solution was a scratch on the surface it was a process to provide water, sustain it and improve the process by extending it. This project will be run by the water authority with the co-operation of the people. When it came to the construction of the kiosks, plans were prepared keeping in mind that the building must be of a permanent nature, functional economical. To ensure it was permanent the building was of brick on sound foundation with a concrete plank roof. To be functional it had to be big enough to hold eight water taps, and to accommodate eight people with large buckets and 25 litre plastic canister. Further it needed to accommodate an operator who could sit comfortably and collect tickets and monitor the people entering and exiting. For security purposes air bricks were provided instead of windows. To prevent people hustling and bustling and to control unidirectional entry, turnstiles at the entrance and exit were provided. (Figure 3). This plan was approved by the community with a request to install wider turnstiles to allow easier access for those with large receptacles, and to improve visibility to help the safeguarding of personal items left outside such as wheelbarrows.

To follow the community's request to use local contractors for the construction of the kiosks, the department proposed to identify contractors within the area. A programme to recruit and train contractors was launched. The first meeting was attended by 50 people. Those who turned up were mostly semi-skilled labourers who preferred to sell their expertise. However, four contractors were identified after the meeting. They were recommended to the tender board as suitable contractors. The tender board accepted the recommendation.

The contract was to be managed as a normal civil engineering project. Several meetings were held to explain the tender procedure and the general conditions of contract that governs the way a contract is managed. Aspects highlighted were the retention period, interim payment certificates, penalties for late completion, surety and insurance. Also explained was the process of pricing a tender. Tender documents were prepared which included a material list to help pricing of the schedule of quantities. Tenders were called for in August 1993. Four contractors submitted tender for the seven kiosks. The evaluation showed an overpricing of the tender. It was decided to renegotiate with the prospective tenderers. During negotiations the department waived the provision of surety as none of the contractors had access to underwriters. Tender board approval was obtained for three contractors as one withdrew. The three shared the seven kiosks.

As the contractors were not financially strong, suppliers were reluctant to supply on credit. This could have delayed the start of the project. The consulting engineer took it upon himself to negotiate with the suppliers to supply materials on credit to the contractors. With the department's agreement he undertook to ensure payment by retaining the contractor's monthly payment cheque if he did not settle his account with the previous cheque. The occasion did not arise as the contractors promptly paid the suppliers.

The department normally takes 30 days to pay a claim. This was not suitable in respect of this contract as the contractors depended on the payment to overcome cash flow problems. It was decided that the consultant would collect the certificate and check and approve and deliver it to the department in Mmabatho 350km from Winterveld the next day. The department would process it immediately and pass it for payment. The account section would have the cheque within a week. The consultant would then collect the cheque and deposit it into the newly opened account of the contractors. This worked very well.

The construction items were:

- Foundation including drains
- Ironmongery
- Construction of walls to roof including air bricks
- Installation of turnstile and roof.

The setting out was done by the engineers representative. The work progressed satisfactorily. At one site the walls built to 1m height were demolished at night. It was suspected that a water vendor in the vicinity could have done it as the building of kiosks would be detrimental to his business. Further problems were encountered with the supply of the turnstiles. The construction of the kiosks went much faster than the local subcontractor could deliver turnstiles. The taps could not be installed until the turnstiles were in place. This seriously hampered the handing over of the kiosks. However water was provided and the kiosks became operational with minimum delay. This project not only provided water it also implemented capacity building and training. This process would be used in future projects.

To run the kiosks it was agreed with the community to employ young persons, both female and male. To avoid transport problems those close to the kiosk would be employed. Two such persons in each kiosk would operate in shifts from 6.00 hrs - 10.00 hrs and 15.00 hrs - 18.00 hrs every day. To avoid handling of money by the operators, tickets were sold at the office of the water authority. To avoid fraud, tickets of different colours are issued at intervals. Each ticket would purchase 25 litres. The operator for each shift would read the meter before opening and after closing. Once a week the operators met at the office of the water authority and handed over the tickets and meter readings to the supervisor for checking meter reading versus collection of tickets. The discrepancies were negligible. It was found that the female operators proved to be better than the males in their accuracy and discipline. The operators at the end of the day locked the kiosks and closed the supply valve with a special key.

This project is a good example of how the community helped to protect assets that they felt belonged to them and helped to make the project successful. The new Government of Unity under the Reconstruction And Development Programme (R.D.P.) has already identified the need to provide water to Winterveld. Under the Presidential special R.D.P. R23 million has been set aside for the provision of water to the whole of Winterveld i.e. both north and south of Winterveld. The first phase is to provide water taps at 200 m intervals. This is the basic minimum standard set in the White Paper of the Department of Water Affairs and Forestry. The taps will be managed by water committees. In the area discussed in the paper the taps would be placed at the edge of the plots. The water would be managed by water committees. The experience gained from the operation of the water kiosks could be used by the water committees. Under the new dispensation, those in a plot could group together and obtain a loan. With this loan they could reticulate the plot and have individual connections.

References

Construction of Winterveld Water Kiosks (Consultburo November 1994).

Case Study of Informal Water Supply in Winterveld Report 2. (Palmer Development Group Oct. 1993).

Winterveld Structure Plan and Development Guidelines. (Taylor and Associates April 1994).

Averting shallow-well contamination in Uganda

Richard G. Taylor and Dr Ken W.F. Howard, Canada

DESPITE AN ABUNDANCE of surface water in Uganda (18 per cent of the land area), the predominantly rural (>90 per cent) population relies almost exclusively on groundwater for a potable water supply. This dependence arises from the more widespread occurrence, superior quality and reduced susceptibility to contamination, of groundwater supplies compared to surface-water sources. As a result, provision of safe water to rural communities in Uganda has depended primarily upon the construction of wells and protection of spring discharges.

In Uganda, as with other regions in equatorial Africa featuring extensive, weathered crystalline rock, often referred to as the 'basement complex', groundwater development has targeted two main aquifer units: a deep aquifer of fractured bedrock and a shallow, muddy-sand aquifer comprizing detrital bedrock and alluvium. Particular attention has recently been directed at developing the shallow aquifer since the formation is less costly to develop and a recent study (Howard and others, 1994) has found it is more productive than the deeper, bedrock aquifer. However, monitoring of water quality in south-eastern Uganda, a region of intense shallow-well development, shows that within months of installation, shallow groundwaters commonly exhibit levels of coliform bacteria and nitrate exceeding WHO health guidelines.

Human and livestock waste excreted in pit latrines, over land or in open-pit wells, called 'scoop wells', may contain worms, protozoa, bacteria and viruses that, if consumed, can lead to the contraction of hepatitis, typhoid, cholera and a variety of diarrhoeal diseases. Wells and springs harvesting shallow groundwaters are generally protected from these pathogens by a granular soil matrix which both filters bacteria, protozoa and worms due to their relatively large diameter (>0.5µm) in relation to the aquifer material, and adsorbs smaller viruses (0.07µm to 0.7µm) on account of their strong, negative surface charge. Despite this cleansing capacity, the presence of coliform group of bacteria in groundwater indicates that faecal contamination has occurred (Lewis and others, 1980). High nitrate concentrations also indicate contamination from sewage sources since nitrogenous material, which is uncommon to the subsurface mineralogy, forms a significant component of human and animal waste, and is oxidized to nitrate under the aerobic conditions of shallow groundwaters. The risks associated with elevated nitrate levels (>50mg/L) include methaemoglobinaemia in young infants and the development of gastric cancer.

Contamination of the shallow, weathered aquifer from domestic sewage has been observed across equatorial Africa. In Nigeria, large nitrate increases in shallow wells demonstrate strong correlations with denser human settlements and hence, the number of waste facilities (Langenegger, 1981; Malomo and others, 1990). This pattern has similarly been noted in northern Uganda by Howard and others (1994). In The Gambia, Barrell and Rowland (1979) found dramatic increases in faecal coliforms coincident with the onset of monsoonal rainfall and surmized that deposited faecal material was being flushed either through the weathered soil or directly round poorly sealed well shafts. Such contaminant pathways are possible in Uganda where subsurface infiltration (i.e. recharge) has been shown to coincide with monsoonal rainfall (Howard and others, 1994).

One method of reducing well and spring contamination is to ensure that waterpoints and pollutant sources (e.g. pit latrines, scoop wells) are sufficiently separated to minimize the migration of pathogens into a pumping well or discharging spring. This region around a waterpoint is known as a wellhead protection area (WHPA) and may be defined in a variety of ways. In this paper, we present evidence of shallow well contamination from domestic sewage in Mukono District of south-eastern Uganda (Figure 1) and, equipped with a recently-gained understanding of the shallow, muddy-sand aqui-

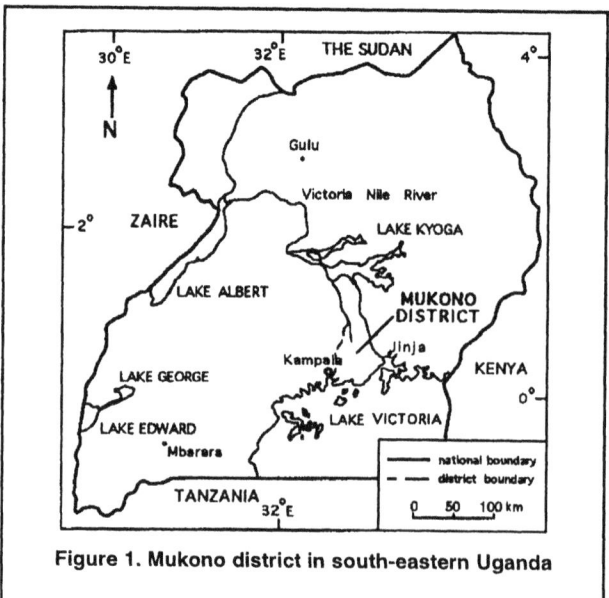

Figure 1. Mukono district in south-eastern Uganda

fer (Howard and others, 1994), delineate WHPAs using simulations of groundwater flow with FLOWPATH (Franz and Guiguer, 1994).

Regional hydrogeology

Shallow unconsolidated formations in Mukono District are derived from the prolonged weathering of Precambrian crystalline bedrock of the Granulitic-Gneissic complex, which covers much of central and northern Uganda, and the Buganda-Toro system of mica schists, acid gneisses and quartzites. Quaternary sediments line the Victoria Nile river and Sezibwa swamp as well as the north shore of Lake Victoria (Figure 1). Grain-size analyses of soil, weathered from the granulitic-gneissic complex in northern Uganda, show the shallow aquifer to be composed of a muddy sand. Water well records and geophysical surveys reveal an aquifer thickness of at least 10m (Howard and others, 1994). Analysis of pumping tests conducted at 60 shallow wells in Mukono indicates the aquifer is largely unconfined with an arithmetic mean hydraulic conductivity of 0.2m/day. Well construction commonly occurs near scoop wells and swamps because the presence of a shallow water table in these areas inhibits the formation of duricrusts, which are impenetrable by hand-drilling, and virtually guarantees water will be found. However, with an average depth to water of just 2.6m, the length and time (in some cases as little as two weeks) during which the granular medium is able to remove surface wastes before they enter the groundwater system, is limited. Pumping tests achieved an average, steady-state drawdown of 4.5m using a mean pumping rate of 12L/minute, a value which is similar to the capacity of most handpumps. Consequently, steep hydraulic gradients can develop between shallow wells and the sources of pollutants (scoop wells and swamps).

Shallow-well water quality

The biological and chemical quality of water from 10 shallow wells in Mukono District was evaluated at the beginning of the first rainy season in April (1994) and three months later during the short dry season in July. Site selection depended upon the presence of an adjacent scoop well which was also analyzed in July, 1994, for its biological and chemical quality. Results of the biological tests are presented in Table 1. Only total coliform counts were considered since false positive readings for faecal coliforms have been observed in tropical environments using standard methods (Barrel and Rowland, 1979).

All of the scoop wells exhibit severe faecal contamination with total coliform counts well in excess of 100 per 100mL. As such, they clearly constitute a potential source of contamination to adjacent shallow wells. Significantly, at the three sites where the scoop well had either been filled in or dried up, total coliform counts in the shallow wells declined dramatically and in two instances fell to within acceptable levels (L10 count/100mL; World Health Organization, 1985). At the remaining seven sites with an operating scoop well, six shallow wells show unacceptably high coliform counts ranging from 12 to 97 per 100mL. At four of these sites, total coliform counts have risen since initial testing in April. With respect to nitrate levels, the average concentration in the seven shallow wells having an adjacent scoop well is considerably higher (11mg/L) than the average amount recorded in 60 shallow wells at the time of their construction (1.0mg/L).

Both the total coliform and nitrate data show deterioration of shallow-well water quality in the presence of a polluted scoop well. No apparent relationship exists, however, between the magnitude of contamination and the distance separating scoop wells from shallow wells. The possibility that surface waste is being flushed by heavy rains through lateritic soils is unlikely since background nitrate levels in the shallow aquifer, measured at the time of well construction, were low. Contaminant migration down poorly-sealed well casings is also unlikely since this pathway would fail to explain the improvement noted in coliform counts at shallow wells where the scoop well had either filled in or dried up. Although inconclusive, the total coliform and nitrate evidence strongly implies nearby scoop wells are a key threat to shallow-well water quality. Delineation of a safe distance between shallow wells and point sources of faecal contamination such as scoop wells and pit latrines, is necessary in order to ensure the sustainability of this potable water supply.

Delineation of wellhead protection areas (WHPAs)

A wellhead protection area (WHPA) is the region around a well where contaminant sources could pose a threat to drinking water drawn from the well. Determination of WHPAs requires both an understanding of the aquifer's hydrogeological characteristics and the selection of appropriate criteria to delimit WHPAs such as the time for

Table 1. Distance between shallow wells and their adjacent scoop well, and total coliform levels recorded in scoop wells (July 1994) and shallow wells (April and July, 1994).

Shallow well #	Scoop well distance (m)	Total coliform scoop well	Total coliform April 1994	Total coliform July 1994
AW057	10	600	167	31
AW091	4	>1000	31	17
AW136	20	900	4	58
AW137	10	413	39	61
AW191	filled in	–	41	1
AW193	50	>1200	2	0
AW194	dried up	–	61	0
AW197	35	119	0	103
AW220	dried up	–	>300	53
AW251	100	>1200	0	97

Total coliform: total # of coliforms in a 100ml sample.
Scoop well: adjacent scoop well.

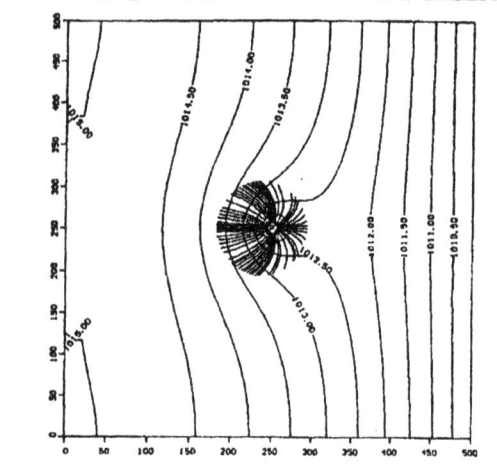

Figure 2. Flowpath simulation of a shallow well pumping under a uniform hydraulic gradient of 0.01. The hydraulic head contour interval is 0.5m.

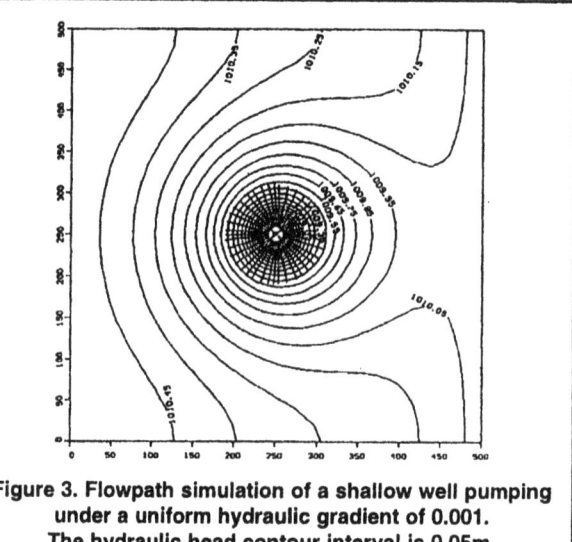

Figure 3. Flowpath simulation of a shallow well pumping under a uniform hydraulic gradient of 0.001. The hydraulic head contour interval is 0.05m.

a contaminant to reach the pumping well or the extent of hydraulic depression caused by the pumping well. In this paper, WHPAs were defined using two-dimensional, groundwater flow models developed with the finite-difference code, FLOWPATH (ver. 5.11) (Franz and Guiguer, 1994). Flow within an area of 500m x 500m was simulated with a well, positioned at its centre, pumping at a rate of 10L/minute for a desirable well lifetime of 10 years. In addition to the hydrogeological parameters stated earlier, an effective porosity of 35 per cent was assumed for the muddy-sand formation. Hydraulic gradients tend to follow the typography of weathered soils within the East African plateau resting between 0.01 and 0.001.

Figure 2 shows equipotential lines (lines of equal hydraulic head) and pathlines of groundwater flow toward a shallow well pumping over a 10-year period. Despite the asymmetry caused by the direction of the hydraulic gradient (0.01 from left to right, prior to pumping) the simulation shows that over a 10-year lifetime, a shallow well draws water from up to 60m away. In two years, groundwater over a 25m radius is pumped. In a uniform flow field with a reduced hydraulic gradient of 0.001 (Figure 3), the pathlines exhibit improved symmetry around the pumping well but extend similarly 60m from the well. Although not presented, a reduction in the pumping rate to 4L/minute decreases the length of pathlines to 40m, over a 10-year period, and to 15m, in two years. In all of the above simulations, pathlines reveal the extent of a pumping well's influence over time and so represent the distance a non-reactive pollutant, like chloride, would travel over that period to reach the well. Nitrate, though susceptible to denitrification processes, also behaves conservatively. Biological pathogens, on the other hand, move more slowly and have a limited life expectancy. Presented pathlines, therefore, serve as generalized conservative estimates of the wellhead protection area.

Conclusions and recommendations

The practice of siting shallow wells in the vicinity of existing scoop wells has been identified as a probable source of faecal contamination to shallow wells in Mukono District of southeastern Uganda. Simulations of groundwater flow in the shallow aquifer indicate that a wellhead protection area of 60m between wells and contaminant sources such as scoop wells, pit latrines and swamps is required to ensure the sustainability of this vital, potable source of water to rural communities. The impact of site variations such as the hydraulic gradient (local slope), as well as the rate and duration of well pumping which are critical for effective planning and surveying of groundwater development activities, have been evaluated. Continued monitoring of shallow groundwater quality is necessary in order to evaluate whether the suggested minimum separation (60m) between wells and contaminant sources, known as a wellhead protection area, is adequate.

The occurrence of swamps and scoop wells coincides with the presence of a near-surface water table. As a result, the institution of WHPAs in Uganda will lead to the construction of shallow wells away from these pollutant sources, in areas where the water table is deeper and the lateritic crust may be impenetrable by hand drilling. In these situations, machine drilling can assist in boring through the crust.

Acknowledgements

The authors gratefully acknowledge the assistance of the Water Resources Unit of the DANIDA-sponsored RUWASA (Rural Water and Sanitation) project in providing water quality and pumping-test data. During the preparation of this paper, the principal author benefitted from a Young Canadian Researcher's Award furnished by the International Development Research Centre, Ottawa, Canada.

References

Barrel, R.A.E., and Rowland, M.G.M., 1979. 'The relationship between rainfall and well water pollution in a West African (Gambian) village'. *Journal of Hygiene*, Vol. 83, pp. 143-50.

Franz, T., and Guiguer, N., 1994. FLOWPATH v.5.11, A steady-state two-dimensional horizontal aquifer simulation model. Waterloo Hydrogeologic Software.

Howard, K.W.F. and others, 1994. A hydrogeological and socio-economic examination of the regolith and fractured-bedrock systems of the Aroca catchment in Apac District and Nyabisheki catchment in Mbarara District. *Final report to the Directorate of Water Development, Ministry of Natural Resources, Republic of Uganda* (May, 1994).

Langenegger, D., 1981. 'High nitrate concentrations in shallow aquifers in a rural area of central Nigeria'. *Quality of groundwater*, Studies in Environmental Science Vol. 17, pp. 135-140.

Lewis, W.J., Foster, S.S.D., and Drasar, B.S., 1980. The risk of groundwater pollution by on-site sanitation in developing countries. *International Reference Centre for Waste Disposal Report No. 01/82*.

Malomo, S., Okufarasin, V.A., Olorunniwo, M.A., and Omode, A.A., 1990. 'Groundwater chemistry of the weathered zone aquifers of an area underlain by basement complex rocks'. *Journal of African Earth Sciences*, Vol. 11, No. 3/4, pp. 357-371.

World Health Organization, 1985. *Guidelines for Drinking Water Quality*. Vol. 3, Drinking Water Quality Control in Small Community Supplies.

SECTION C

RURAL WATER SUPPLY AND SANITATION

Reconstruction development plan — Hlanganani

R. Burgess and M. Slabbert, South Africa

THE MANAGEMENT OF South Africa's water and the equitable distribution of this scarce resource are tasks delegated by the Department of Water Affairs and Forestry to various provincial water supply authorities. In the province of kwaZulu Natal, Umgeni Water plays a major role in the management and distribution of water. Umgeni Water was formed in 1974, to supply bulk water to the cities of Durban and Pietermariztburg and other towns in kwaZulu Natal but in recent years has been working towards the concept of 'total water management'.

In 1989 a major infrastructure study of the Umgeni Water 7000km² supply area was completed. The findings of this study focused on the fact that vast inequities in the provision of services existed within this supply area.

In order to address these inequities a further study was commissioned in 1991 that resulted in the Rural Areas Water and Sanitation Plan (RAWSP) being formulated. This plan made recommendations with estimates of costs for the supply of water to the communities within the aforementioned rural areas, representing a total population of 500 000 people.

In 1994 the Umgeni Water supply area was extended to include five further rural areas. As a continuation of the RAWSP and in order to assist with the aims of the Reconstruction and Development Plan, Umgeni Water Commissioned a study in each of these five areas, one of which is Hlanganani.

Locality of the study

The province of kwaZulu Natal lies on the eastern shores of South Africa and the area of Hlanganani lies within the province. It comprises six geographically separate blocks of 1280 square kilometres.

The study area fits broadly between latitudes 29°30'S and 30°15'S and the lines of longitude 29°25'E and 30°15'E.

History of the area

The South African land act of 1913 and 1936 led to the *de jure* definition of black and white rural areas with the highest potential agricultural land being made available to white farmers. This legislation was instrumental in destroying the black farming class in kwaZulu Natal and contributed to the deterioration of both material and environmental conditions in kwaZulu Natal. Further this legislation exacerbated the distorted pattern of urban settlement in kwaZulu Natal and helped to shape the settlement pattern which is now found in the study area.

These historical influences effected the quality of life in the rural are of Hlanganani. This can be illustrated by the following statistics:

- Population densities in kwaZulu Natal are six-and-a half times those in the old Natal Province;
- Between 40 per cent to 60 per cent of all households in peri-urban and dense rural areas in kwaZulu Natal receive no direct income from wages;
- Half the households in the area earn less than the household subsistence level;
- The quality of physical infrastructure/services and social facilities/programmes tends to be poor in the rural areas.

Objectives of the study

The objectives of the study were as follows:

- To evaluate the best water supply options for the area;
- To evaluate the provision of water in the context of integrated development proposals for the area.

Situational analysis

A detailed situation analysis was carried out. Existing information was used but additional data, particularly population statistics, was obtained by means of field surveys and the use of aerial photography. The situational analysis in summary comprized the following:

- A study of the demographics of the area.
- A compilation of the socio-economic information comprizing education levels employment, income and expenditure, standard of dwellings, access to water and related problems and the identification of basic needs and related priorities.
- An assessment of socio-political status in the area primarily identifying and understanding the main players, power groups and stake holders in the area.
- A summary of existing infrastructure and development plans.

Demographics

The current population (190 500) of the area was calculated by means of homestead counts using aerial photography and field surveys to assess the average homestead size. The field surveys revealed that the average homestead consisted of eight people. It was realized during the course of the study that the growth populations were subject to significant margins of error depending on what method is used to derive them.

It was found in all the areas bar one that females are in the majority. This is a reflection of the migrancy patterns prevalent in the area and the necessity for the economically active portion of the population to seek work in the industrial sectors of the kwaZulu Natal province.

The age distribution of the population displays the skewed demographics pyramid typical of Third World communities: very large youth cohorts (< 18 years) and a small aged cohort (> 64 years) making for high dependency ratios on the economically active sector of the population. Household data collected during field surveys show that the average household size was eight and that children comprize 50 per cent of the household numbers in the area. Moreover, in the more rural areas between 20 per cent and 30 per cent of the household may consist of grandchildren of the household head. This confirms the observed phenomena of parents working in urban areas and sending their children to their grandparents in the rural areas.

Population densities varied greatly from 1500 people per km^2 to 50 people per km^2. The mean population density was calculated in 1993 as being 147 persons per km^2 in contrast to a density of 24 persons per km^2 in the white district of nearby Richmond.

Socio-economic information

To all intents and purposes the economy of the district has been dominated by subsistence agriculture and remittances from wages earned elsewhere. The dependency ratio throughout the area is approximately 50 per cent and only 16 per cent of the population are self-employed. Surveys show that approximately 40 per cent of the adult population are illiterate (21 years of age with less than Std. 4 education).

Sub-regional economy is generally dominated by farming, particularly stock ranching, although dairy is also an important sector.

A study of the household economic profile shows that the mean household income per month was well under R1 000.00. Thirty per cent of the population surveyed have a household income of less than R250.00 per month with only 4.3 per cent having an income greater than R1 500.00 per month.

Socio-political information

Political dynamics over the past five years in the district have been dominated, as in much of the kwaZulu Natal area, by the battle for supremacy between the Inkatha Freedom Party and the African National Congress.

There are 14 tribal authorities in the area. Given the dominance of traditional customs tribal authorities feature prominently in local affairs and in development matters.

There are innumerable small, local organizations or special income groups at the level of burial societies, saving clubs, sewing and candle-making groups, farmers associations, creche committees, school committees etc.. These groups are geographically extremely localised and are insignificant as representative groups able to negotiate on behalf of communities. It is considered that they could be important in terms of mobilizing communities around a particular project.

Population growth and water demand

Population projections

The current population, having been determined by homestead counts and field surveys, was the initial input to the population growth model. Two population growth models were used. The first one used a constant growth rate over a 25-year time span at 2.5 per cent per annum. A more complicated growth model using a varying growth rate over the 25-year life span of 1.1 per cent to 2.92 per cent was used as a comparison. Growth projections were compared and it was accepted that the population would grow over the 25 years from 190 000 to 350 000.

Water demand and levels of service

It is anticipated that the level of service to the rural communities will vary between a centralized community handpump or standpipe and private house connections. Final design life consumption figures (10 - 20 years) for rural areas was taken as 50l/capita/day for the mixed rural and peri-urban areas and for the peri-urban area a consumption of 70l/capita/day was used.

Growth in demand for higher levels of service

Cost recovery is considered a major necessity for the sustainability of the water supply systems to the area. Provision was made for the growth in demand for the higher levels of service. The growth in demand scenarios assumed a straight line relationship from 19 per cent of the final demand in year one to 100 per cent of the final demand in year 2020.

Technical alternatives considered

Development of surface water alternatives

To evaluate the possibility of utilizing surface water resources per district, the quaternary catchment boundaries were used to model the hydrology of the area. Suitable abstraction points from nearby perennial rivers were identified to supply the proposed pipeline networks. Possible storage reservoir sites were located on high ground near to the identified communities.

Pipeline routes were identified running predominantly along roads and ridges. Using the quaternary catchments the flow in the rivers was modelled and tables of monthly flows according to a percentage rate of failure were obtained for each of the proposed abstraction points. The monthly flows for a two per cent risk of failure were selected. The communities supplied from an abstraction point were then grouped and the population count and water demand relating to each abstraction point was calculated for the present and future scenarios. Downstream compensation was calculated for present and future scenarios and allowance for downstream irrigation requirements was built into the calculations.

Once a suitable abstraction point had been established based on the hydrology of the area and the practicality of conveying water to storage reservoirs and secondary distribution networks, the scheme was costed.

Using the growth in demand model and the water demand figures a discounted cash flow analysis was conducted on the scheme using varying discount rates and design parameters. Using this analysis the break-even cost of water was calculated. The capital cost of the works, the capital cost per capita and the break-even cost of water was then used to rank the schemes.

Development of groundwater alternatives

An evaluation of the groundwater potential was undertaken of the entire district of Hlanganani making use of aerial photography. Based on lithological principles, categories of groundwater potential were established and mapped. These groundwater potentials ranged from very low to very high (five groundwater potential categories). Tectonic structures such as faults, dykes, shear zones and fractures were identified on the maps and circled. Potential target drilling sites were considered in conjunction with accessibility.

The areas of high groundwater potential were then superimposed on the existing road network and the spatial distribution of the communities.

Three categories of groundwater service levels were applied to the various districts of Hlanganani. These were:

- Handpumps
- Motorized boreholes
- Well fields using motorized boreholes.

The groundwater proposals were then costed and discounted cash flow analyses were carried out. The schemes were then compared with the surface water proposals.

The way forward

The output of this study represents strategic development information for this area. This information will be disseminated as widely as possible.

The findings will be presented to various audiences concentrating specifically at local level as certain actions, issues and priorities recommended in the study will need community input. Where possible short-term action will be implemented immediately while medium- and long-term proposals are developed. A ten-year programme of implementation to serve _most_ people in the area with services has been set as a challenging objective by Umgeni Water. Considerable outside funding support will be required to achieve this programme. Detailed feasibility studies have been commissioned for the most promising proposed schemes identified in the study. These further studies will provide more accurate costs necessary when approaching donors.

Conclusion

In order to promote the aims of the Reconstruction and Development Plan in Hlanganani with respect to water supply, there is a need to establish a partnership with all the participants. The partnership should be based on trust and close communication during the formulation of all further stages. This requirement is seen as being fundamental to the effective implementation of the plan and its success.

Sustainability with large communally-owned systems

Brian Copeland, Uganda

THE KEY TO the successful sustainability of a system is the mobilization of public awareness and co-operative spirit to the needs of maintenance, hygiene, sanitation and costs, and the matching of the system to the specific community, or in the case described, the several disparate communities. With large systems covering a large area and with public access to standpipes, this presents special problems due to complexity, population size and institution building, increasing the load on mobilizers progressively as the system grows.

In 1992, WaterAid, with initial funding from DANIDA took on the reconstruction and enlargement of the Bwera Water Project, begun in 1987 to a Carl Bros plan and built by DWD. It was far too small and had broken in many places.

After further survey, the mainline was relaid, a proper intake built at the source and a further 16 reservoirs of 70-100 000 l built, and some hundreds of kilometres of pipe laid. Still under construction (in May 1995 11 out of 16 parishes had been completed) there will be about 900 standpipes in 16 parishes covering perhaps 250km^2.

We employ 25 salaried local staff and had originally 64 (four from each parish) volunteers to be trained in maintenance. Of these only a few can now be relied upon as they were never paid, but once a parish is 'on line' then they are paid by the community for repairs. The parishes also supply community labour for trenching etc., locally available materials such as sand and meals to work crews.

Bwera is in west Uganda, Bukunjo County, and the River Lubiriha, from which the water is taken, forms the Ugandan/Zairean border: at this point 20 1/sec are diverted to a population of 60 000 and the system is designed for 80 000 by 2001 providing 20l/h/d. Organization reflects the Ugandan RC system of government of participation through elected representatives at different administrative levels (a bit like the Poder Popular of Cuba). Each parish has a reservoir and distribution system for which it is responsible. There are five elected committee members and a further one from each parish elected to the central committee, which therefore has 16 members of which again five form the executive. Each tapstand has a committee of three, for maintenance, hygiene and rate collection (receipts given), and each parish decides its own constitution. The central committee is responsible for repair and maintenance to the main supply line (common to all), payment of fees/salaries to permanent or hired staff, upkeep of central office, monitoring performance and arranging audits. Of the present monthly rate of 400/1 (30p) per household 20 per cent goes to the central committee. The Bwera Water Association is now a registered indigenous NGO, and its patron the Rt. Hon. Crispus Kionga, Minister of Internal Affairs, who was the original government initiator of the project long before WaterAid arrived.

Problems foreseen were a belief that water is free and a resistance to regular payment, the lack of existing grassroot consequent organizations with which to work, the belief that donors not only provide but should also maintain, and the generally low educational/income level of this poor but developing area. The concept of community ownership was difficult to explain and devise as it would have been in Watford or Dallas, since, like us, they expect 'top down' provision. Not foreseen were:

1a The arrival and rapid growth of the customs market and its future development as a duty free zone at the border trading point
b. The planned 200-bed hospital, funded by EADB, with staff quarters, which alone will take as much water as a parish
c Immigration to the area due to trade, at present estimated at 50/month in the town alone, and further immigration from the mountains to the plains now supplied with potable water, to exploit the high coffee prices
d. The amount of water abuse for car washing, brickmaking and construction in a booming area, and irrigated gardens.

These are problems of rapid development and apart from the latter beyond the commitment of WaterAid. They will however shorten the useful life of the system.

Mobilization difficulties

As usual, the devil is in the detail.

2a The system is too large to be comprehensible to the layman and there is a total lack of awareness of the technical and administrative interrelatedness of its constituent parts. Explanations are involved and technical. The wananchi are only interested in the bottom line.
b. The general attendance at meetings is about two per cent, and usually no more than five per cent even at handover ceremonies. Even elected representatives

won't attend unless we feed them. People of course have other things to do, but it makes communication and the dissemination of information difficult.

c. Mistrust of money collectors. This is well placed, as some elected rate collectors and representatives have absconded with funds and even the local bank has stolen from the parish accounts which took 18 months to resolve. Low educational levels make accounting procedures incomprehensible to the wananchi and difficult for committee treasurers.

d. Elected members of committees volunteered their services in the erroneous belief that there would be a salary or fee when WaterAid depart. They will not continue to work for nothing, therefore allowances must come from rates. Ergo, rates must rise.

e. It was only after two-and-a-half years into the project when we had five parishes 'on line' that we had payment registers, which might be relied on. Although beginning well at around 90 per cent they soon fell to an average of 23 per cent in Oct. 1994. After a serious effort by mobilizers they then rose a bit, but in May 1995 are again falling to a level too low to maintain the system.

f. At the outset, only one mobilizer was needed to organize the pilot community for labour; trenching, backfilling, soakaways, pipeline marking, hygiene and sanitation. As the number of parishes increased, it was still necessary constantly to return to ones considered complete to reinforce messages, sort out problems at tapstand level etc., while at the same time mobilizing for construction many other parishes being constructed in parallel. The load on mobilizers was therefore greatly underestimated, even though we were uniquely lucky to find a partner organization in Kasanga CBHC to undertake health and sanitation aspects. It had been hoped that committee members would themselves be active in mobilization but again, without recompense, they had other things to do. They need to earn a living, and so not surprisingly regard such duties as employment. Altruism is an unaffordable luxury.

Other worries

3a. There had been problems of our workers 'moonlighting', by fixing private connections. This is now forbidden, but when we leave and they no longer have a source of income, it is unlikely they will restrain themselves. If the better off begin installing showers and baths, consumption will quickly rise again.

b. Most of the pipe laid was HDPE, not manufactured in Uganda. Both Kenyan and UK pipes face import surcharges and procurement difficulties. DWD were excluded from maintenance because of the accompanying loss of public accountability and the difficulties they have in maintaining their present workload.

c. That demand will exceed supply very quickly leading to water shortages and a further fall-off in rate payment. There is no understanding of the carrying capacity of the 6" main, which was not the result of design, but left to Uganda on the break-up of the EAF.

d. That our best trainees and technicians would sell their skills elsewhere at a rate unaffordable by their committees. They also know how to manipulate the system for sectional interests if pressure or inducement is sufficient.

Attempts to solve these problems

1. Supply problems caused by points 1, a, b, c are a future problem for the development of the areas, beyond the committment of WaterAid. Local government has been informed of our concerns but seem unlikely to revise their plans. Point 1d will be addressed by having bye-laws passed, regarding the use and abuse of potable water. We count on the co-operation of the Combolo chiefs and RC system for enforcement.

2a Continued repetition of the message that all leaks and breakdowns must be reported immediately to parish trainees or committee members, followed by shutdown of affected area until repair. Hammer home need to pay water rates.

b. A small budget of 50 000/- (£32) per quarter was set aside for food for important meetings to encourage attendance. This too will have to be funded from the water rate when we leave.

c. A training programme in bookkeeping, budgeting and management will commence in June 1995. A bit too late maybe, but there were many difficulties encountered. The almost cultural pursuit of embezzlement will remain a problem.

d. A system of attendance fees and allowances was worked out with committee members. People will not take long-term responsibility without recompense. Salaries/fees for future permanent staff agreed between central committee and trainees at a locally affordable rate. (Much lower than the NGO rate).

e. We hope that the enforcement of bye-laws, though coercive, will be seen as a necessary part of a 'carrot and stick' approach.

f. The number of mobilizers was increased to three, then to five. Our programme support unit helps Kasanga CBHC for a couple of days each month and has trained some of our mobilizers, but we cannot claim to have solved the difficulties of community mobilization for payment of water rates. The level of resources allocated to this aspect has to be much higher with 'open access' systems and community management, and our mobilizers who are necessarily local Bakonjo speakers have no engineering or other training, but fly by the seat of their pants.

3a We hope that bye-laws will prevent this, but 'money finds a way'.

b. A stock of spares left with the central committee and tool kits with each parish. WaterAid's continued presence in Uganda will facilitate overseas procurement if necessary, but again this will have to come from water rates.

c. Repetition of the limitations of the supply system, and the setting of inlet valves to reservoirs at design population flow rates and then padlocked. A weak point since so many people are now trained in the system that it can be manipulated for sectional interest and destroy the balance of supply.

Results

As of May 1995, rate payments are still too low to maintain the system satisfactorily. Bye-laws are still pending although passed at RC5 level and there is still some local political in-fighting over who controls the system and its assets to be ironed out. Such a large system potentially generates a large cashflow and employment opportunities. Mobilization will continue for a year after the construction phase has finished. We await further data once bye-laws are in place.

Recommendations and lessons learned

1. With hindsight, it would have been simpler and would have required less social engineering if water shops had been set up at agreed points and fitted with meters. The attendant would then be paid a percentage of the rate collection measured by the meter, and payment to committees could also have been checked against measured delivery. However, the original system had open access via standpipes and I presume that this was simply continued.
2. Professional agencies such as WaterAid, which have large local salaried staff, have inevitable cost ceilings and time horizons. Engineering planning, while attempting critical path analysis, faces procurement problems common to the continent which turn ETA's into no more than hopes, while system software, ie. the social engineering must be opened, varying according to regions, peoples and local experience. The pressure for 'top down' solutions increases with the size of the project and the financial implications of over-run. Volunteer agencies without local salaried staff, whose only cost is capital expenditure on hardware and freight may well be more effective where systems are smaller or time horizons indefinite.
3. Other areas or countries may well provide a different experience. The Bakonjo are a self-reliant people with little co-operative organization or institutions. The socio-political groups of societies which have undergone popular armed struggle may well provide better vehicles for co-operation and organization. The RC system, while admirable, was not the result of grassroots experience. This should be taken into account when designing systems and service delivery.
4. It is now realized that mobilization is a far larger component of sustainability than was believed. The chief and RC system were not invited to become involved until it was clear that rate payment was below that necessary to maintain the project. Such organizational and legal aspects should be anticipated and form either part of the information provided, or ideally arise from participatory organizational design.
5. It was later realized that a significant part of default was unintentional but the result of seasonal crop payments. A larger part of default was embezzlement by collectors (many have been dismissed or have absconded).
6. Reticulation was designed to make maximum use of supply potential without other reserve than population growth. This may not have been a good idea, as large systems are likely to generate their own growth factors.
7. The necessity of common accounting systems and training in budgeting, bookkeeping and management.
8. The WaterAid PSU unit was not constituted until the project was well underway. In future they should be incorporated at the earliest opportunity and with adequate resources for training trainers, especially in such large public systems requiring rate payments and large area consensus. A more participatory approach could then be implemented in which solutions to anticipated problems would arise from within the community. Project completion dates seem to argue for a more didactic approach.
9. WaterAid local staff are paid at the going NGO rate, which is many times the commercial labour rate. This sets a benchmark expectation on our departure which cannot be fulfilled from community resources. We should consider carefully the inflationary implications of our belief in 'a decent living wage' as in the long run it is the poor who suffer the worst of its effects. A larger social wage might be an alternative. Our best technicians and fieldworkers will be lost to the system when we stop paying them.
10. The problems caused by embezzlement are likely to continue in this area, and at standpipes, with 1000 people handling funds, it seems inevitable that the mice will nibble the seedcorn, while meticulous policing would have further costs which would have to be reflected in the water rate if implemented.
11. Development is a long learning process in which the lessons learned are not universally applicable and formulae which are not flexible should be avoided. However I realize that in order to convince a people that we seriously intend to proceed with a project, they must first see pipe being laid, but that construction quickly outruns social organization unless far greater effort is put into this area.

Village level operation and maintenance

C.B. Jespersen, Uganda

IN APRIL 1984, the Government of Malawi requested the Danish International Development Agency (DANIDA) to finance a groundwater project in the northern district of Karonga. An important aspect of the project was the introduction of a community-based (village-level) operation and maintenance (VLOM) system for the water points.

The Karonga Lakeshore Integrated Rural Groundwater Supply Project (KIP) completed its construction phase on 31 March, 1991, with the installation of 300 water points, 295 of which were fitted with Afridev deep well handpumps and concrete structures i.e. a pedestal for the pump, apron, washing slab and a spillway.

In the last month of the construction phase, all water points were handed over to the recipient communities. This marked the actual commencement of the operation and maintenance (O and M) phase, of which the first four years (1991-1994) were financed by DANIDA on a declining scale.

The concept of VLOM varies depending on who is using the phrase. The handpump producers utilize the acronym as an addition to their trademark to indicate that their product is fit for the most remote communities, for which it will ensure water for years on end as only a few parts need to be changed and this can be done by the users themselves. Planners see VLOM as a way to privatization, thereby reducing the burden on government expenditures; government institutions directly responsible for rural water supply regard VLOM as a means of reducing pressure on already overburdened public maintenance teams.

All of these viewpoints are true, but none of them take into consideration the full range of structures needed to ensure that VLOM creates a sustainable water supply. Further, none recognize that VLOM is not only a technical concept but more, a socio-economic concept that has a large amount of community development attached to its introduction and function.

Once introduced, VLOM is a dynamic process, needing constant development and refinement to cater for the increased skills obtained by the communities, thus increasing the possibility of having the users take further responsibilities within the system and, ideally, takes ultimate charge of it all, through private business structures.

The main conclusions of four years of introduction of O and M are:

- It seems possible to establish a sustainable rural groundwater supply based on users' own organization and manpower (VLOM) with spare parts supplied through private outlets (a one-tier system as an addition to the two- and three-tier systems generally in operation).
- A basic requirement for the function of the system is user confidence in their own abilities to manage VLOM respect to organization, finance and technical aspects.
- Creation of confidence can only be reached through training and support for a minimum of three to four years, longer if possible.
- Support can only be given through knowledge of users' demand of, and reactions to, the structures and function of the VLOM system introduced.
- Knowledge can only be obtained through social and technical monitoring. By far the greatest amount of attention should be paid to socio-economic factors. Intensity of monitoring will be highest in the first two to three years after which it can be reduced and finally cease.
- Ownership of water points, community participation and self determination will reduce possibilities of funding agency preferences in relation to system capacity, distance requirements and selection of technology.
- Utilization of monitoring as a management tool requires funding agency flexibility and acceptance of immediate project shifts from one budget line to the other. In some cases monitoring will reveal the need for additional budget lines and related funding above the original budget. This could be covered by a certain percentage of the original budget set aside and only utilized if a definite need is identified by monitoring.

The sections below discuss specific issues:

Community institutions should be developed early and before sites for the water points are identified. In this way, the institutions can be incorporated into the planning process from the very beginning and thus avoid resistance full community responsibility.

Linkages between the community institutions must be maintained; this will serve to strengthen those at the bottom, who need it most and render them more capable of responding to unexpected or unusual events.

It is important to take the cultural context into account when designing or developing training needs. For example, the contradictions inherent in trying to make women active in all phases and aspects of VLOM in a society where women are not known for their community management roles need to be explicitly addressed. In KIP, instructions as to the proportion of women in institutions went some way to ensuring their participation, but the project needed to go further to ensure that women were able to participate in all aspects of VLOM, including the technical, and to counter the natural conservative tendency within communities to confine women to their usual roles.

Similarly, the attempt to be participatory also needed to address the tendency for village headmen to dominate discussion and activities.

In connection with HESP, training of trainers, where the trainers are village leaders, has failed. A direct approach to water point users, through training and drama and sanplat casting done by village contractors, connected to health centres, showed better results. Further, by having sanplat customers delivering basic materials, i.e. sand, stones and gravel to the site of casting, demand-driven production and high percentage of installation is ensured. As for the sanplat technology the project has had success with pit latrines with a sanplat (with a lid) and without a vent pipe.

Water maintenance funds (WMF) were part of the established procedures for maintenance. However the project has questioned this and now seeks to instill into the communities that responsibility for collection of funds is theirs. How and when funds are collected and kept is up to them.

There must be a mechanism whereby individuals who embezzle funds from committees can be dealt with by users. The safeguards seemed to be in place and were generally followed but some thefts will occur, therefore sanctions must exist.

The importance of the project personnel, particularly those responsible for the transfer of technical skills and community development, should not be underestimated. The messages they convey to communities, either explicitly or implicitly have a powerful impact on the eventual success of the project. Their training and orientation should be given emphasis and re-training and re-orientation should be built into the project plans to ensure they continue to give out the appropriate messages.

The community development assistants (CDA) have a special role to play. They are the first to get in contact with project communities. As such they form the foundation of trust on which future interaction between recipients and project is based. Therefore CDAs must identify themselves with their communities and speak the local languages. Also important is the continued service of the same individuals throughout the project period, and that they represent both genders.

In relation to large rehabilitation programmes being implemented nationwide, the KIP experience suggests that concentrated programmes covering a district or part of a district are preferable as they:

- reduce transport costs.
- increase efficiency of supervision.
- increase efficiency of training programmes.
- increase the possibility of inter community support.
- increase the possibility of privatization of spare part distribution and sales.
- avoid social tension in villages as all water points are covered and not only one or a few.

The traditional model for the design and implementation of rural water supply schemes has the following sequence of activities:

- Preparation
- Mobilization
- Construction
- Handover to users
- Operation and maintenance.

In this sequence, users are not involved in the construction of the water points but simply taught to maintain them after they have been constructed. This sequence does not allow communities to develop a strong sense of ownership of and responsibility for the water points. The sequence should be changed to:

- Preparation
- Technical and social mobilization
- Establishment of operation and maintenance (VLOM) system
- Construction and simultaneous handover to users.

This will slow down construction activities but ensure community participation throughout and in this way prepare for sustainability.

Choice of technology must be related to the society in which it is being introduced. In areas where various technologies can be maintained and spare parts obtained through already established mechanical enterprises and shops, the users should be given a choice. However, this requires educating the users on the pros and cons of various choices in regard to spare parts, repairs and price. In areas where there is no tradition for mechanical repairs it is a long process to establish privatized O and M. In such areas only one specific pump should be introduced. And only one type regardless of depth. The advantages of a unified O and M system, stock of spares, tools and training programmes does far outweigh the economics of different pumps for different depths. With the acquisition of user confidence in handling one technology and the establishment of general mechanical repair skills, additional types of pumps can be introduced. By then communities do possess practical experience and are then in a position to make an informed choice among alternatives.

In the introduction of a spare part distribution system, distinction should be made between fast and slow moving spares. In societies with no tradition for mechanical repairs, sale of fast running spares should be introduced into already existing village shops, but in consultation with the local communities. Preference of shop and location is important. Shop owners' local standing and social engagement and their own dependence on the water supply are deciding factors in ensuring the continued stock of spares. Project support in supply of the initial stock should be considered with funds for replenishment of stock to come from the shop owner's sales of the initial supply.

With regard to wholesale supply of both fast and slow moving spares, large shops that cater for the general supply to village shops should be selected. Initially, they might require spares on commission from project or government with later resumption of full responsibility for both purchase and sales.

Ownership of the water points must be clearly defined, not only ownership of the installations and their downhole components and the land upon which they rests, but also a piece of the surrounding land for possible use for irrigated gardening.

The question of vegetable or other production around the water point must be very carefully planned. For remote areas this production has no market and can therefore not be suggested as a possible means of income generation.

Livestock is another question of concern. In areas of high density their demand on water will influence choice of technology. Also access to water point, share of livestock owner contribution to water point maintenance and provision of a watering trough should be decided by each community in the preparation phase. The possibility of increase of livestock due to water now being available should not be forgotten.

References

Gaynor, C., C.B. Jespersen and G. Banda. 1992. Village
   Level Operation and Maintenance: First Sociological and Technical Monitoring Report. Centre for Social Research, Zomba.

Gaynor, C. and C. B. Jespersen. 1992. Village Level Operation and Maintenance: Second Sociological and Technical Monitoring Report. Centre for Social Research, Zomba.

Hyde, K.A.L and C.B. Jespersen. 1994. Village Level Operation and Maintenance: Third Sociological and Technical Monitoring Report. Centre for Social Research, Zomba.

Singida integrated rural development project

Peter H. Killewo, Pontain Ruta and Edward Lungwa, Tanzania

SINGIDA IS A semi-arid region located in the central part of Tanzania. It receives a mean annual rainfall of about 700mm. The population of this region is about 940 000 people. The region lacks access to potable water for the rural community which accounts for 90 per cent of the total population. It is estimated that only 40 per cent of the rural population has access to improved water supply. In some areas women have to walk up to ten kilometres daily for domestic water needs. The quality of water obtained from these sources is very poor and contributes to the prevalence of waterborne and water-related diseases. Environmental degradation is quite severe. In the more populated areas soil erosion is a common problem. Overgrazing, deforestation and poor land management practices are rampant in this region.

The Singida Integrated Rural Development Project (SIRDP) started in October 1984 in an effort to address the fundamental problems facing the rural community in Singida region. The project is being implemented by Tanganyika Christian Refugee Service (TCRS), a non-governmental organization which is operated by the Lutheran World Federation (LWF) Commission of World Service. Although the basic function of TCRS is to provide assistance to refugees who have found asylum in Tanzania, it is also involved in a number of programmes for development work as for the case of SIRDP. The project is mainly funded by Danchurch Aid through LWF. The main components of the project include water supply, environmental health, agriculture, natural resources management and community development. This paper however highlights mainly the water and sanitation components of the project.

Objectives
- Raising villagers' awareness to enable them to participate fully in development activities and providing them with a stimulus to pursue such activities on a self reliant basis: improving the quantity, accessibility and safety of village water supplies.
- Arousing villagers' realization of the health benefits achieved through the use of improved water supplies, latrines, proper sanitation and hygiene.
- Raising community awareness of the severe consequences of environmental degradation and assisting them in reversing this trend.

Approach
In order to ensure proper implementation and sustainability, integration between project components and among government departments is emphasized. Technical staff have been seconded to the project from all involved departments. Community awareness-raising and mobilization involves the community development staff working in close collaboration with the village governments and field extension staff.

The project has a regional steering committee comprizing the relevant heads of departments. The committee is the co-ordination mechanism for the project. The districts have consultation committees which perform the same function at district level. The project is implemented in a group of villages located in the same locality or 'village clusters'. Village selection is based on a **demand - driven** approach. Requests for water supply and sanitation assistance are channelled through respective ward development committees and district councils. Final selection however, is made during a joint meeting between the project and district officials. Apart from facilitating easy logistics, this approach ensures higher cost effectiveness. Base line data collection is carried out by a social survey team before implementation. The beneficiaries are fully involved in all stages of project planning, implementation, operation and maintenance in order to assure a sustainable development. This conforms with the national water policy which emphasizes sustainability of projects through full user involvement.

For the project to create impact on the community, full involvement in the course of implementing the project has been given a top priority.

The project gives first priority to development of shallow wells. Where shallow wells are not feasible, medium depth boreholes are drilled. In both cases handpumps are installed. As for sanitation, the project has opted for development of improved pit latrines with unreinforced dome cover slabs for households and ventilated pit latrines for institutions. The main consideration in making the choice of technology is sustainability.

The project avoids the use of a wide variety of hardware in order to facilitate smooth operation and maintenance. Two types of handpumps have been adopted in the project namely NIRA AF 85 for shallow wells and AFRIDEV for medium depth boreholes. Both of these pumps are locally manufactured and conform to VLOM.

Water component
After a village has been selected, a written **contract agreement** is signed between the project and the village

concerned after a communal meeting attended by both parties concerned. In the contract, the community is informed and has to agree that within a time frame, it is supposed to provide free labour security to technicians/contractors, also contribute a specified amount of money towards construction of the wells whereas the project will provide technical staff, equipment/tools, transport and materials.

In addition to existing **water sources** as identified through social surveys additional/new sources are identified during auger surveys for shallow wells and geophysical surveys for medium depth boreholes where auger surveys have failed. During auger surveying, the communities are involved in selecting places to be surveyed which will determine positions of the wells. They are also fully involved in carrying out actual survey work.

In order to develop more sense of ownership and responsibility, also future sustainability, from July 1994, beneficiaries have been asked to contribute a certain amount of money towards construction of wells.

During the first year (July 1994 - June 1995) it was agreed that user contribution be 20 000/= (40 US$) per well. This contribution will be raised gradually towards full construction cost. In the following year (July 1995 - June 1996) the contribution is set at Tshs. 100 000/= (200 US$) per well. Response from the communities has been encouraging.

All construction of shallow wells is now carried out by **sub contractors** who have good working experience. A contract agreement is made between the project and sub contractor specifying contract regulations, conditions of terminating contract and implementation costs. While the sub contractor will be engaged in technical and supervisory duties the beneficiaries' participation still remains the same. A project shallow wells construction co-ordinator checks on the work of sub contractors and approves every steps of construction.

Before a shallow wells project is completed, the village concerned appoints four people (men and women) to be **trained** as pump attendants. During pump installation a trainer from the project trains village pump attendants on pump operation and maintenance.

The villages also appoint well caretakers (mainly women) staying closest to the wells whose duty is to remind others of proper use of the pumps and keeping environment clean. In most cases pump attendants and well caretakers are not paid any allowances but are exempted from other communal duties.

All completed wells are officially **handed over** to the beneficiaries concerned. During handing over certificates are awarded. On these certificates the beneficiaries are reminded in writing of their responsibilities to take good care of their wells, to continue to collect money to maintain village water funds, to request water rights and to buy basic spanners for maintenance of the pumps.

All completed wells are **monitored** each month so as to keep records of general problems affecting them especially on the pumps. This helps in advising villagers on what spares should be stocked in their stores for simple maintenance. Required information is filled in special forms by village pump and supervisor goes around to collect them at the end of each month.

The supervisor also helps out where village pump attendants have failed to do a repair.

Achievements

Since this project started, 312 new shallow wells have been constructed, 130 medium depth boreholes have been drilled and 230 malfunctioning wells have been rehabilitated. Also 230 pump attendants and 1132 well caretakers received training.

Problems and solutions

A few wells dried up due to drought. This has especially affected shallow wells more than medium depth boreholes. More emphasis has been put on thorough surveys during dry season.

Sometimes poor village leadership leads to poor community participation. Where such situations cannot be rectified in spite of constant follow up, the project is forced to pull out. In all cases higher district officials are asked to assist.

It is still customary for me to dominate all activities except collection of water from the wells. Sometimes separate meetings are held for women to put across their opinions.

Sanitation

In order to ensure long lasting health benefits brought about by improved water supply a sanitation component which deals with construction of improved latrines and hygiene education is being implemented in villages supported with water supply. The main objective is to ensure that every household in project villages is using a sanitary latrine which can last for a minimum of five years before it is filled up. This also includes primary schools and dispensaries within the villages. Alongside latrines construction village health workers (VHWs) are trained in basic hygiene measures. In turn these VHWs carry out health education activities with fellow villagers through small gatherings and home visits.

Latrine construction

Implementation of the programme starts with motivation and awareness-raising seminars for ward and village leaders, extension staff, influential people and the village populace. During these meetings the role of each party involved in the programme is clearly explained. This is followed by mobilization of the needed materials for casting of slabs. Each household is also supposed to contribute 1000/= Tshs. (2 US$) as part payment for the construction costs.

TCRS supplies cement, working tools and pays for sub-contractors. Each household is responsible for curing and transporting the casted slab to construction site, digging the pit and building the superstructure. Primary schools are assisted with at least eight VIP latrines. Parents produces burnt bricks and dig the pits whereas the school children collect sand, gravel and water. TCRS supplies cement, weldmesh, fly screen and pays for the subcontractors.

Achievements

The programme has attained some remarkable achievements, one of them being reduction of diarrhoea diseases and associated deaths. A study carried out in 1987 in nine pilot villages indicated 26.4 per cent diarrhoea incidence among under fives and seven years later after assisting these villages with improved water supply and sanitation the diarrhoea incidence dropped to 17 per cent. Also diarrhoea associated deaths during the same period dropped considerably.

Increased demand for latrine slabs from villages indicates the acceptability of the technology. This is mainly due to the sturdiness of the slabs and to a lesser extent the health benefits associated with the use of the slabs.

Reports from the field show that slabs from filled up pits have been shifted to new pits. This indicates that the technology is permanent.

Problems and solutions

Although assistance with latrine coverslabs has in some villages been up to 100 per cent there has been a very big problem with the use of the squatting hole lids; most slabs are not regularly cleaned and lack of routine maintenance of the latrine shelters has led to some of them collapsing. In order to curb these problems the project has plans for intensifying hygiene education activities and placing emphasis on regular checking of the superstructure so as to build up repairing habits.

Decrease in subsidy for slabs has resulted in decrease in the number of households acquiring the slabs. This is mainly affecting the rural poorest who are in most cases in need. This implies that when the subsidy is eventually removed very few households will be able to possess concrete slabs.

In order to solve this problem emphasis will be placed on each household using a latrine which fulfills basic health requirements.

Lack of motivation and support from village governments has resulted in many village health workers (VHWs) dropping out and some of the remaining are not as active as expected. Frequent changes of leadership at village level have also contributed to this problem. Village leaders have to be constantly made aware of the importance of the VHWs so that they can give them the necessary support.

Other project components

Apart from water supply and sanitation, the project incorporates natural resources management, agriculture and community development. Afforestation and soil conservation promote conservation of water sources and soil fertility. Improved methods of agriculture gives rise to higher crop yields, improved nutrition and improved income for the rural community. Community development activities include among others the promotion of income generating groups. These are provided with soft loans, the amounts of which depend on the nature of activities planned. The primary objective of these components is to create an environment conducive to promoting water supply and sanitation by building up a higher capacity for the users to contribute towards a sustainable development.

Conclusion

TCRS is now in the last year of the third phase and there are already plans of extending into a fourth four-year phase (1996 - 1999). This will be a phasing out phase whereby TCRS will gradually hand over its activities to the local NGO yet to be identified. Privatization of activities, increased user financial contributions, women's involvement and user training will be the main focus of the fourth phase.

Sustainability of community water supplies

J.S. Mukhwana and J.J. Hukka, Kenya

THE KENYA FINLAND Western Water Supply Programme (KFWWSP) started in the Western Province of Kenya in February 1981 with the 'supply driven approach' (SDA). The SDA was latter found to be unsustainable in the long run since beneficiaries were merely passive recipients of externally funded projects.

During the SDA, a lot of work had to be done to set up structures which could deal with issues that were important to the beneficiaries. This included siting, construction, O&M and actual ownership of the water supplies. To reduce this burden, the approach was gradually changed to 'demand driven approach' (DDA).

DDA was started in May 1993. Under this approach, communities contributed 30 per cent of the total cost of the piped water supply project in terms of labour, material and cash (minimum two per cent of total cost of the project). There has since been a lot of awareness creation and the programme soon found it difficult to cope with the demand.

It is expected that the community water supplies (CWS) implemented by the programme will continue to be operated, maintained and managed in a self sustaining manner even after the programme ends in December 1995. Some of the CWS implemented under the SDA (especially pumped systems) have already started experiencing serious operational problems. Therefore training, especially in financial and other management affairs, will be essential, if they are to be kept operational.

Programme achievements

The programme has constructed/rehabilitated/augmented 46 institutional and ministry water supplies (MWS). Fourteen CWS have been implemented and handed over while two are still under construction. Of the 16, eight are gravity and seven are pumped systems using groundwater. One CWS using surface water has a treatment plant. These systems will serve about 130 000 consumers.

Twelve projects have been implemented under SDA while four are on DDA. Of the four, two are still under construction. Total community contribution is about US $ 300 000 while the programme has contributed US $ 600 000.

Operation of CWS

The 16 CWS are managed by the community through water committees. Each committee comprizes members served by the water supply and it includes a chairperson, secretary, treasurer, committee and co-opted members. They are elected at a general meeting and serve for a specified period of time depending on the constitution of the water supply but usually for a maximum of three years according to the regulations of the Ministry of Culture and Social Services (MoCSS) with which the committees are registered. The committees do not have a legal status. The role of the water committees is to:

- Authorize expansion of and/or improvements of the water facility and supply of spare parts, extension of services, and maintain a true and accurate account of all money received and spent.
- Decide the charges, fees and contributions for services provided to the members and recommend for their approval at a general meeting.
- Employ extra staff to reinforce the operation and maintenance of the water supply.
- Identify the training needs of the community and organize ways of achieving this.
- Sign contracts of agreement with external agencies on behalf of the community.
- Look into ways of reinvesting project funds and tap the existing community resources for the project's sustainability.

Out of the 14 completed projects, nearly all of them have serious problems which can be classified as **financial, management, technical and social/political.**

(i) Financial problems:
- Inadequate revenue collection.
- Misappropriation of revenue collected.
- Poor record keeping.
- Unsuitable tariffs.

(ii) Management problems:
- Unsuitable committee members (could be illiterate or over qualified). This has led to poor planning for most of the CWS.
- Inadequately qualified staff mainly as a result of poor remuneration.
- Inability to follow constitutions (by-laws).

(iii) Technical problems:
- Inappropriate technology used.
- Inadequate tools and equipment.
- Lack of routine and corrective maintenance.
- Poor quality of works.

(iv) Social/political problems:
- Interference by politicians and other influential people in decision making.
- Inter-clan rivalry.
- Inability and/or unwillingness to pay.

Steps to enhance sustainability

Emphasis has been laid on training of the committees and their assistants (employed staff) on both technical and financial management. In particular, the following steps have been taken:

- Information package was prepared and sent to all CWS. The package has eight modules comprising DDA in water supply development, general information and procedures for the development of community based water supplies, technological options, community managed piped water supplies, health education, self management support, handpump maintenance and spare part distribution system and training.
- Training has been carried out for revenue clerks and/or system managers on:

  - Roles of management committees.
  - Revenue collection.
  - Tariff setting.
  - Bookkeeping.
  - Budgeting.
  - Meetings.

- Model by-laws were developed from the existing by-laws of the various CWS and copies were sent to all the CWS.
- The decision support system (DSS) has also been prepared and sent to all CWS. Training in its use will be arranged. The DSS manual comprizes, among other aspects, the following:

(i) Elements of successful community water system management. These include:
- Technical characteristics which describe the general scope of a given water system.
- Population and business characteristics whose data is used to calculate several performance indicators and to estimate the future demands and the investment requirements accordingly.
- Personnel characteristics which describe the staff composition.
- Water audit characteristics.

(ii) Performance management monitoring aspects which include:
- Economic performance measures
- Efficiency measures
- Service level measures.
- Capital projects progress report.
- Technical operations report.
- Billings and collection report.
- Statement of operating expenditure.
- Principal financial ratios.
- Other financial statements, e.g. balance sheet.
- Annual report.

Umbrella Water Users Association (UWUA) is to be established to give technical and financial management assistance to the member CWS and possibly water point source committees. Through this UWUA, it is expected that there will be sharing of knowledge and pooling of resources which will create a system that will fill the vacuum left by the programme.

- The UWUA should work more or less like a co-operative society with individual CWS being the shareholders.
- Activities of the UWUA could include monitoring, collection, dissemination of information and training of the communities to ensure sustainability of the CWS. Assistance in the form of loans based on shares could also be given to enable emergency repairs.
- The UWUA should be manned by a team of qualified staff with experience in co-operatives, management and in O&M and technical/financial management of water supplies. Experience in writing project proposals to attract loans for extensions etc. and in establishing income generating activities will be necessary.
- The provincial water engineer's office may look after but not directly control the activities of the UWUA.
- Technical assistance may be requested through the UWUA from the government or private consultants as deemed necessary.

In addition, the transfer process, where the MWS are handed over to the consumers' has been started. This process together with the given institutional and management development support aims to improve the sustainability of water supplies in Western Province of Kenya.

Spring protection - sustainable water supply

J. Mwami, Uganda

WATER SUPPLIES ARE a vital element of rural infrastructure and are an important area for government action. Most Ugandans live in rural areas and are confronted with high mobility and mortality rates due to disease caused by unsafe water, improper sanitation and immunizable disease.

Rukungiri in south western Uganda is one of the most densely populated districts in the country with 200 people per square kilometre. Like most rural areas in Uganda the people earn a living through subsistence agriculture. The main water sources are rivers, springs and rainwater. There is a minimum average annual rainfall of 1500mm distributed throughout the year. Drier seasons are not as pronounced and regular as elsewhere in Africa but can last for three or four months with only light rains. With good climate, food production is successful and consequently in 1991 the per capital income of the local people was US$ 61.19 which was higher than the national average of US$ 49.18. Prices in this report are given in Ugandan shillings and the exchange rate in April 1994 was US$ 1.00 to 1000/=.

History of spring project

Since 1985 the church of Uganda North Kigezi Diocese in Rukungiri has run a water programme funded by Water Aid, a UK charity.

Initial projects included rehabilitation of hospitals, spring protection and also rainwater collection systems for clinics, schools and churches. These projects involved the construction of large tanks, and installation of plastic guttering imported from the UK.

Within the first two years, half of the rainwater projects were in a very bad shape. Communities were not keen to maintain them because they provided only a limited amount of water from an intermittent supply. On the other hand the pumped schemes were 'off and on' due to the high running costs. The only project which was working as designed was the spring project.

For these reasons pumped schemes and rainwater collection systems were discontinued in order to concentrate on water sources that benefited more people at a lower cost.

The spring programme

Community mobilization
The use of spring water is not a new idea in village life in this part of the country. Traditionally people collect spring water which may either be in a pool (collected by dipping in a collection container) or by use of a banana fibre in the form of a gutter (for springs from steep slopes).

Taking advantage of the socio-acceptability of the spring water, the spring project was encouraged. This was done by mobilizing people using church leaders who talked to people during Sunday services about the advantages of safe drinking water. The church here is a very strong indigenous organization whose involvement helped the project achieve the intended impacts. The church leaders are very respectable and their words are taken seriously. This implementation strategy has two advantages: one is that it is much cheaper than employing a separate mobilizer (since they do it as part of their work) and the other is that the impact is permanent as the church is also permanent.

Community participation

A definition of participation is a necessary point for a strategy on achieving sustainability. Participation is the learning process by which communities control and deal with technology, change and development. It is a very necessary component of every water supply project that has maintenance and long-term sustainability as its objective.

The spring project has been implemented in line with the above definition of participation. Initially the communities were always expected to provide the following to have their sources protected:

- Manual labour.
- Stones and sand for constructional work.
- Feed and house the 'Fundi' (artisan) during the construction.

The project input was limited to cement and paying of wages for the fundi. As communities got more mobilized, the community contribution was increased to include half of the fundi's pay. There are undoubtedly some rural areas where cash is simply not available but even in these areas very poor households usually have some resources in particular their own time to contribute to constructing and maintaining service improvements.

This contribution can often be important; the community contributions were reduced to half in some areas but well organized self-help labour was used. So far 950 springs have been protected in the district serving about 56 000 people, thus making 14 per cent coverage.

Indigenous water use

Quantity and quality
For such a wet area the quantities of water used in the average rural household are surprisingly low. In a survey during a dry spell it was found that the average daily water consumption in the district was 5.7 litres per person per day. But when sources are protected the consumption increases due to ease of drawing and improvement in quality.

There was a marked improvement in quality after protection of sources though contamination was taking place in both the collection and storage containers. The socio-economic status of a household had a direct effect on the quality and quantity of the water at the household concerned.

Below is a sample of the results of socio-economic, quantity and quality parameters of some of the 100 households surveyed.

On average there were 12 counts of coliforms in samples taken from a protected source and 150 counts for samples from unprotected sources.

Financial matters

Affordability
The total cost of materials for the protection of a spring is based on the cost of cement as the local materials are relatively cheap. On average it needs 12 bags of cement to protect a spring. The other materials needed are a lorry load of stones, a lorry of sand, a metre of 2" GI pipe, a square metre of polythene or terram.

The total cost is therefore:

Cement ush	168 000
Sand ushs	15 000
Stones ushs	20 000
GI pipe ushs	4000
Polythene ushs	1000
Skilled labour ushs	50 000
Unskilled labour ushs	120 000
Supervisory work ushs	32 000
Total ushs	410 000

Thus the community input is Ushs 180 000= as they provide sand, stones, half of the pay for skilled labour, and unskilled labour, let alone feeding and housing the fundi. Supervisory work include the time and fuel for the engineer and the supervisor. The project input therefore is Ushs 230 000=. On average a single protected spring has 60 beneficiaries, giving a community input per capital of Ushs 3000= and hence a project input per capital of Ushs 3833=. We have been improving on the design to achieve better ones and reduce the total cost by cutting down the amount of materials used. However, the latest design which includes a big spring box to act as reservoir has raised the total cost. The design allows for the storage of night flow (for low yield springs) and the tank is fitted with a tap, a washout and overflow. We have started building this type of spring only where the low yield spring is the sole source for a population of at least 60 people. The total cost for this type of spring is about 42 per cent more than that of an ordinary spring but it is shared between the communities and the water programme.

Material availability
Cement is available locally in Rukungiri for less than at trading centres. The cement is manufactured and is priced at around 14 000= per 50 kg (April 1995). Good quality sand is found within the district but is located in the rift valleys; in some areas the available sand is very poor.

Good stones are also available in most parts of the district but occasionally we provide transport for areas where it is not available.

Maintenance and sustainability
Before constructional work begins for any spring, there must be in place a water and sanitation committee which is charged with mobilizing the people before and during construction. They are also charged with maintenance of the spring. The committee is formed from the beneficiaries. Day-to-day maintenance is performed by a caretaker.

Every spring has a caretaker. The caretaker is not paid for his work but is exempt from the normal bulungi bwansi (communal work) which is carried out every Wednesday. Each caretaker has a manual which guides him during the maintenance. These manuals are given to them after attending a workshop or during the construction of the spring.

As the input from the community is being increased gradually, there is hope that in future the communities will be able to meet the full cost. The technology being simple and requiring only an artisan the communities will be able to use their own local people in future.

Conclusion
- For any rural water supply project to be sustainable, governments and external agencies must establish the environment in which communities can construct, operate and manage improved facilities.
- Communities should not be underrated in terms of their contribution to the costs of the chosen services.
- The most appropriate technology should always be given first priority for a given community for a lasting solution.
- Involvement of indigenous institutions in the implementation of projects should be encouraged for sustainability.

References

1. Briscoe J. and Ferrant D. 1948. Water for Rural Communities. Helping People Help Themselves. The World Bank Washington, D.C
2. St Gall 1985. Manual for Rural Water Supply. Swiss Centre for Appropriate Technology at ILE, Switzerland.
3. Wash Technical Report No. 62 1990. Steps for implementing Rural Water Supply and Sanitation Projects. U.S Agency for International Development U.S.A.

Table 1. Results from protected sources

Number of people in a household	Daily demand (litres)	Capacity of collection containers (litres)	F.C/100ml	Socio-economic
7	75	35	250	Below average
7	90	85	150	Average
9	90	80	5	Below average
7	60	60	65	Average
7	100	50	8	Average
9	90	50	3	Average
7	60	30	65	Above average

Table 2. Results from unprotected sources

Number of people in a household	Daily demand (litres)	Capacity of collection containers (litres)	F.C/100ml	Socio-economic
12	50	30	350	Below average
10	120	25	380	Average
4	80	50	35	Above average
8	40	5	410	Below average
5	75	50	250	Above average
5	75	55	310	Average
6	70	60	350	Below average

Ferrocement water storage tanks

Brian Skinner, WEDC

FERROCEMENT IS A form of thin concrete reinforced with layers of continuous and relatively small diameter mesh. It is usually made from a mortar of Portland cement and sand applied to steel reinforcement which is often provided in the form of small aperture wire mesh and/or closely spaced small diameter bars or wires. In conventional ferrocement this relatively close spacing of reinforcement throughout the mortar creates a composite material which behaves almost homogeneously; very differently to the way reinforced concrete behaves. However, many so called 'ferrocement tanks', although using small meshes, do not have reinforcement widely dispersed through the mortar, but they still function successfully. Although, perhaps, such tanks should strictly be referred to as 'wire reinforced mortar tanks', in this paper they will be included within the term 'ferrocement tanks'.

The aim of this paper is to publicize the advantages that ferrocement has over other materials commonly used for constructing water storage tanks. It also aims to give basic information on the different construction methods which can be used for ferrocement tanks. Further references are suggested for readers who want to examine some published tank designs and to experiment with using this material.

Because of the lack of space, this paper has focused on cylindrical tanks. A hemispherical excavation lined with ferrocement and covered with a domed roof is one cost-effective alternative (Nissen-Petersen 1992b). For smaller storage volumes jar shapes are appropriate.

Comparison of ferrocement tanks with other types of tank

Most medium and large above-ground tanks around the world are made from one of the following:

- Conventional building materials, particularly concrete and brickwork (both reinforced and unreinforced) but also stone masonry.
- Steel (flat or corrugated sheets, welded, soldered or bolted together).

Advantages of ferrocement

This cost-effectiveness of ferrocement over conventional materials results from some of the following factors:

- Ferrocement tanks are usually cheaper than tanks of fibre-reinforced plastic, steel etc. because these other materials have high manufacturing costs. Ferrocement has better corrosion resistance and lower maintenance costs than steel.

- Ferrocement tank designs usually make more effective use of cement and aggregate than tanks built using conventional materials. A number of well tested ferrocement designs for capacities between 20 and 50 m^3 use less than 1.3 bags of cement per m^3 of water stored. Capacities of between 5 and 20 m^3 can be built with 1.5 bags/m^3 or less. (Unfortunately, in some situations the sand needed for ferrocement may be more expensive than that used locally for bricklaying or concrete, reducing these cost savings.)
- For ferrocement tanks there is no need to purchase and transport large quantities of masonry stones, aggregates or bricks. (However there will be the additional expense of purchasing reinforcing mesh for the ferrocement.)
- The cost of reinforcing bars needed for large concrete and brickwork/blockwork tanks will be saved and this money can be used towards the purchase of wires and meshes for the ferrocement tank.
- Ferrocement has other advantages over reinforced concrete. Some of these arise from the differences between these two materials which are listed in Table 1 and/or described in the next section.
- Although ferrocement construction is labour-intensive it requires relatively low levels of skill and few tools. Thus it is ideal for use in many developing countries.
- The tanks can be rapidly constructed. Typically, a 30m^3 tank can be completed in 10-13 days with a team of 10 or less workers.
- The raw materials (steel wire and mesh, sand and cement) are widely available.
- It produces much lighter structures than those constructed from brick, stone or concrete and is cost-effective for elevated tanks if a suitable support structure (usually steel or concrete) is provided.
- It is suitable for prefabrication either in panels (joined together on site using ferrocement), or for smaller sizes as complete tanks carefully transported and moved into place.

Parameters for ferrocement

A number of parameters are used to characterize ferrocement. The suggestions in this sub-section are from ACI (1993a) except where another ACI publication (ACI 1993b) is referenced.

Volume fraction: This is the volume of reinforcement per unit volume of ferrocement. A value of at least 5.1 - 6.3 per

Table 1. Differences between ferrocement and concrete	
FERROCEMENT	**CONCRETE**
Coarse aggregate is not used, only sand.	Uses coarse and fine aggregate.
Thin sections are possible (mostly less than 50 mm thick) saving raw materials, particularly cement.	Sections are rarely as thin as 50 mm.
Only a thin mortar cover depth is required to the outermost layers. Depths of cover of as little as 2 mm can be used when crack widths are carefully controlled.	Larger depths of cover are required, usually more than 40 mm for water retaining structures.
It has superior cracking resistance making it ideally suited to water retaining structures. The well distributed wires ensure that any microcracks which develop during shrinkage, or strain under load, do not propagate and widen to a size which results in water leaking.	Does not have very good resistance to cracking caused by tensile strain under load or by shrinkage, unless closely spaced bars are used. A large depth of cover exacerbates this problem.
Can be placed to form the final desired shape without the need for shuttering forms. This is very useful for cylindrical tank walls since the fabrication of curved shuttering is expensive.	Concrete walls need inner and outer shuttering to contain the wet concrete.
It is useful for the construction of lightweight thin domed roofs to tanks.	Construction of domed roofs is difficult. Flat roof alternative is heavy and may need beams and/or column supports.
Has a high tensile strength to weight ratio which leads to lighter sections and the possibility of prefabrication.	It has low tensile strength to weight ratio.
It is has fairly good flexibility, elasticity and impact resistance mainly due to the relatively large amount of small diameter, closely spaced, two way reinforcement.	It is not very flexible.

cent is given as typical (this is equivalent to 400 -500 kg/m^3). A minimum total value of 1.8 per cent in both directions is recommended. The author of this conference paper has discovered that this value is not reached in most of the available 'ferrocement' tank designs in use in developing countries. The volume fraction in these tanks is only around one per cent but the tanks have still performed well.

Average spacing: The average spacing between reinforcing element is of the order of 5 - 10 mm.

Specific surface: This is the bonded surface area of reinforcement per unit volume of composite. A minimum value for ferrocement recommended by one author is quoted as 0.2 mm^{-1} (i.e. mm^2/mm^3) but ACI then gives a minimum value of 0.08 mm^{-1}, with a recommendation that twice this value is used for water-retaining structures.

Depth of cover: The recommended average net cover to the reinforcement is only 2 mm. In water retaining structures a lesser value is accepted if crack widths are limited to 0.05 mm and the reinforcement is galvanized. The present author had found that in most of the available tank designs used in developing countries the cover depth is much greater than 2mm, at about 20 mm.

Mix proportions: The desirable mix proportions (by weight) for mortar for ferrocement are:

Sand: Cement between 1.5 and 2.5
Water: Cement between 0.35 and 0.5

The higher the sand content, the higher the required water content to maintain the same workability. For watertightness ACI (1993b) recommended that the water-cement ratio should be kept below 0.4. The natural moisture content of the sand should be included in this calculation. This ratio had an important effect on the shrinkage potential but shrinkage is also dependent on the sand gradation (excessive fines should be avoided).

The mix should be as stiff as possible, provided this does not prevent full penetration into the mesh. Normally the slump of fresh mortar should not exceed 50 mm (ACI 1993b). Mixing mortar for ferrocement using conventional concrete mixers (rotating drum mixers with fins attached to the sides) is discouraged since the mortar is usually too dry to produce a homogeneous mixture using this method. Hand mixing if carefully carried out is satisfactory.

Sand: To achieve a workable, high-density mortar mix well-graded sands are desirable (i.e. with a wide range of particle sizes). ACI (1993b) gives the following recommended grading:

US Sieve No.	Standard square mesh size (mm)	Percentage passing by weight
8	2.36	80 - 100
16	1.18	50 - 80
30	0.6	25 - 60
50	0.3	10 - 30
100	0.15	2 - 10

Reinforcement

Wires and meshes can be galvanized but with good quality mortar, good crack control and reasonable depths of cover this is not necessary.

Meshes: Fine meshes with small apertures are used in ferrocement to distribute the reinforcement throughout the mortar but the mesh is often also needed to hold the mortar in place when it is first applied. Where multiple layers of mesh are used it is best if the wire grids are offset to produce more widely distributed wires. Figure 1 shows the five main types of mesh in use.

Hexagonal mesh is particularly suited to double curved sections. *Welded mesh* is relatively stiff and is best suited to singly curved sections, although when cut into pieces it

Table 2. Schematic diagrams and descriptions of methods of ferrocement tank construction

METHOD	STAGE i	STAGE ii	STAGE iii	STAGE iv	STAGE v	STAGE vi
1a USING FIRM INNER MOULD						
1b USING FIRM INNER MOULD						
2 USING FIRM OUTER MOULD						
3a	USING MOULD FIXED TO OUTSIDE OF SKELETAL STEEL Stages i to vi will be similar to Method 2					
3b	USING MOULD FIXED TO INSIDE OF SKELETAL STEEL Stages i to v will be similar to Method 1B					
4 USING NO MOULD						

	METHOD 1a Using firm free standing absorbent inner mould
i)	Erect inner formwork (mould).
ii)	Plaster first layer of mortar onto mould (mould needs to be absorbent to hold mortar in place).
iii)	Tie reinforcement around first layer of mortar.
iv)	Plaster second layer of mortar through reinforcement onto first layer of mortar.
v)	Remove internal formwork and apply finishing coat of cement slurry if used.
	METHOD 1b Using firm free standing inner mould
i)	Erect inner formwork inside mesh (if mesh is not self supporting it can tied to the shutter).
ii)	From outside the tank plaster first layer of mortar through mesh and against shutter.
iii)	Let mortar harden. Remove inner mould.
iv)	From inside the tank plaster second layer of mortar against the inner face of the first layer.
v)	Apply finishing coat of cement slurry if used.
	METHOD 2 Using free standing outer mould
i)	Erect self supporting mesh (or fine mesh and supporting skeletal steel).
ii)	Erect self supporting formwork outside mesh.
iii)	From inside the tank plaster first layer of mortar through mesh and against shutter.
iv)	Let mortar harden. Remove outer mould.
v)	From outside the tank plaster second layer of mortar against the outer face of the first layer.
vi)	Apply finishing coat of cement slurry if used.

METHOD 3a Using mould fixed to outside of free standing mesh (or fine mesh and skeletal steel)
As for method 2 but formwork is tied to outside of mesh for support.
METHOD 3b Using mould fixed to inside of free standing mesh (or fine mesh and skeletal steel)
As for method 1b but formwork is tied to inside of mesh for support.

	METHOD 4 No mould used. Mortar held in place by fine mesh supported by skeletal steel frame		
i)	Erect self supporting frame of rods and fine mesh.	iii)	Apply additional layer(s) of mortar, at least one from opposite side.
ii)	Push mortar into the mesh from one side (with hand held support behind if necessary). Let mortar harden.	iv)	Apply finishing coat.

can be used for domed roofs. Strong, large aperture welded meshes (e.g. 6 mm diameter bars at 150 mm centres) are often used to form a skeletal framework to support finer meshes. *Woven mesh* is more flexible than welded mesh. Fine woven meshes are suitable for construction method 4 (see Table 2). *Chain link fencing mesh* is a special type of woven mesh which is occasionally used. *Expanded metal* is a mesh formed by slitting thin gauge sheets and expanding them in a direction perpendicular to the slits; it has very good mortar retention properties so is ideally suited for construction method 4; it is not suitable for doubly curved sections.

Wires: *Plain wire* can be wrapped circumferentially around tanks to provide wires at closely spaced centres. In addition wires can be also be connected to base reinforcement and be carried vertically up the walls to form an in-situ mesh. Some tanks in Thailand use only plain wires (e.g. 3.25 mm diameter) in this way to reinforce tank walls built using construction method 1a. *Barbed wire* is used in some designs because it is more readily available than plain wire. *Binding wire,* an ungalvanized plain soft wire, usually about 1.63 mm in diameter, is used to tie reinforcement together and to hold finer meshes firmly in place so that they do not move during plastering. Like larger diameter plain wires it can be used circumferentially to resist hoop tension.

Bars: Bars or strong welded meshes are necessary to support the finer meshes used in construction methods 2, 3a, 3b and 4. It is important in methods 3 and 4 that the skeletal frameworks of bars or mesh are stabilized by wooden braces and/or inclined ropes tied to pegs driven into the ground.

Moulds: A variety of materials can be used for moulds for cylindrical tanks. For construction method 1a it is important that the mould is slightly absorbent because the mould alone has to hold the first layer of mortar. Segmental steel framed moulds, faced with split bamboo or basketwork, and plastered with clay are used in Thailand for this method of construction. Method 1b and 2 can use a variety of materials including, prefabricated steel or wooden moulds. Often in Nepal small diameter polyethylene pipes are coiled in a horizontal spiral around a vertical wooden framework to form an inner mould for method 1b. Methods 3a and 3b allow the use of flexible sheets of steel or plywood tied to the skeletal steel. Other materials used for the mould for method 3a are a fence of poles or bamboo, or matting or sacking, held in place outside the mesh by spirals of rope.

Typical tank designs

Most of the designs examined by the author have capacities of 30m^3 or less. Many are reinforced with one layer of skeletal steel bars or mesh (typically 6 mm bars @ 150 mm centres) covered with one layer of chicken wire (typically with 25 mm apertures). The larger tanks in this range also use additional circumferential spirals of wire to hold the mesh in place and/or to add additional hoop strength. Wall thickness is typically 40 or 50 mm. Domed ferrocement roofs are often used, sometimes with a central prop.

Conclusion

Ferrocement tanks have many advantages. These can not be fully appreciated until the technique has been used in a particular region. Readers interested in constructing ferrocement tanks are encouraged to obtain Watt (1978), which gives brief details about many methods, or Nissen-Petersen (1992a) which is an excellent photo-manual for tank construction using sacking for a mould using method 3a. Information about other designs which are not so readily available can be obtained from the author at WEDC.

References

ACI (1993a) State-of-the-Art Report on Ferrocement, Reported by ACI Committee 549, Publication ACI 549.R-93, American Concrete Institute, Detroit, Michigan 48219, USA

ACI (1993b) Guide for the Design, Construction, and repair of Ferrocement, Reported by ACI Committee 549, Publication ACI 549.1R-93, American Concrete Institute, Detroit, Michigan 48219, USA

Nissen-Petersen E. (1992a) How to Build Cylindrical Water Tanks with Domes, Volumes 23m^3 and 46m^3, ASAL Consultants Ltd., PO Box 867, Kitui, Kenya.

Nissen-Petersen E. (1992b) How to Build an Underground Tank with Dome, Volume 80m^3, ASAL Consultants Ltd., PO Box 867, Kitui, Kenya.

Watt S.B. (1978), *Ferrocement Water Tanks and their Construction*, Intermediate Technology Publications, 103-105 Southampton Row, London WC1B 4HH, UK.

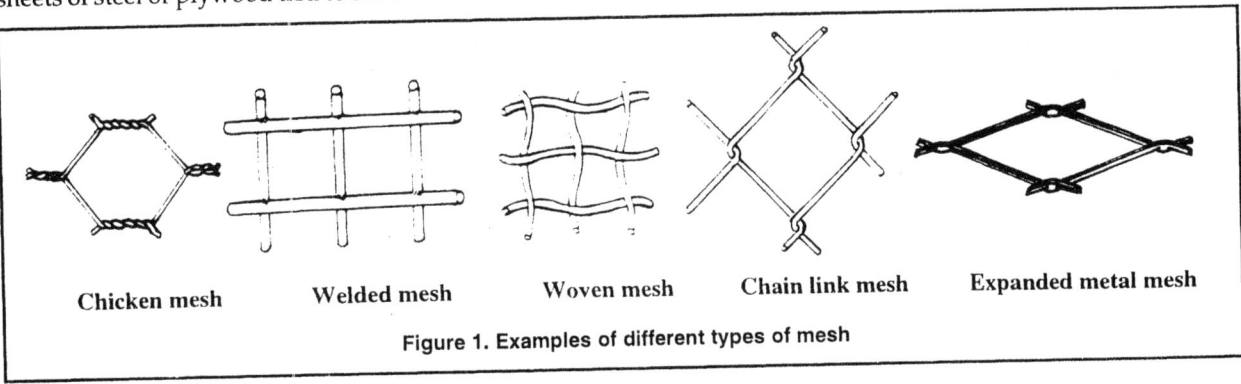

Figure 1. Examples of different types of mesh

Sustainability of Kabarole shallow wells

Mtwalib Walude, Uganda

KABAROLE SHALLOW WELL programme started early 1993 with WaterAid as its sole supporting agency. It is located in Kabarole District in western Uganda. The aim of the programme is to help about 550 communities improve on their existing water sources and hence bring safer water close to their homes.

Some handpumps have been earmarked for use on shallow wells in Uganda. The Nira AF85, the Tara and the Consallen are being tried out in the country. WaterAid has been asked to install 250 Nira handpumps in the country. The handpumps are being monitored by the Departments of Water Development to determine the one that best suits village level operation and maintenance.

For the improved water sources in Kabarole District, the mode of protection is a hand-dug well near an existing water source installed with the Nira AF 85 direct action handpump.

Up to date, about 100 wells have been sunk in Kitagwenda county in the southern part of the district. There has been a series of stages that have been established to ensure long-term sustainability of the installed water supply facilities. The paragraphs that follow attempt to explain the stages that have been developed.

Technology

The technology used is basically a hand-dug well of up to 7m deep with at least 3m depth of water in it. It is lined with cement blocks for durability and the lining sits on a concrete strip foundation. Within the water table, the space between the lining and earth cutting is filled with hard-core to stop well collapse. The pore spaces within the hard-core and the bottom of the well are filled with 6mm granite stone chippings to check silt ingress into the well. The space above the hard-core is filled with clay to prevent inflow of dirty water from the surface into the well. The well is covered with a reinforced concrete slab which has a provision for installation of a handpump. The cover slab has an access hatch provision which can be used for inspection, silt removal from the well, deepening the well in case it dries or use of a bucket pump in case the community is unable to afford a handpump. Around the wellhead is the capping which checks the flow of dirty water into the well. A waste water drain of about 6 - 10 m leads away from the apron to an existing storm drain or soak away pit. Grass is planted around the well compound to make the soil firm and flowers to make it beautiful. A fence is also planted around the well compound to stop animals from entering the compound and damaging the apron. A storm drain is provided around the compound to stop the inflow of runoff water close to the well.

Originally, the handpump had a large spout which wastes water while drawing using a jerrycan of a much smaller inlet diameter, a very common container used in Uganda. The handpump body height was such that there was little clearance between the spout delivery point and the jerrycan inlet.

The spout diameter has now been reduced and the handpump body height increased by the manufacturer to cater for all these anomalies.

Service level

The idea of service level has been considered as an important aspect of sustainability. Consideration has been centred around village, parish, sub county and county level.

The number of wells at village level is an integer multiple of 250 people, and depends on the number of people in the village. It has been realized that most families in Kabarole district live in families of 5 - 10 people and wells allocation considers the number of families per well. For any well, the number of families should not be less than 25. The more the number of families, the less the cost of spares per family.

At parish level (a collection of villages), the greater the number of wells, the bigger the catchment for spares, the bigger the responsibility for an area mechanic and the parish water committee and the smaller the distance there is to cover to execute joint community work and hence the greater the commitment. Most parishes have about 20 wells. Also, the greater the number of wells, the fairer the representation at parish water committee level.

At sub county level, the larger the percentage of parishes with wells, the easier it is to form a well-represented sub county water committee, the bigger is the catchment for spare parts supply and the more chance there is of guaranteeing a spare parts depot.

Originally, none of the above factors was considered. Now the concept has been achieved up to parish level and it is hoped that it will fully apply in the north. It is important to note that the nature of technology does not allow for bigger service coverage in parishes or sub counties.

Community participation

Community participation has been identified as an important prerequisite for sustainability of the wells. Before a community participates actively, visual aids are used to make it clearly understand what well improvement is about and the costs involved. Responsibility charts are drawn and circulated at parish and sub county level to show the commitment of the users towards meeting some of the costs. This makes them a little more responsible over their water facilities.

Communities are helped to review their existing water sources. This makes them understand the state of the sources of water in their villages and identify improvement needs. It is a useful tool for the agency to determine what kind of improvement choices exist for a village or parish. For villages where it is possible to sink shallow wells community leaders participate fully in siting and trial boring to determine the location of a well before actual construction starts.

Construction of a well sees division of responsibility between male and female community members. The male team takes on heavier activities while the female team takes on lighter ones. Working in shifts is encouraged to save time for other family activities.

After construction, a trained handpump mechanic from within the parish installs the handpumps on the wells in the parish so the community can identify him as the nearest able member of their community. He moves around with the parish water committee members, who introduce him to the community before a handpump is installed. After installation there is joint monitoring of the installed facilities by the community representatives and the agency staff to introduce the members to monitoring and evaluation.

Institutional capacity building

Institutional capacity building entails selection, working relationships and job satisfaction, community empowerment and financial management.

Selection of fundis (masons) and well committees is carried out just before the beginning of construction with the help of local leaders and the community. All well committees in a parish meet to form a parish water committee. The parish water committee together with the local leaders meet to select a suitable handpump mechanic. Training of local leaders, masons and well committees takes place just before the start of construction. That for parish water committees, caretakers and handpump mechanics takes place after construction of the wells. Well committees take on the responsibility of daily planning and management at all levels before, during and after construction. Masons are foremen of all construction activities and repairs in a parish. Parish water committees are in charge of the overall management at parish level. Handpump mechanics remove the installed handpumps and clean them once every three months (servicing) and carry out the actual repairs in a parish.

To ensure job satisfaction, parish water committees are elected once every year, and caretakers and handpump mechanics are exempted from contributions for spares.

The mechanics charge a small fee per well for each service to keep them on the job before the actual repairs are required. During handover all trained members receive certificates and each parish receives a bicycle, some stationery and handpump tools to facilitate their administration. Visits within and outside the locality are encouraged at all levels to exchange new ideas.

Handpump spare parts

The overall management of spare parts is the responsibility of the community. The cost of handpump spares to be replaced over a period of 10 years is estimated at $450. This is referred to as a direct cost. Indirect costs to be met by the community include income tax (I), cost in freight (CIF), percentage depreciation (D) and local administration costs (L). For ten years, the total cost (TC) of spares is given by: $TC = \$450 + I + CIF + D + L$. Indirect costs per well can be made very small if orders for many wells are made at once.

If a bucket pump is chosen, the cost of maintaining it will be very small compared to that of the handpump since it can be fabricated in the country. However it offers low service levels.

It is important to mention the costs involved in maintaining an installed water supply facility before, during and after construction to the community so that they either choose to use a handpump or a bucket at the beginning of construction or at the end.

Financial management and record keeping

Financial management is a very crucial issue in ensuring that spare parts are available for use at the time when they are needed. A lot of training preparations have been identified as a requisite to this.

Training involves: budgeting for the total spares needed in a village, parish and sub county; estimating the total cost of spares at each level; collection mechanisms of money for spares (monthly, quarterly, biannually or annually, whichever is suitable for the community); payment for money (cash or in kind/through fines or fund raising drive); introduction of banking procedures to communities and the value of banking; identification of rural development banks close to the communities and helping them to open up accounts in the identified bank; demonstrating and encouraging public accountability; and an efficient supply of spares as a back up for community satisfaction and their willingness to pay.

Keeping records of well repairs, spares supply and sales and user comments is a very big financial management tool.

Conclusion

In general, most of the important aspects for Kabarole wells sustainability have been considered.

The aspects include: technology used, service level, community participation, institutional capacity building, spare parts, financial management and record keeping.

A lot of effort is being made to drive the issues to a reality. It is however early to determine any long-term success achieved.

The gravity flow schemes programme in Uganda

N. Wobusobozi, R. Pieter and N. Herbert, Uganda

IN 21 DISTRICTS of Uganda the altitude of the land especially in the highlands and the availability of sufficient rains offers the opportunity to develop spring sources and rivers into gravity flow schemes to benefit large rural communities.

The primary objectives of the gfs programme is the improvement of the quality of life of the rural population by providing clean water and promoting of sanitation facilities and hygienic practices to ensure a safe water 'chain', in addition, successful gf systems have been associated with many other indirect benefits for the community. Due to their scale gf systems encourage social integration as a result of communities coming together to form committees to manage the different components of the system. Once the communities become aware of their potential as an organized group they can easily be mobilized to initiate other community based development programmes.

The operation and maintenance

Preparatory steps
The community involvement starts during the identification of the scheme, when their role throughout the different phases and their ultimate responsibility for the completed facility is made clear. It should be well acknowledged that a user community will only maintain their facility when they are convinced that it will improve on their living conditions.

Before actual construction of the project starts an agreement of co-operation between all the partners including the community should be signed. The agreement identifies the respective roles and functions and specifies the contributions in cash or in kind.

A water and sanitation committee from among the user community should be appointed which during the implementation of the project will be transformed into an O & M committee.

In conclusion, the following are the main elements in planning for the O & M phase:

- The preparation of the community for O & M of the scheme;
- The design of the most appropriate O & M structure; and
- The community capacity; technical knowledge, and financial ability.

The preparation of the community for O & M of the scheme

A gf scheme often supplies large communities with drinking water. Therefore to ensure consensus of views on the development and the future operation and maintenance of the scheme extensive consultation should be made with the entire community right from the beginning.

It is acknowledged that the involvement of the entire user community during the preparatory period will create a stronger base for future O & M activities. Therefore, while in the construction stage the community should have their role in the day to day management of the scheme after completion explained. The community should also be made to understand the work expected of the O & M committee and the scheme attendant.

Training of user communities
People elected to water committees often have limited knowledge of financial management and many of the technical issues related to the operation and maintenance of the gravity systems. Therefore, as construction begins the training needs of the community should be carefully defined.

Fairly large groups should be trained in the user community, to increase capacity and to reduce the risk of losing the knowledge. There are a good number of training programmes already in place which can be adjusted to meet the specific needs of the user community. Training at community level should, whenever possible, be conducted in local languages. Exchange visits to other existing gfs projects have been shown to be very useful for Watsan/O & M committee members. To increase the impact of these visits the committee members should give feedback to the community.

The design of the most appropriate O & M structure

Harmonizing of existing O & M structures
Many gf schemes have been implemented without proper guidance, which resulted in different O & M structures. In order to come up with an O & M system manageable for the user communities the different existing systems/structures should be first assessed and afterwards analyzed. The analysis should provide a framework to which different organizations should refer when they assist the community in putting up an O & M structure.

Proposed structures

A community-based O & M structure will be appropriate for small-and medium-scale schemes. In the case of large-scale schemes technical assistance from an external service (e.g. commercial enterprise, district water office)should be sought. Instead of setting up an O & M structure for one water facility a structure at sub/county level covering all the water facilities should be considered.

A community-based O & M structure should be flexible enough to accommodate the involvement of the private sector. Initiatives such as water kiosks, commercial O & M services which contribute to the maintenance of the systems should be encouraged.

During the planning and the implementation of the project the project staff supports the user community in many different ways. Too often this support ends abruptly after handing over the project to the community. To ensure continuity a follow-up structure should be put in place, e.g. extension of project duration period by a follow-up phase. In this phase the county water officer should play a facilitating role. Before implementing a water supply project an organization structure should be in place.

Monitoring

Monitoring the operation and maintenance of a gf scheme will improve on the continuation and thus the reliability of the scheme. Monitoring activities should cover:

technical aspects, water quality and quantity, assessment of constructions, reliability of the scheme

performance aspects, of scheme attendant, committees, etc.

development aspects, purpose water is used for, the quantity of water used, etc.

organizational aspects, frequency of water committee meetings, who is participating, content of the meetings, etc.

financial aspects, accountability, use of water fees, financial organization.

Monitoring of O & M activities should be recorded and analyzed periodically. The records could facilitate a transparent structure, and ensure a more controllable O & M committee.

The community capacity; technical knowledge, and financial ability

Role and tasks of the community and its committees

The daily running of a gravity flow scheme can not be done on an ad-hoc basis. Clarification of the role and tasks of the user community in general and the committees in particular should be in place which in turn should lead to consensus on responsibilities of the O & M committee.

The compilation of an O & M manual, covering description of activities (preventive and curative), tool manual, work manual for the scheme attendant, breakdown of items to be replaced, the lifetime and costs involved in case of replacements, recording formats for malfunctioning, repairs, replacements, etc. will be of great assistance to the planning capacity of the O & M committee.

Involvement of women

Since women play an important role in the welfare of the family the reliability and the quality of the water facility is of prime interest to them. Women should therefore be involved in the decision making process during the planning and implementation of the project and actively participate in the operation and maintenance of the water facility.

Financial capacity of the user community

It is necessary to make an assessment of the financial capacity of the community. Based on the outcome of the assessment, realistic contributions can be requested from the community during the implementation of the project.

At the same time it indicates whether it will be feasible to expect the community to cover the operation and maintenance costs of the scheme. For the latter detailed cost estimations about financial requirements of O & M are to be established. During the assessment of the financial capacity recommendations on how and when to raise water fees should be established. Below are some of the recommended ways of raising funds for O&M.

- Ways of water costing
  - public standpipes, flat rate per user
  - private connections, flat rate per tap, metered
  - water selling points, amount per jerrycan
- fundraising options
  - taxation
  - public rallies, auctions
  - water fees

Sustainable rural WATSAN management in Bolgatanga

George Aduko Yanore, Ghana

THE GWSC, UNDP/WB water and sanitation programme together with some local agencies including the Department of Community Development, Environmental Health Division of the Ministry of Health and Department of Social Welfare assumed responsibility for executing the Bolgatanga Community Water Supply and Sanitation Pilot Project, otherwise called 'The 50 Well Project', in July 1988 with funding from CIDA.

The Bolgatanga Community Water Supply and Sanitation Pilot Project was designed to find out whether communities were willing and able to take responsibility for managing their water supply and sanitation systems. The project objectives were therefore to develop a strategy for transferring maintenance responsibilities to the communities with fund mobilization, saving and spare parts distribution as important elements.

The project was also to promote the installation and use of household latrines and help to promote general hygiene and sanitation in the project area.

The other objective was to emphasize the involvement of women in playing lead roles in the community management concept.

The project was therefore by nature a multi-sectoral one with a high integration of its components (i.e. community management, hygiene and sanitation, water supply and women development activities).

What has been done

The project had over the three-year period (1988 - 1991) accomplished its main objective of transferring management of water and sanitation to the communities. The nature of the pilot project permitted an intensive testing of the following:

- Communities' willingness and ability to manage on a sustainable basis with fund mobilization, saving and management of funds collected as important elements.
- The technical capability in pump maintenance and repairs.
- Improvements in hygiene and sanitation practices.
- The involvement of women in water/sanitation management in co-ordinating income generation activities to supplement maintenance funding.

Community management

The main task of the project was to transfer management responsibilities for maintenance to the community. It was therefore imperative to develop strategies that would enhance capacity building in knowledge, skills and problem resolution methods at the community level.

The primary focus was the pump community using a combination of recognized traditional, political and social organizations as entry points. It was necessary for each community to establish a seven-member water and sanitation management committee (WASAMC). The WASAMC had the responsibility for the day-to-day running of the water or sanitary facility. Women being the traditional providers of water in the project area took lead roles on the committees.

The committees were provided with back-up support by village extension workers (VEWs) who were paid a small allowance by the project. Each VEW supported an average of 15 communities. The VEWs were nominated by the communities and liaised between project, the committee and the community.

Community participation is the pivot upon which the success of any community activity hinges. The communities were therefore initially assisted in organizing themselves to participate actively in planning the operation of the water points. The task of communities organizing themselves to deliberate regularly on issues of management became a tradition through the efforts of the village extension workers. The WASAMCs utilized the traditional leadership of the village chiefs and elders in resolving problems encountered amongst themselves and other community members. A sense of belonging and ownership developed amongst the people and helped towards the achievement of positive results.

Financial management deficiency is one of the main obstacles to the smooth functioning of decentralized water systems. Thus fund mobilization and sound financial management methods were of great importance. As a result of taking control of management of funds and improved bookkeeping skills introduced by the project, all communities collected sufficient monies for maintenance during the three-year period of the project.

One case of financial mismanagement was however reported and a few more individuals defaulted on payment of pump maintenance funds. In some cases the recalcitrant individual was prevented from having access to pump water.

Water supply maintenance

Experience over the years in the Upper Regions had shown that centralized maintenance and repair of rural water handpumps were not only cumbersome but costly and therefore unsustainable. The dispersal of the water systems meant a high outlay of equipment as well as high running cost.

During the pilot project, the prospects of sustainable maintenance therefore favoured a simple and easy to maintain Village Level Operation and Maintenance (VLOM) handpump. For the first time in Ghana, three types of VLOM handpumps, Afridev/Aquadev (similar but different manufacturers), Nira AF-85 and Volanta were installed on 50 boreholes for community self management.

Maintenance is an important requirement of any system based on mechanical technology. Preventive maintenance was therefore introduced and performed by trained village mechanics chosen from within the WASAMC. They dealt with about 50 per cent of the repairs and reported those beyond their capability to the area mechanics.

Hygiene and sanitation improvement

The activities of the hygiene and sanitation component were complementary to the provision of potable water to the rural population. Community-based education was considered appropriate towards achieving the complementary role of hygiene and sanitation. Hygiene education was carried out during community training workshops organized for community health workers.

Areas covered included:

- Proper use of water.
- Pump site sanitation.
- Compound cleanliness.
- Food hygiene and nutrition.
- Personal hygiene.
- Causes and prevention of common diseases such as diarrhoea and malaria. Most of these information-sharing activities with adults and children were done through the medium of songs.

The selected trained health workers carried out pump site and home visits to share their knowledge with pump users.

Women involvement and activities

Women represent over 50 per cent of the population in the Upper Regions of Ghana. They are also the main providers of water in the household. Women's involvement in the rural water system was a prerequisite for the achievement of any meaningful goals. The main thrust became the integration of women in activities aimed at the acquisition of organizational and technical skills in support of community management.

Women played an important role in hygiene and sanitation as representatives of the WASAMC on the promotion of hygiene and sanitation. They taught other women simple methods of preventing diseases, pumpsite cleanliness and household sanitation using illustrated picture books designed for the purpose.

The project location is characterized by prolonged dry season. Innovative income generation ventures such as irrigation farming and basket weaving improved women's socio-economic status and made funding available for pump maintenance.

The women's activities also extended to the provision of social infrastructure and environmental management. Women from five of the pump communities came together to initiate the construction of a community clinic, which was identified as a pressing need of the community. The women solicited technical assistance from the Department of Community Development whilst some building materials were provided by the Adventist Relief Development Agency (ADRA) and the Ministry of Health.

Realizing the role of environmental conservation in preserving water supplies, the women also initiated tree growing at their various pumpsites.

The active involvement of women in the project activities disproved an earlier notion that in a male dominated society, response by women may be slow.

Achievements

Some major achievements were realized towards the overall objectives of the project. These include:

- Developed sense of ownership over water point, enhancing the spirit of self reliance.
- Developed skills for community self management.
- Developed relevant technical skills for maintenance and repair.
- Funding and fund mobilization for water supply became a tradition of the communities particularly with women's groups.
- Although the latrine promotion strategy was unsuccessful, the awareness had been created and the demand for latrines was on the increase after the completion of 32 demonstration latrines scattered in the project area. The target was 100 demonstration latrines.
- Pumpsite sanitation and hygiene education prospered well in the communities, demonstrated by the window dressed pumpsites of the area and improved hygiene practices of the women. Although the impact of the latter could not be measured, there were visible signs of improvement in household sanitation in particular.

Current status

Towards the middle of the third year of the project, support for the communities was being deliberately withdrawn. The aim was to monitor the communities' own performance in the various aspects of self management. By then all the committees had participated in 17 management training workshops each lasting between two to seven days.

Findings reported here are taken from random visits and a survey carried out in the communities in April 1995 to assess the successes and failures.

Community self management

Although some were dormant, all the WASAMC formed six years ago were still in place to provide leadership in community action.

- The committees met five times per year on the average, but minutes of meetings were not kept, because the committees were predominantly illiterates.
- Decisions and actions taken were mostly on money collection and pumpsite sanitation.
- Most committees expressed difficulty in organizing money collection.
- All communities maintained bank accounts although 70 per cent of them were woefully insufficient for any meaningful maintenance, let alone future pump replacement.
- Committees were capable and able to carry out maintenance and repair work on handpumps.

Handpump performance

Generally, the pumps performed well. The weak points were recorded in terms of rod breakages, perforation of rising main and leakages from the riser main coupling, and foot valve failures.

The Afridev

The plastic bearings, bobbins and plunger seals were found to be most frequently used. It was observed that they were mainly used for annual schedule maintenance as recommended by manufacturers, and that the wear was usually slight.

The rod connections used are quick disconnect types and do not require tools. However, rust builds up quickly on the welded parts of the hook and eye. At the only deep setting borehole (39m) the rods broke at the hook end. In one particular case the rods broke four times in two months.

The Aquidev

The difference in diameter between rod centralizers and the rising main is about 3mm; the centralizers sometimes rub the rising main during operation. The ribs on the outer surface of rod centralizers have perforated the rising mains on four occasions causing leakages.

The foot valve attached to plunger with a nylon cord sometimes snaps during pull out. With the slightest disturbance, the foot valve moves from its vertical position causing leakages.

Volanta

The volanta rising mains can leak through the separate pieces of coupling glued together. Two instances of this were observed. The foot valve assembly sometimes disconnects from the threaded portion of the cylinder. This happened in four out of 12 pumps.

Nira AF85

Unlike the other VLOM pumps the foot valve is not extractable without removing the rising mains. The T-handle of the stainless steel handle wear and even perforate after four years of use. Five of the eight pumps developed the problem.

Despite these failures in some of the pumps, about 75 per cent of them are still in proper operation after six to seven years of installation. The poor performance of the 25 per cent of the pumps may be attributed mainly to the reluctance of communities to spend money on preventive maintenance.

Lessons learned

Many of the lessons learned from the 50 Well Project are centred around the human institution, finance and a few technology failures. Perhaps the most single important lesson learned endorses the fact that sustainable community management hinges on capacity building of the water committee which also depends on resources, time and the effort put into extension work. Training and confidence-building of the water committee to act on issues of management is time consuming and requires not less than (at least in the Upper Regions) five years for communities to become managers rather than users of water systems.

Regular meetings and decision making is difficult; so raising the level of service is a very slow process even when the demand is there.

In some cases of the 50 Well Project, only part of the community have a felt need for a handpump. Ensuring the availability of sufficient funds for maintenance is difficult especially in cases where there are alternative water sources (e.g. hand-dug wells). Interestingly, communities are generally reluctant to utilize mobilized funds for preventive maintenance unless there is need for a major intervention.

Sanitation issues, particularly the latrine, was regarded a secondary issue.

The sale of handpump spare parts seemed to be an unviable business. The average annual sales for the spare parts agent in the 50 Well Project is around 150 000 cedis (US $136) due to few part failures and reluctance of communities to spend money on preventive maintenance.

Conclusion

Experience from the 50 Well Project indicates that consultation and joint decision making, where roles and rights are agreed upon with the communities as partners, generally provide more realistic solutions to sustained self interest in management.

Sustainable community management is easily realized where the community and their selected committee members have a common motivation factor (e.g. where water is scarce or the value of clean water is appreciated), without which awareness creation through training is usually a process of many, many years.

An important factor inhibiting sustainable rural water supply is the lack of private sector support due mainly to economic interest. Major players (government, ESAs) in the sector's development will need to demonstrate their support by relaxing import and export regulations and also channelling more resources through the private sector (NGOs) to enhance sustainability of rural water and sanitation facilities.

Although community management seemingly experiences some bottlenecks, it is probably the only known sustainable arrangement for ensuring uninterrupted water supply and sanitation in the rural areas of Ghana.

SECTION D

SANITATION AND WASTE

Community initiatives in solid waste

Mansoor Ali and Darren Saywell, WEDC

OVER RECENT DECADES, one of the commonest characteristics in developing nations has been the disparity between rapid urban population growth and infrastructure provision. The product of this mismatch, described as 'urbanization without health' [1] is the catalogue of overcrowding, growth in illegal settlements, uncollected household waste, and the absence of water, sanitation and other basic facilities which are typical of many urban centres in Africa, Asia and South America. As a result many millions of the urban poor live in neighbourhoods which are hazardous to health and well-being.

Uncollected or improperly disposed-of wastes can serve as breeding grounds for disease vectors, especially vermin, flies and their associated pathogens. Poor management of solid wastes thus presents serious health hazards to all urban inhabitants, but most especially those in low income communities (which suffer most from poor infrastructure provision) and the young (who play on streets or ground earmarked for dumping). The identification of waste management as integral to sustainable urban development is increasingly recognized by the international aid and development community. The United Nations Conference on Environment and Development stressed that '...solid waste production should be minimized, reuse and recycling maximized, environmentally sound waste disposal and treatment promoted and waste service coverage extended'. [2] UNCHS Habitat emphasizes environmentally sound and resource-efficient approaches to the problem of growing solid waste quantities, and considers waste management as a crucial component of human policies and programmes.[3] What these examples illustrate is the rising importance that solid waste management has amongst advocates of sustainable development.

The nature and operation of solid waste management varies significantly from nation to nation. Distinctions such as these are not limited to the national scale however, and can be seen at the city and neighbourhood level. Regardless of scale, these differences are to some extent attributable to prevailing socio-economic, financial, legal and political variables at that level. There is a clear requirement to reconcile the need for more effective waste management with the constraints that are faced by local municipalities or national governments.

Community involvement, or its absence, is in part both the problem and potential solution of this dilemma. The health hazards faced by many low income urban communities from improper collection and disposal of refuse are a function of their exclusion from traditional waste management avenues. Factors including illegal status, geographical marginalization of poor communities, and difficult terrain tend to detach many urban inhabitants from waste management services. However, recent changes in attitude by waste management professionals have placed community initiatives and participation at the heart of sustainable urban development. The main shift in thinking has been twofold: the need to develop local solutions which match local needs and options (often in contrast to professional training); and the identification of neighbourhood refuse collection schemes, based on community participation, as a cheap and effective methods of addressing the solid waste problem.

Community involvement in waste management streams is strongly represented through informal sector activities such as sorting, picking, managing and collecting waste. Recent work by WEDC in low to middle income urban communities in Karachi, Pakistan, reveals the extent of these community's intervention in the provision of primary collection services.

Cases of community involvement

The case studies discussed in this paper demonstrate the potential of community involvement in the planning, operation and implementation of solid waste management. Most of the data and information was collected during 1994-95.

Many urban inhabitants are involved in privately-run recycling systems. The other functions of solid waste management, namely collection, transportation and safe disposal are normally the responsibility of municipal authorities, a responsibility which many are failing to provide adequately. [4,5] The widespread lack of environmental awareness, little understanding of the health consequences of poor solid waste management practices, and inadequate financial resources all serve to reduce public concern about the impact of poor waste disposal. By contrast, there is increasing attention given to the immediate residential environment, a trend which is particularly visible in middle and high income areas of Karachi, where communities are increasingly co-operating in order to plan and manage the waste management system at the neighbourhood level (typically ranging between 50 to 1000 houses). Common to all of the case studies is that middle and high income area communities share similar objectives, which are:

- A reliable and regular service of waste collection from the residence;
- A system of street sweeping in the neighbourhood;
- Reducing pollution in the neighbourhood through removal of waste transfer points or containers;
- A system for the collection of garden waste and construction debris generated in the area.

In a number of Karachi's neighbourhoods, communities have organized their own waste management systems which satisfy one or more of the above objectives. Although seeking similar goals, organizational patterns and system details vary significantly. Analysis of these case studies *may* provide a model for other urban communities to manage their own waste collection systems, and for municipalities to incorporate community initiatives into their operations.

Case studies

House-to-house waste collection in F. B. Area [6]

In this example, residents were consulted about the possible introduction of a house-to-house waste collection system in their neighbourhood, and asked to comment on the plan, which included details and costings for the scheme. In total, 1000 letters were sent to houses situated in blocks 10 and 11 of the area, and 90 per cent of residents voted in favour of adopting the system. Two second hand Suzuki pick-up trucks were purchased and a door-to-door collection system was started. The collection system is based on pick-up trucks (capacity 500 kg) which cover a predetermined route. Collection crews stop at various points along the lanes to load waste from bins before moving to the next house. When the pick-up truck is full the collected waste is disposed of at a central point, from where the municipal vehicles collects the waste for final disposal. Under the system, each house was charged a monthly fee of Rs 25 over the first four years, rising to Rs 30 per month during the last two years. [7] All operation and maintenance costs are paid from the collected revenue. Additional income is raised through the resale of separated waste such as glass, plastic and metal. Although initially operated under the auspices of a municipal councillor, dissolution of local authorities in 1989 meant that the collection system has since run as an independent enterprise.

Evaluation by WEDC in early 1994 showed that the system worked effectively: the community contributed a regular amount for waste collection, the system was self financing, and significant gains had been made in the provision of a reliable and regular waste collection service. The main constraints that were identified included disruption to the formal collection system forcing municipal sweepers to move to other, more profitable areas, lack of will to support and replicate the programmes elsewhere in the municipality and irregular operation of the pick-up trucks. Despite these problems, the system continues to operate and is currently collecting waste from 800 houses daily.

Karachi Administration Women Welfare Society (KAWWS) [8]

The KAWWS is a group of housewives from a higher middle income neighbourhood of Karachi, known as Baloch Colony. [9] The area is characterized by a number of yet undeveloped open plots, which have become *de facto* a site for household waste disposal. In 1988, KAWWS formed a group with the objective of collecting money to purchase waste collection bins, which would help address the problem of improper disposal on open plots. KAWWS charge a monthly fee of Rs 100 from each participating housewife. Although in this scheme bins were purchased for the neighbourhood, the collection and disposal of the waste remained a problem, there was no formal agreement between the municipal corporation and KAWWS to collect waste from the transfer points. KAWWS subsequently negotiated with the municipal refuse vehicle driver in the area to arrange for waste collection for a set fee.

The arrangement worked well, and in 1994 KAWWS received funding from UNICEF in Pakistan to establish a revolving fund to provide additional waste bins in the area. Following consultation with local shopkeepers and other residents, bins have been placed at appropriate sites in the neighbourhood. Evaluation by WEDC in 1994 showed that the programme had substantially improved cleanliness in the area. The main constraints included low levels of participation (restricted to about 50 housewives), residents' perception of the initiative as a service delivery programme (many residents prefer a cleaner environment and a regular service for waste collection, but few are interested in contributing their time in arranging the systems); increasing housing density has made the siting of bins a long-term problem; and the municipal sweeper system has been disturbed with workers moving to other profitable areas. Despite these constraints, KAWWS is still active in the area and has expanded its work into other environmental improvement projects such as tree plantation, park development, etc..

Organized waste collection by C. P. Berar Society [10]

This is a relatively new programme (late 1994) initiated by a long-established association, *Anjuman e Falah o Bahbood* (Welfare Association). Funding (Rs 35 000) for proper management of solid waste in the area was received from UNICEF, and was used to buy tools, equipment, training and education materials. The cost of operating the collection system was born from the community. Phase I of the programme involved waste collection from 1000 houses. Wheelbarrows and shovels were used by the municipal sweepers, who collected waste from the houses and swept the streets. The community has organized itself into groups of 20 households, each with a volunteer to monitor the system for that grouping. For every five volunteers there is a group leader. The community association maintains links between the group leaders and volunteers.

Further detailed investigations are required before conclusions can be drawn from the programmes' experiences. Preliminary evaluations conducted in May 1995 indicate that the programme has not disturbed the existing municipal system, and sweepers continue to work in the area. The community association has developed a healthy relationship with municipality supervisory staff which helps improve the efficiency of the existing arrangement. This is an interesting model of community participation, in which community involvement is limited to the role of watchdog.

Street sweeping and waste collection in Gulshan e Iqbal, block 7 [11]

Waste collection in this higher middle income area is organised through an informal group of housewives known as *Falahi Tanzeem*. The group charges monthly fees of Rs 100 per house, Rs 500 per month from established schools and Rs 250 per month from newer schools. Contributions are collected by a staff member specifically appointed for this task. The association also employs eight sweepers, five of whom are seconded from the municipal authority. The association's revenue is divided between the seconded and employed workers. The sweepers use their wheelbarrows to carry waste to municipal containers which are approximately 2 kms distance from the neighbourhood. Further investigations are planned to establish how the desire for a cleaner environment balances with willingness to pay and the perceived (low) priority of waste management services in many parts of Karachi.

Analysis of the case studies

Opportunities and constraints

There are several points which can be raised from the case studies described:

- It is clear from the programmes that there are dedicated activists within the community who 'own' the initiatives and direct and guide its operation. Does this diminish the notion of community involvement? Although being derived from individual(s), the ideas do not remain their sole provenance, with the community typically initiating, and taking charge of improvements as and when they occur.

- The problems of urban areas in developing countries are typically distinct but similar. Community initiatives, if properly understood and fully incorporated into the municipal system have potential to improve system efficiencies and reduce expenditures. Community groups in higher and middle income areas have shown their ability to solve the problems of street sweeping, household waste collection and the transfer of wastes to central collection points within walking distances in the neighbourhood.

- Although municipal authorities can focus their attention on the development of appropriate transfer points, improving waste transportation and development of disposal sites, many fail to encourage community efforts, instead typically planning for privatization, without understanding the social and economic consequences of this intervention. Pre-qualification notices published in Karachi's daily newspapers in April 1995 illustrate the top-down nature of this intervention: although experience is one of the requisite criteria asked of firms, the notice does not mention the type of work involved or the areas in which it will be carried out. Community groups are effectively excluded through the narrow interpretation of pre-qualification criteria.

- Another crucial point drawn from the case studies is that of enterprise development in waste management. Case study 1 is a good example of a community-based enterprise, in contrast to the other examples where sweepers or collection crews are paid a fee to operate the system. Community groups, municipal authorities and donor agencies should focus their attention on developing grass root enterprises for waste collection and street sweeping. The community groups can establish a contract with such an enterprise, monitor its activities, negotiate rates and educate the community. Payment for the service may be direct from the household in the case of household waste collection and through the association for street sweeping. Municipal authorities can play an enabling role by placing the sweepers and making them directly accountable to the community groups. Case study 4 closely mimics this arrangement.

Encouraging community initiatives

Municipal authorities can take the following steps to encourage popular participation in the waste management process:

1. Publicize in local newspapers that those groups willing to assist municipal authorities in improving environmental conditions in their area should come forward to the relevant municipality office (or administrator).

2. The municipal authority transfers sweepers to the representative community organization. Sweeper attendance should be verified jointly by an area supervisor and a community organization representative.

3. The community group can decide and plan their own internal system of waste collection from houses to the transfer points (*katchra kundi*), street sweeping and collection of garden waste and construction debris.

3. The community group decides the rate and frequency of additional payments made to the sweepers. This may be from a centralized money collection, or a decentralized system in which residents pay directly for waste collection while the association pays for street sweeping and collection of garden waste etc..

4. The community group provides and maintains all necessary tools and other safety equipment for the sweepers.

5. The community group should check that municipal sweepers are not involved in work other than that for which they are paid.

6. Collected waste should be brought to a single point decided mutually by the municipal authority and the community. One collection point should serve at least 500 houses and a system should be devised by which the municipal authority ensures a timely and regular collection of waste from the transfer point. One way of doing this is a ticket system, in which a certain number of tickets are given to the community group which are redeemed by the driver following collection.

From transfer point to the disposal site, the waste management should be the responsibility of municipal authority or their designated contractors. Thus, Karachi Municipal Corporation can utilize the appropriate methods for all these tasks.

Summary

Although describing the experiences of middle-upper income urban communities in Karachi, these case studies illustrate the potential that exists for closer integration of the community with solid waste management practices, as a way of stretching scarce resources, to improve the health and well-being of urban inhabitants and to encourage grassroots enterprise development.

References

[1] Hardoy, J.E., Cairncross, S., and Satterthwaite, D. (1990) *The Poor Die Young* Earthscan Publications, London.

[2] Quarrie, J. (Ed) (1992) Earth Summit '92: The United Nations Conference on Environment and Development, Rio de Janeiro, 1992. Regency Press Corporation, London.

[3] UNCHS Habitat Improving the Living Environment for a Sustainable Future United Nations Centre for Human Settlements HS/270/92 E. UNCHS (Habitat), Nairobi, Kenya.

[4] Shenk, H., and Baud, I., (1994) 'Solid waste management in Bangalore: reflections, assessments and suggestions'. In *Solid Waste Management: Modes, Assessments, Appraisals and Linkages in Bangalore*. Manosher Publishers, New Delhi, India.

[5] Lardinois, I., and Van de Klundert A., (1993) 'Organic Waste: Options for Small Scale Resource Recovery'. Technology Transfer for Development and WASTE Consultants, Amsterdam, The Netherlands.

[6] For details contact Mr Pirzada M. Rafi, B-218, Block 11, F.B. Area, Karachi, Pakistan.

[7] 1 US$ = Rs 31. The average family income per month in the area is Rs 8000 - 10 000, and average plot size is 400 sq yards.

[8] For details contact Ms Sara Siddiqui, C-32 Block 2, Karachi Administration Employees Co-operative Housing Society, Karachi - 75350.

[9] This area is among higher middle income groups in which 64 per cent of households have an income level greater than Rs 5000 per month, against average incomes in planned areas of Karachi of Rs 4930 per month (Applied Economic Research Centre, University of Karachi, 1988).

[10] For details contact Mr Shafi ullah Khan, House No. 70, Block 7/8, C.P. Berar Housing Society, Karachi.

[11] For details contact Ms Nishat Zafar, 183-D, Block 7, Gulshan -e-Iqbal, Karachi.

Increasing sewer longevity by septicity control

Dr Karim Alibhai, Arthur Boon, Ms Alison Vincent and Ms Jenny Williams, UK

SEPTICITY WITHIN A sewerage system occurs when micro-organisms present in sewage and adhering to submerged surfaces have utilized all the dissolved oxygen and any nitrates that may be present in the sewage (derived from groundwater infiltration or present in the water supply). When anaerobic conditions have developed, bacteria in the sewage reduce the organic compounds of sulphur to sulphide and subsequently the sulphate-reducing bacteria utilize sulphates, as an alternative electron acceptor for the dissimilation of organic matter, and form sulphides. The consequences of sewage septicity are important for two critical reasons:

1) The formation of noxious odours which can give rise to a public nuisance; and

2) The corrosion of the fabric of the sewerage system by hydrogen sulphide including its biological oxidation to sulphuric acid which can result in the complete destruction of concrete pipes and mortar joints, particularly in warm climates where rates of sulphide formation and oxidation will be very high.

Sewage by its nature has an unpleasant odour which is made obnoxious when it becomes septic. Typical compounds present in odours from sewage include: organic sulphides and H_2S with odour thresholds within the range 1 to 4 ppb (these are acidic odours); and ammonia and amines (including other organic compounds such as skatole, indole and diethylamine) which have much higher odour thresholds than the acidic sulphides but are more persistent (these are alkaline odours).

Problems of odour and corrosion which can arise from sulphide formation will depend on the amount of hydrogen sulphide which escapes into the sewer atmosphere, and this will depend on the pH value of the sewage.

Hydrogen sulphide is a flammable and very poisonous gas with a characteristic odour of rotten eggs. Its threshold odour concentration is very low — between 1 and 10 ng/l — and it is potentially very dangerous because its smell is quickly lost as the concentration increases; unconsciousness followed by death can occur suddenly from about 300 ppm by volume in air. It can transfer into the sewer atmosphere where sewage turbulence occurs, for example in wet-wells, back drops, manholes and in gravity sewers. Its smell is made worse by the presence of other malodorous compounds, particularly mercaptans (or thiols) which may be formed in anaerobic sewage.

H_2S corrodes copper, copper-based alloys such as brass, some bronzes and Monel metal and silver to form black metal sulphides. As a result, it can have a disastrous effect on electrical equipment at pumping stations. Metalwork, such as step-irons, ladders, manhole covers and penstocks, unless made of corrosion-resistant materials, will be destroyed by prolonged exposure to hydrogen sulphide particularly in damp conditions. Even cast iron and some grades of stainless steel will be corroded (or pitted).

It is, however, through the corrosion of concrete sewers, manholes, and Portland cement mortar by the acidic products of H_2S oxidation that the prime consequence of septicity is well known. If oxidation occurs while H_2S is dissolved in sewage the products are harmless. At pH values between 6 and 7, chemical oxidation in sewage produces sulphur, while at higher pH values (between 7 and 9) dissolved H_2S would be oxidized to sulphurous compounds and finally to sulphate. However, H_2S in the damp, warm atmosphere within a gravity sewer, manhole, or wet-well will be oxidized to sulphuric acid by various autotrophic thiobacilli which grow successfully on exposed walls and other surfaces.

Problems associated with corrosion (and odour) caused by septicity occur in many parts of the world and particularly where sewage temperatures are high. Total collapse of eight-year-old concrete and asbestos-cement sewers has been recorded in South Africa, and concrete sewers have failed after only six years in the Middle East. However, problems also exist in temperate climates as well.

In nearly all cases cited in the literature, the effect of septicity has been most serious downstream from rising-main sewers, in locations where debris can accumulate, and in circumstances where excessive turbulence (back-drop, cascades, inverted siphons etc.) allows previously formed H_2S to be emitted into the atmosphere.

Gravity sewers should be designed to ensure that self-cleansing velocities are maintained at average flow-rates and that debris deposited at lower flow-rates will be eroded in order to prevent excessive accumulation. If such debris were retained within the sewerage system for long periods between peak flow-rates it would inevitably result in sulphide formation within the sediments which could cause odour and corrosion problems. A self-cleansing velocity of about 0.75 m/s should be adequate to keep sewage aerobic and this should prevent sulphide formation within the sewage but may not completely avoid sulphide being formed in accumulated debris and released as H_2S at points of turbulence.

When sewage is pumped up a rising-main sewer, out of contact with the atmosphere, the dissolved oxygen which may be initially present will be rapidly used by microbial activity and sulphide formation will start. The effect of temperature on the formation of sulphide (i.e. the rate of formation should double when the temperature increases by 10°C within the range 5-25°C).

Prevention of septicity
Inhibition
It is possible to inhibit the activity of the micro-organisms responsible for sulphide formation by addition of bactericidal chemicals. Such chemicals include chlorine, sodium hypochlorite or a range of organic chemicals (mostly chlorinated hydrocarbons) which would need to be added continuously in order to remain effective and may require high dose rates. The high cost of such continuous additions, together with possibility of problems with biological treatment processes downstream (particularly anaerobic digestion of sludges) caused by residual chemicals or byproducts, are likely to preclude the widespread use of such bactericidal chemicals for total prevention of sulphide formation.

Maintaining aerobic conditions
Sulphide will not be formed in sewage if dissolved oxygen (DO) is present. In a rising-main sewer, sewage is kept out of contact with the atmosphere and soon becomes anaerobic, particularly in small-diameter pipes with a large internal surface area per unit volume. Injection of air into sewage entering a rising-main can be used to reduce the period for which anaerobic conditions may develop and hence minimize sulphide formation. Use of commercial oxygen allows the saturation concentration of DO to be increased about five-fold, and potential problems associated with residual nitrogen gas can be avoided.

Maintaining anoxic conditions
In the absence of dissolved oxygen, nitrate can be an alternative to sulphate (as an electron acceptor) for dissimilation of organic matter, as the bacteria involved function at a higher redox potential than the proteolytic bacteria (which reduce organic sulphur) and sulphate-reducing bacteria. The condition under which micro-organisms utilize nitrate for the dissimilation of organic matter in sewage is termed anoxic. In recent years, various proprietary chemicals, which contain nitrate, have been used to prevent sulphide formation in rising-main sewers in the UK. Some of these chemicals contain an oxidized iron salt (Iron(III) sulphate) and nitric acid, and will be effective provided that the nitrate is not totally used by the micro-organisms. However, when the nitrate has been used by the micro-organisms, septicity will recur (enhanced in rate by added iron ions) and Iron(II) salts will be formed which are corrosive to steel, copper, brass, bronze, zinc and silver. The sulphate anion of the added Iron(III) salt will also be available for reduction to sulphide, so the overall effect may be to increase odours and cause greater corrosion particularly at the end of a long rising-main.

For nitrate addition to prevent completely sulphide formation, it is necessary to calculate how much will be required and this will vary according to the following characteristics of the sewage: Oxygen demand (including slimes growing on the walls); temperature; and flow-rate of sewage (which will vary between night and day and also dry and wet weather).

Chemicals to remove H_2S
Addition of lime (or preferably sodium hydroxide) to increase the pH value of sewage, and so reduce the proportion of sulphide present as H_2S, will reduce the emission of H_2S and can inhibit bacterial action. Alkali addition, to increase the pH value above 9 at all times, would probably be more expensive, and difficult to control effectively, than available alternatives. It would also result in release of alkaline odours which could cause odour nuisance. However, in some cases, such as small-diameter rising-mains, in which sewage is retained for long periods (possibly greater than 18 h), the cost of alkali might be similar to oxygen injection, chlorination, or the addition of other chemicals such as hydrogen peroxide, nitrate salts or bactericides.

An alternative to oxygen injection into sewage entering a rising-main would be to inject oxygen into sewage before it leaves the discharge end of a main and so oxidize previously-formed sulphide. Such a method could be used where sewage was pumped infrequently into a rising-main thus resulting in long retention periods. A simple system would involve recirculation of sewage contained in a relatively short length of the main near to its discharge end. A small pump would be needed to operate continuously and which would be capable of recirculating several times the sewage contained in the short length of main, both during the period that sewage was being pumped along the main and when it was stationary.

Mathematical modelling to control odours and minimize corrosion (SPACA)
The need to prevent and control septicity of an entire sewerage system, which may contain numerous gravity and rising-main sewers, may be complex with preventative actions taken upstream having an effect on odour formation and release downstream. In order to provide an effective logical and systematic approach. Acer have produced a computer-based mathematical model, consisting of Septicity Prediction And Control Algorithms (SPACA), which will estimate sulphide production and concentration throughout a network of sewers (either existing or proposed) in order to develop a strategy for sulphide prevention. The model can be used to assess the effectiveness of various methods of control, including oxygen injection, or the addition of nitrate, chlorine or

hypochlorite, hydrogen peroxide or iron salts. This allows the establishment of a least-cost option, to provide an effective resolution to potential or existing odour problems over a wide range of operating conditions. Inputs to the model include sewage flow-rate, temperature, COD, pH value, respiration rates, dissolved oxygen, sulphate and sulphide concentrations as well as sewer sizes, including lengths and types (gravity or rising-main).

The mathematical model utilizes empirical equations. The computer programme is Windows based and written in Visual Basic which ensures excellent user interface, rapid calculation and good presentation of results. In order to reduce the complexity of the model, it runs under steady-state conditions. To enable the effects of diurnal flow variation in the sewerage system to be taken into account, model runs can be performed on the system at a number of flow conditions which allows a sensitivity analysis to be carried out.

The sewerage network is represented by a number of 'nodes' and connecting 'sewer-pipes'. Each significant junction between sewers in the system can be represented by a node. All pumping stations, manholes at sewer intersections, or changes between gravity and pumping mains, are included into the model network as well as the final treatment works. Each connecting pipe must be specified as gravity or rising main and have its physical parameters (diameter, length and gradient) defined. Each node has its position in the network defined (at the periphery, middle or ultimate end) and the necessary information on flow, temperature, respiration rate and composition of sewage entered, or calculated, to enable sulphide production to be estimated.

It would be unrealistic and uneconomic to attempt to limit sulphide production to zero at all times, in all conditions. Sulphide concentrations can be tolerated in sewage if corrosion is not accentuated and odour nuisance does not occur. The required level of control of sulphide formation was based on two factors, firstly levels required to avoid corrosion and secondly levels required to avoid odour nuisance. (a) Corrosion - sulphide levels above 1 mg/l are likely to be a problem with respect to corrosion, although corrosion has been known to occur at concentrations of 0.5 mg/l in turbulent conditions[5]. Sulphide concentrations were therefore controlled so that they should not exceed 0.5 mg/l at any time. (b) Odour nuisance can be estimated by calculating the odour radius resulting from release of H_2S. The odour radius gives the estimated area from the odour source within which odour complaints could be expected.

Running the model

Once an adequate calibration is achieved, results can be analyzed to highlight the sites which require immediately treatment and those which require no, or minimal, action. The model output shows both sulphide concentrations in the sewage and sulphide production rates in each pipe. Control measures, such as addition of oxygen, nitrate or other chemicals, can be activated at every node and the quantity introduced into the system to prevent sulphide production can be user-specified or automatically calculated. Implementing only one treatment measure at a time allowed analysis of the impact that each would make to the system as a whole and so to build up a step-by-step control strategy which was both effective and economic.

In conclusion it should be emphasized that there is no single simple solution to sewage septicity, which can give rise to the need for odour control and the prevention of corrosion within a sewerage system or at a treatment works, because no two systems are alike. It is necessary therefore to examine fully the causes of septicity, prior to taking any action to prevent or control its formation. In most circumstances, this may be done using data and equations available from the literature, although there is no substitute for obtaining recent data from the system to be investigated.

Prevention of septicity by oxygen injection, nitrate addition or adequate aeration within the sewerage system is likely in many cases to be more economic and effective than to add chemicals to remove sulphide after formation, particularly, as such prevention will result in partial treatment of the sewage. Such pretreatment can have significant benefits of reduced capital and operational costs for the treatment works downstream.

To reduce the operating costs for chemical addition to sewage, it may be possible to use waste industrial effluents which contain the appropriate chemicals, such as nitrates from meat preservation, sodium hydroxide from the textile industry and iron salts from steel manufacture or from steel products. Care would need to be taken to avoid introduction of wastewaters which could be harmful either to the fabric of the sewerage system, to the downstream sewage treatment works, to the receiving water quality or to the operations staff involved.

Because the complete assessment of the consequences of septicity within a sewerage system may be complex, Acer has developed a mathematical model to enable such assessment to be carried out systematically. The results of such a mathematical assessment should enable potential problems of odours and corrosion to be minimized, or avoided, at minimum cost using effective measures of prevention and control that have been outlined in this paper.

Controlling septicity in the rising main can also be a form of treatment where soluble BOD is converted into sludge (insoluble SS), particularly at higher temperatures. Tables 1 and 2 show results of such trials for comparison. This illustrates that at higher temperatures with particularly oxygen injection, a high percentage reduction in BOD is achievable, which in some cases could eliminate the need for secondary treatment altogether. It should be emphasized that such a system will not nitrify or remove phosphorous and if higher degree of treatment is required secondary and/or tertiary treatment may be necessary.

Table 1. Treatment of sewage in the rising main.

SAMPLE OF SEWAGE ANALYSED	FLOW OF SEWAGE	RATE OF INJECTION OF OXYGEN	TEMPERATURE OF SEWAGE	CHANGE IN BOD OF SEWAGE DURING PASSAGE THROUGH THE MAIN		
	(m³/h)	(kg/h)	(°C)	(mg/l)	(%)	(kg/h)
Raw	1373	Nil	14	+3	+1	+3
Settled				-	-	-
Raw	1524	54	21	-13	-6	-21
Settled				-70	-23	-107
Raw	1640	Nil	14	+3	+1	+4
Settled				-19	-9	-30
Raw	1510	51	13	-5	-13	-11
Settled				-39	-14	-67

Table 2. Primary sedimentation tanks.

CONDITIONS OF OPERATION			PERFORMANCE					
Flow	Retention Period	Overflow Rate	Crude Sewage		Settled Sewage		Percentage Reduction	
			BOD	SS	BOD	SS	BOD	SS
(m³/h)	(h)	(m/h)	(mg/l)		(mg/l)			
WITH OXYGENATION OF SEWAGE								
2325	2.0	3.2	163	212	34	46	79	78
858	5.3	1.2	246	262	60	38	76	86
1129	4.0	1.5	187	212	70	50	62	76
NORMAL OPERATION								
792	5.8	1.08	200	230	130	104	35	55

Solid waste management in Addis Ababa

Paul Arnold, Ethiopia

THE POPULATION OF Addis Ababa was estimated at 2.63 M in 1993 and growing at a rate of six per cent per annum (BCEOM/GKW 1993). Most of the houses in the city are unplanned and very densely sited with average residential densities up to 326 people/ha. These areas have narrow and unmaintained access roads which greatly limits the population that can be served by refuse collection vehicles or who are within reasonable distance of a communal storage facility.

The last major study on solid waste management for the city of Addis Ababa was carried out in 1982 (Norconsult A.S. 1982). Updating the population figures in this study provides an estimate of the solid waste production of the city as given in Table 1. From the records kept by the municipality at the landfill site in 1991 and 1992 the percentage of solid waste collected is between 35 per cent and 40 per cent of that generated. The industrial waste is mostly generated from beverage, food, shoe, textile factories and tanneries.

In 1993 the Addis Ababa Municipality was reformed into Province 14 Administrative Region and the responsibility for solid waste management (SWM) passed to the Health Bureau. This bureau has inherited an ageing fleet of 26 'roll-top' trucks, four compactor vehicles and 11 container-hoist vehicles. From discussions with the responsible personnel at the Health Bureau, approximately 25 per cent of these vehicles are nonoperational at any one time. The development and expansion of the SWM system is at present still in the planning sage. However, the arrival in 1994 of 28 new container-hoist vehicles, financed by the World Bank, is expected to improve the collection system.

Collection systems

There are currently four types of collection system: a communal system which requires the delivery of wastes by the householder to a storage confiner; a block collection system where the householder delivers the wastes to the vehicle at the time of collection; a company/institutional system whereby a 4 or 6m^3 capacity container is placed in the organization's compound and emptied for a fee of 11 Ethiopian Birr (EB) (£1.4 1993)/m^3. Street cleaning is carried out manually using a handcart which is periodically emptied into the nearest communal storage confiner. With the exception of the company/institutional system all other collections are carried out free of charge.

There are 174 containers or skips of 8m^3 capacity distributed throughout the city for communal storage. This system is used for low and medium income (<1000 EB/household/month (£133, 1993)) areas and suffers from the problem of too infrequent emptying with the spillage of waste on the ground creating a health hazard. The block collection system is operated by the 'roll-top' trucks and compaction vehicles. This collection system is used mainly for high income (>1000 EB/household/mth) areas which have good access roads, as well as for market areas with a high waste generation rate.

Disposal site

There is only one disposal site for the entire city of Addis Ababa. This is sited at Repi, 12km south west of the city centre. This open dumping site is very poorly equipped, with only two ageing bulldozers and one roller compactor. The road to the site is in a very poor condition and becomes virtually unusable during the heavy rains. Hence there are often days when no waste can be collected from the city. Rapid urbanization around the site and the lack of any segregation of different types of waste results in over 100 people, including children, scavenging through the refuse with all the associated health risks. With no engineering control measures contamination of ground water through leaching and surface water through runoff is highly likely, especially during the heavy rainy season in July and August.

To reduce transportation costs at least three new disposal sites are required to serve the expanding city. These should be sanitary landfill sites, designed to minimize any detriment to the environment.

Pilot study

A pilot study was carried out in a residential area, Kebele 29, close to the large commercial market of Merkato. The community of 955 households were participants in an integrated urban development programme by OXFAM (UK) started in 1987. Resource constraints limited the pilot study to 200 households which were, however, representative of the main socio-economic groups within Kebele as described in Table II. In a World Bank report (1990) the subsistence level for the city was assessed to be an income of 236 EB/household/month (£63 1990). In Kebele 29, 87 per cent of the households have an income of less than 200 EB (£53 1990) and therefore represent the most disadvantaged socio-economic group.

Each householder was interviewed, to seek their participation in the survey and to obtain some information about the household and their existing practises in SWM. The community is served by one 8m³ skip sited at one corner of the Kebele, too far away from the majority of the population and therefore discouraging community participation. Hence only 28 per cent of the population use this facility. The block collection system is only occasionally used in Kebele 29, serving 12 per cent of the population. The majority of the population (60 per cent) use the river as a dumping place, since its course forms a boundary to the kebele. This practice, however, has a serious detriment to the water quality of the river, which has effectively become an open sewer.

Earlier in their six-year development programme, OXFAM had tried to improve the SWM system in the community. They issued each household with a 100 litre container made from an old oil drum. These containers were painted and marked with the household number. The idea was that by providing these large primary storage containers households would be encouraged to dispose of their solid waste within their compound before carrying to the communal container. However, within a week of issuing these containers it became obvious that the residents considered these clean watertight containers to be far too valuable for the collection of rubbish. Instead the containers are used for washing clothes and fermenting barley.

Sampling procedure

Black plastic bags, 0.5m square, were supplied to each household for collecting their solid waste. The sampling programme took place over seven consecutive days commencing 29 July 1993. The sampling procedure generally followed recognized practice (Flintoff 1984). The weighing device readily available was a spring balance type with a capacity of up to 50kg. This relatively small capacity, together with an absence of any lightweight wood made the recommended 500 litre box too heavy to weigh. Instead 64 litre boxes were used. These proved to be a more appropriate size in view of the relatively small sample size and the very low level of waste generation.

It was not possible to collect samples from about 25 per cent of the households. This was due to the householder not being at home or the household waste not having been put in the collection bag provided.

Results of sampling

A summary of the results of the sampling work is shown in Tables III and IV.

A comparison of the average generation rates measured in the pilot study with other studies on SWM in Addis Ababa is shown in Table V. The reason why the pilot study results are at the lower end of the range of rates may be due to the extreme poverty of the study area, and a reluctance of the people to send all their waste to be analyzed.

The reason for the high percentage of grasses and food wastes in the study area is the cultural practice of using grasses to cover the mud floors of the houses in general and also during the daily coffee ceremony. Such type of wastes are very suitable for either composting or the manufacture of briquettes for fuel, both of which need only require low-cost technology. The composting option is unlikely to be sustainable at a community level in the capital city, where the transportation costs to agricultural land will be high. The composting would need to be undertaken by me formal sector at processing sites on the outskirts of the city adjacent to agricultural land. The manufacture of briquettes for fuel is more promising for community participation, as there is a large market within the city. Their use as an alternative to firewood is especially important in view of the severe deforestation in the region. Further research is required to assess the sustainability of these two options. The extremely low amounts of salvageable constituents reflect the small amount of goods passing through each household and the minimal amount of packaging materials used for these goods.

The average density of the solid waste collected in the study area was 230 kg/m³ from a range of 180 - 380 kg/m³ and is considerably lower than the value of 500 kg/m³ given by Norconsult. The densities from the pilot study were measured prior to the disposal of the wastes into the communal storage containers. Hence the increase in density reflects the consolidation that takes place in the containers during storage and transportation. These densities compare to values of 570 kg/m³ for an Indian city and 277 kg/m³ for Ibadan, Nigeria. (Holmes 1984).

It is very interesting to note that in a socio-economic survey of the city carried out by the Addis Ababa Water Supply and Sewerage Authority in 1990, 52.3 per cent of households have an income of less than 200 EB(£53 1990)/month. Hence the solid waste from the study area is representative of the type of waste generated by about half of the households in the city.

Conclusions

The study highlighted the inadequacies of Addis Ababa's existing solid waste collection system, which collects less than 40 per cent of the waste generated. This lack of coverage is due to the rapid unplanned growth of the city and severe resource limitations. The existing disposal site is an environmental hazard and should be replaced by three new sanitary landfill sites.

The high proportion of grasses and food wastes (70 per cent) suggests that much of the waste from Addis Ababa could either be composted and used as a fertilizer or manufactured into briquettes for fuel as an alternative to firewood for cooking. Further study is needed to explore the sustainability of these two options.

Improvements in the collection and treatment of solid waste could be initiated by a community-based, low technology approach. The sale of briquettes to a large readily available market would provide the financial incentive for the sustainability of this approach.

Acknowledgements

The author acknowledges the contributions that Diro Dibaba, Getaneh Mekonen and Nigussie Kidane made to the pilot study which were in partial fulfilment of their degree in Civil Engineering at Addis Ababa University. He is also grateful to OXFAM (UK) for sponsoring the study and their Ato Girmaye Kahessaye for his enthusiastic support. He also acknowledges the support and co-operation of Ato Haile Wubneh and Dr Abera Kume from the Region 14 Health Bureau.

References

BCEOM/GKW. Master plan study for the development of wastewater facilities for the city of Addis Ababa. 1993.

Flintoff, F. *Management of solid wastes in developing countries*. WHO S-E Asia Series No 1, 1984.

Holmes, J.R. (Ed) *Managing Solid Wastes in Developing Countries*. Wiley, 1984.

Norconsult, A.S. Addis Ababa Solid Waste Management Master Plan Study, 1982.

Sir William Halcrow, Integrated Urban-rural Development Project, 1989.

Table I. Estimated solid waste production of Addis Ababa 1993

Source	Solid waste generated (tonnes/day)	Percentage
Household	454	67
Commercial	61	9
Industrial	41	6
Hotels	27	4
Hospitals	14	2
Street	81	12
TOTAL	678	100

Table II. Division of population of Kebele 29 into socio-economic group by income levels

Ref	Socio-economic group	Monthly Income/household	
		Ethiopian Birr	Equivalent in £ Sterling, 1993
A	Poorest of the poor	0-100	0-13
B	Very poor	101-200	14-26
C	Poor - Low	> 200	> 26
D	n/a	Residential shops/offices	

Table III. Generation rates by socio-economic group in Kebele 29

Generation rate	Socio-economic group			
	A	B	C	D
kg/person/day	0.093	0.076	0.100	0.159
kg/household/day	0.522	0.525	0.831	0.826
Households	57	42	29	21
Population	320	290	242	109

Table IV. Constituents of wastes by socio-economic group in Kebele 29

Constituent	Socio-economic group and average % by weight			
	A	B	C	D
Grasses & Food wastes > 50 mm	30	35	30	27
ditto 0-50 mm	31	30	38	35
ditto < 10 mm	10	9	7	7
ditto sub-total	71	74	75	69
Paper	3	4	5	6
Metals	1	1	1	1
Glass	0	0	1	0
Textiles	2	2	2	2
Plastics & rubber	2	1	2	1
Bones	0	0	0	5
Misc combustible	1	0	0	1
Misc non-comb'le	0	0	0	0
Inert mat'r <10mm	20	18	14	15
TOTAL	100	100	100	100
DENSITY kg/m^3	218	228	246	220

Table V. Comparison of generation rate in Kebele 29 with previous studies

Area	Generation rate (kg/person/day)
Pilot Study, Kebele 29	0.10
Low rise densely housed area	0.14[a]
City centre area	0.13[a]
Single dwelling housing area	0.25[a]
Block of flats housing area	0.25[a]
Akaki development	0.20-0.31[b]

[a] Norconsult 1982 [b] Halcrow 1989

Sustaining quality by control of industrial discharges

Derek Harrington and Dr Karim Alibhai, UK

THIS PAPER SUMMARIZES the progress of an ongoing project carried out by Taylor Binnie and Partners (TBP) (a joint venture of two UK consulting engineers, ACER Consultants and Binnie and Partners), on behalf of the European Investment Bank (EIB), the Cairo Wastewater Organization (CWO) and the General Organization for Sanitary Drainage (GOSD) for the protection of this enormous investment.

The project has focused on the study, management and control of industrial discharges for the Shoubra el Kheima district of Cairo, that:

(i) Exceed existing legal requirements,
(ii) Damage the sewer fabric,
(iii) Produce hazardous conditions within the sewer network,
(iv) Produce odour or accumulate debris within the sewers,
(v) Interfere with biological treatment processes,
(vi) Compromise the efficient re-use of the treated effluent and sludge.

The benefits accruing from the implementation of an effective effluent control programme include:

- Protection of the environment and public health,
- Maximizing the use of water resources,
- Improvements in sewer capacity,
- Reduction in sewer maintenance,
- Improvement in river drainage quality,
- Reduction in costs to industry.

Work undertaken by CWO and GOSD over the last decade has involved the design and construction of an extensive sewerage network and six major treatment plants to serve Greater Cairo and Helwan. This study area covers approximately 875 square kilometres and serves a population of about 15 million people. These plants are already significantly reducing pollution levels within Cairo and are providing the potential for effluent and sludge re-use in agriculture. The total treatment capacity of these plants is 3 280 000 m³/day.

Like all major urban areas, Greater Cairo and Helwan have locations which may be wholly industrial, commercial, residential or mixed. Some districts are also centres for specific types of industry, such as the tanneries, which can cause significant problems in the sewer systems and treatment works and therefore need to be monitored and controlled. An extensive literature review was carried out to ascertain progress to date on industrial effluent control initiatives and to establish baseline data for the Cairo Project. The conclusions of this review were that:

- Information on quality and quantity of industrial effluent is sparse,
- Industry is reluctant to control its pollution,
- Access to sampling locations is often refused,
- High levels of toxic materials may be discharged to the sewers,
- Legislative controls although in place are not implemented,
- A comprehensive database of polluting industries does not exist.

The first step in the development of an industrial database for the project area was the preparation of a comprehensive list of industries. A number of sources of information were identified. However, much of the in-

Table 1. Average water consumption, effluent volumes and polluting loads for industry throughout Egypt (Source GOFI)

DATA	NOs	WATER	EFF	POLLUTION LOADS (t/DAY)				
Industry		Use mill.m³/yr	mill. m³/yr	BOD	COD	Oil	SS	Metals
Chemical	53	127	98	26	178	23	33	0.94
Food	119	296	227	182	142	110	168	0.17
Spinning & Weaving	75	114	88	39	47	24	64	0.3
Engineering	39	13	12	5	7	2	3	0.03
Metal/Metallurgy	11	69	60	15	14	8	24	0.2
Mining	33	19	14	3	1	1	4	0.01
TOTAL	330	638	499	270	389	168	296	1.65

formation was available only as the address, telephone and industrial activity with little or no data on effluent flows, concentrations and loads. However information that was useful is summarized in Tables 1 and 2.

The food and chemical industries discharge the greatest volume of effluent and the oil and soap industries were the most polluting with respect to organic material. Oil/grease and solids were noted as a general pollutant from all industries. In a more detailed study in the Shoubra el Kheima area the NRC found that the textiles and metal industries constitute 83 per cent of the total manufacturing base and were by far the most polluting. The above review confirmed the need for; better co-ordination between the government organizations responsible for monitoring of industrial pollution and the production of a single master database of polluting industries.

Industrial pollution may be microbiological, physical, organic or inorganic and hence, a wide range of parameters needs to be monitored. To ensure that sampling costs do not escalate it is normal to tailor the number of samples and types of analysis to particular industries. Table 3 shows the range of analyses used to quantify particular effluents on a routine bases.

A review of the existing legislation in comparison with standards in other countries shows that the standards for some parameters including suspended solids, BOD and some heavy metals are too severe. One example is a BOD value of 400 mg/l which may be less than some strong wholly domestic sewages. With the development of the new extended sewerage system and the construction of treatment works capable of treating most industrial effluents, a review of the discharge standards was recommended and this was later implemented.

One of the key elements of an industrial effluent monitoring programme is the establishment of fully reliable laboratory with trained staff and appropriate equipment and resources. As part of the study, 21 laboratory facilities in Cairo were reviewed. As a result of this review, a recommendation was made that the existing GOSD laboratory at Heliopolis should be used for monitoring industrial effluent, following major refurbishment. It was also recommended that some analyses could be contracted out at suitable laboratories.

A pilot sampling and analytical programme was included in the study in order to provide representative data to gauge the nature and extent of the overall problem associated with effluent quality. Within the short time available a limited sampling programme was completed involving 51 samples mainly from industrial locations. The pilot sampling and analysis programme quantified, to a limited degree, the problems experienced in the operation and maintenance of the Cairo sewerage system.

The analysis of sewage samples from four GOSD pumping stations indicated that the high concentrations of pollutants were diluted to acceptable levels within the sewerage system. However, with regard to effluent and sludge re-use, it is considered necessary to evaluate further the metals content in the final effluent and sludge.

Several of the factories have installed treatment facilities although some are not always in operation. The introduction of an ongoing effective monitoring programme may persuade these factories to utilize their treatment works on a regular basis.

It was therefore concluded that construction of simple treatment facilities at 40 per cent of the pilot sampling locations would significantly improve effluent quality.

Table 2. Effluent characteristics from industries sampled by NRC (Greater Cairo)
(All results in mg/l except pH and flow) Source: NRC

Manufacturer	No. of Samples	Flow m^3/d	pH	BOD	COD	SS	Oil/ Grease	Heavy Metals
Cement	1	320	9.6	5	16	100		
Plastics	4	220-1850	7.1-8.4	5-28	9-95	0-84	44	
Pulp/paper	4	70-950	6.4-8.6	260-450	180-2550	7-2000	15-230	
Iron and Steel	9	300-24000	7.3-7.4	7-140	40-440	100-190	50-175	67
Non-ferrous	7	300-2250	7.2-8.7	15-350	260-1677	55-3044	0-190	3-47
Chemical	4	175-136000	7.4-10.0	30-7500	60-1400	110-1210	43	
Pharmaceutical	4	185-630	7.3	120	760	760	100	
Oil and Soap	3	400-2000	7.2-11.0	850-33000	1900-42000	290-1930	140	
Textiles	19	25-12000	2.2-12.2	3-1080	13-4040	2-3396	29-321	
Food	15	120-792000	3.9-7.0	100-1530	410-10220	60-500	2-80	

Table 3. Industrial monitoring - appropriate deteminands

INDUSTRY	DETERMINAND
Textiles	
Bleaching/Dyeing	Temp, pH, COD, detergent
Wool scouring	Temp, pH, COD, detergent, grease
Knitwear	COD, detergent
Stone Washing	Temp, detergent
Laudries	Temp, COD, detergent
Food	
Processing	pH, COD, nitrogen, solids
Breweries	pH, COD, solids
Restaurants	Temp, grease, BOD, solids
Tanning	Metals, solids, sulphide, pH, COD
Chemical	pH, COD, phenol
Drugs	COD
Electronics } Electroplating } Metal Finishing }	pH, COD, metals, cyanide, solids
Garages	COD, phenol, oil/grease
Printing	pH, metals
Abattoirs/Markets	BOD, nitrogen, solids

Appropriate facilities include neutralization, sedimentation and/or oil and grease traps.

The data gathered during the Study was used to develop a database. Some 50 publications were obtained and reviewed for this purpose, producing more than 4000 records for input to the database. All reliable analytical results, including those obtained during the pilot sampling programme were also loaded onto the database.

Implementation (phase 1) - 1993

An implementation group was instituted under the auspices of the Ministry of Housing with representatives from private and public industrial organisations, GOSD, the Cairo Wastewater Organization and the Egyptian Environmental Affairs Agency. The terms of reference of the group were to recommend changes to Law 93, develop an industrial effluent control agency and raise public awareness of the problem of industrial wastewater pollution. Law 93 was first enacted in 1962 and was considered inappropriate for the current situation. As a consequence, an international review was carried out and changes recommended. The summary of the review and the recommended changes are shown in Table 4.

Implementation (phase 11) 1994

As a result of the success of the implementation group in addressing the various issues EIB commissioned further technical assistance during 1994. One of the many recommendations of the group was to implement a control programme at one particular district in Cairo to show industrialists what can be achieved. Shoubra el Kheima was chosen and EIB agreed to fund a pilot programme. Shoubra el Eheima is centrally located in Cairo and is bounded by the Nile to the west and the Ismailia Canal to the east. It has a population of about one million and is a mix of urban development, agriculture and industry. TBP were asked to appraise the location and recommend a programme of implementation.

The 'way forward'

To develop the initiative TBP recommended there was a need to carry out the following tasks:

- Inform industry on how best to tackle the problem of industrial pollution and to make them aware of the statutory requirements.
- Update the database by continued sampling and including data from other agencies.
- Carry out a selection of industrial audits to ascertain treatment options including 'good housekeeping'.
- Categorize those industries requiring treatment prior to discharge to sewer.
- Identify technical and financial initiatives required to implement the desired changes.

Implementation (phase III) 12/94 - 5/95

The Phase III implementation programme has been divided into two distinct parts. The first has been the identification of priority industries and the choice factories for audit. The second is the carrying out of the audits and the development of the possible subsequent loan/grant arrangements for construction of the treatment plants at individual factories.

The identification of priority industries had the following elements:

- Reviewing and updating the database to include EEAA, GOFI, Federation of Egyptian Industries (FEI), and the GOSD data.
- The introduction of a short intensive sampling programme of selected industries.
- The categorization of priority action industries.
- The selection of criteria and the setting of 'benchmarks' for the priority industries.
- The choosing of factories for audit followed by a short appraisal visit to assess suitability.

Priority industries were chosen by a review from four important industrial sectors that were finally chosen which were the textile, food, chemical and metal industries. Table 5 is a summary of the selected criteria and was used in 'broad terms' to aid the selection of appropriate factories.

'Benchmarks' have been derived for particular industries and are, in essence, a set of expectations and goals. These will become part of the audit protocol document and include the following objectives:

- Many of which are simple 'good housekeeping' initiatives.
- Effluent discharge wherever practicable to the sewer.

Table 4. Proposed guidelines for Greater Cairo for industrial discharges into sewers

Compound	Proposed Limits, Flow <100 m^3/day	Proposed Limits, Flow >= 100 m^3/d
pH	6 to 10	6 to 10
Suspended Solids	1 200 mg/l	800 mg/l
Oils & Grease	150 mg/l	100 mg/l
Cyanide	1 mg/l	1 mg/l
Sulphide, soluble	10 mg/l	10 mg/l
Temperature	43 C	43 C
BOD	1 100 mg/l	800 mg/l
COD (dichromate)	2 200 mg/l	1 600 mg/l
TKN	200 mg/l	100 mg/l
Total Phosphorus	50 mg/l	25 mg/l
Phenol	1 mg/l	0.5 mg/l
Mercury	0.2 mg/l	0.2 mg/l
Cadmium	0.2 mg/l	0.1 mg/l
Lead	2 mg/l	1 mg/l
Arsenic	1 mg/l	0.5 mg/l
Chromium (hexavalent)	1 mg/l	0.5 mg/l
Silver, Copper, Manganese, Nickel, Zinc, Tin, Boron	5 mg/l individually 15 mg/l cumulative	5 mg/l individually 10 mg/l cumulative

Table 5. Criteria for the possible selection of factories for audit

Medium sized 100 - 2 000 employees
Large water users
Produce polluted effluents
Are reasonably modern
Have an enlightened Management
Are happy to have their factory audited
Have available land for treatment plant
Are representative of the type of industry
High potential for effluent minimisation
Site demonstrates potential to develop in short to medium term
(not likely to be closed down)
Representative of the public or private sectors
Representative of the sector operational standards
Representative of the sector effluent characteristics
Potential for substantial cost savings/attractive pay back
through source management and control
Enthusiasm of site personnel to participate in pilot scheme

- Emphasis on 'in situ' treatment of wastewater for water re-use at the factory.
- The reduction in water use.
- The development of source management control.
- Improvement in water use efficiency, including the separation of contaminated/uncontaminated wastewater.
- Construction of bunds and retaining walls to reduce accidental spills.
- For particular industries standard wastewater values have been obtained and typical treatment options will be appraised.
- For textiles these include balancing, fibre separation, cooling, sulphide removal, flocculation and settlement.

A total of 10 factories have been chosen for audit and these are representative of the type of ownership and industrial sector in the Shoubra District. It is expected that the industrial audits will identify the extent of pollution and the remedial solutions for particular industries. To encourage industrialists to embrace the audits it is hoped that financial savings can be recommended by both reducing water consumption and reducing wastage at source. The final objective will be to produce a wastewater which does not exceed the requirements of Law 93 for discharge to the sewer. It is proposed to carry these out during May to June 1995. If successful, it is hoped that the results will be emulated by other industries. The aim will be the development of an efficient control programme, adequately resourced both financially and technically.

Sustainability of rural sanitation in Venezuela

Dr David Holmes, Venezuela

TODAY, SANITARY CONDITIONS in rural Venezuela are typical of those to be found in most developing countries in the tropics. Major infectious diseases, such as malaria, hepatitis, river blindness, leishmaniasis, tuberculosis, Chagas and cholera, are all present, and in some cases on the increase. The majority of the population lacks access to clean drinking water and adequate facilities for excrement disposal contributing to high morbidity rates due to parasitic diseases.

Ironically, in the two or three decades following WWII, a veritable revolution in rural sanitation was achieved under the direction of Dr Arnaldo Gabaldon (1909-90), the internationally-known physician and academic, who created and led an exemplary anti-malaria and rural sanitation programme which became a model for public health administrators all over the world.

Under Gabaldon's tutelage, Venezuela became the first tropical country to apply DDT for malaria control on a massive scale. A newly created army of professional sanitary inspectors and hygienist fanned out, often on mule back or in dug-out canoes, to bring a message of hope and a kit bag of the latest public health measures to the remotest corners of the country.

Initial results were rapid and dramatic. The mortality rate from malaria dropped from more than 100 per 100 000 population to less than 10 within a decade. This same figure was reduced to 0.5 by 1955 (Ramirez, 1987). The combination of this technological breakthrough and Gabaldon's administrative and organizational genius enabled the country practically to eradicate malaria by the 1960s. The same spray that killed mosquitoes also killed flies thereby reducing the transmission of intestinal parasites.

The sanitary engineers soon followed to supervise the construction of latrines, sewers, water supply systems and even low-cost, rural houses. The net result of these and other measures was to reduce the crude death rate from 10.2 per 1000 in 1950 to 5.5 in 1980. This, coupled with a rise in the birth rate, triggered a demographic explosion which caused the annual average intercensal growth rate to rise from 1.7 per cent in 1936 to a peak of four per cent in 1961, one of the highest in the world.

Institutionalization of rural sanitation

To ensure continuity and adequate logistic support, Gabaldon backed up his 'army' of sanitary inspectors and engineers with an elaborate institutional infrastructure including the famous Malaria School in Maracay, and an efficient information network on all important aspects of rural sanitation. Nearly every village and town was endowed with its own resident sanitary co-ordinator.

The Malaria and Rural Sanitation Service was given a privileged status within the Health Ministry. Its nucleus was a group of well-paid and well-trained, public health professionals which constituted an elite corp within the public administration. Gabaldon insisted that even the lowest secretary and fieldworker be indoctrinated in the organization's values and sense of mission.

Collection and treatment of sewage

In 1962, a separate division, called the 'Section for the Control and Disposition of Wastewater' was created within the Malaria Service to manage sewer and latrine construction in the rural areas. Its specific objective was to 'achieve an improvement in health by means of the construction of systems for the collection of waste water, designed and constructed in the rural setting, to avoid the propagation of diseases derived from the incorrect disposal of excrement' (Romero et al, 1985). According to the first national census in 1936, 64 per cent of rural houses did not contain any system of excrement disposal. As a result of the efforts of the Malaria Service, by 1981, this figure had been reduced to 34 per cent.

Sewer construction

In 1960, only 34 out of the approximately 5000 towns and villages (of less than 5000 inhabitants) in Venezuela had a sewer system (Censo, 1990). The coverage of the target population was probably no more than one per cent and certainly less than five per cent. With the impetus provided by the new institutional support, from 1962 to 1985, 509 new systems were constructed by the Malaria Service, many with associated oxidation ponds, raising the estimated coverage of the eligible population to around 30 per cent (Romero et al, 1985).

Latrine building

As a complement to the sewer programme, pit latrines were constructed for the dispersed rural population (see Graph 1). Initially, residents were expected to pay for the latrine by means of long-term, low-interest loans. Most proved to be uncollectable and were eventually forgiven by subsequent governments.

Potable water supplies

As a complement to the improved means of excrement disposal, rural water systems were constructed beginning in the 1940s. Starting from a base of near zero, the coverage of the population living in settlements of less than 5000 had risen to 70 per cent by 1985 (Romero et al., 1985).

Sustainability
Despite these promising beginnings, which set Venezuela apart from most developing countries and seemed to promise the eventual triumph of modern technology and organization over the traditional plagues of the tropics, a process of decay began in the 1980s which reversed many of the earlier gains and seriously called into question the long-term viability of this development model.

Sewer usage
As mentioned, sewer construction advanced very rapidly, extending the potential coverage to 30 per cent of the eligible population by mid-1985. However, only 26 per cent of the houses adjacent to the sewer lines were actually hooked up by this date (Romero et al., 1985) meaning that in reality, less than eight per cent of the eligible population actually took advantage of the service. Thus, in terms of any health benefit, a large proportion of this huge investment was simply wasted.

Sewage treatment
An additional and related problem arose with respect to sewage treatment. A large number of the originally constructed oxidation ponds failed after a few years of service because of poor design, inadequate maintenance and incorrectly estimated sewage flows.

According to Lansdell (1987, p. 56), the principal problems were:

- Vegetation invaded the banks and floor causing smells and vector breeding. Maintenance budgets would not cover the expense of clearing and the lagoon was left to its own devices.
- Initial sewage flow was insufficient to combat evaporation, the lagoon never filled, dense vegetation took hold, increasing losses through evapotranspiration.
- The inlet sewer was badly designed or vulnerable to washout by floods.
- Unplanned urban expansion reached to within 10 m of the lagoon water's edge. The lagoon became overloaded, and smells and insects affected the nearest house.

Latrines
The latrine construction programme declined markedly toward the end of the decade and was all but abandoned by the 1980s. This was due in part to the relatively high cost of the programme (Romero, 1985) and in part to a tacit recognition that latrines came to be regarded by many potential users as ugly, malodorous sources of disease and symbols of underdevelopment.

However, another unstated factor was also present. In the 1980s, the Health Ministry began massively dosing the rural population with low-cost, anti-helminth drugs, such as mebendazol. At a cost of around US $1 per child per year for drug treatment versus a construction cost for latrines of between US $100 and US $200, it is clear why many health officials viewed this approach as a more cost-effective method for attacking the problem of intestinal parasites (Cutting, 1991).

Unfortunately, subsequent research in Venezuela and elsewhere (Maraven, 1990) has shown that medication, while certainly effective in treating patients with intestinal parasites, provides only transitory relief. Unless accompanied by additional measures such as health education, latrines, and improved water supplies, reinfection takes place very rapidly, completely nullifying the initial results in a matter of a few weeks (Tanner et al., 1987). Thus, drugs do not represent a panacea but rather one more tool in an integrated approach. Also, promiscuous use of drugs enhances the risk of developing resistant strains of the pathogen.

Potable water
Venezuela's rural aqueducts, which once set the standard in Latin America, also have deteriorated substantially in the past 15 years. Common problems are:

- Capricious and unreliable water treatment; over- and underdosing with chlorine are common. Water testing frequently reveals the presence of coliforms.
- Most rural water systems rely on diesel pumps which are notoriously difficult to maintain in rural areas, resulting in considerable downtime.
- Administration of rural water systems is deficient. Workers do not get paid on time, supplies arrive late, routine maintenance is not regularly performed, and there is little or no effort to collect water bills.
- Water rates are ridiculously low or nonexistent.

Non-sustainability of the model
Why did the rural sanitation campaign in Venezuela, which showed such promise in its initial stages, prove not to be sustainable in the longer term? Part of the answer lies in the vast shift in the population from rural to urban areas in response to new economic opportunities created by the burgeoning petroleum industry (see Graph 2). This phenomenon forced the government to shift priorities away from the problems of rural development toward the more pressing problems of urban slums. But there is more to the story.

Institutional factors
During the decade of the 1970s, Gabaldon progressively relinquished management and control of the Malaria Service with various adverse consequences for the organization, especially in the area of merit promotion. Increasingly, as in almost all other areas of the public

administration, the Service became less and less professional and more and more politicized. This coincided with increasingly stringent budget restrictions which tended to undermine pride and dedication to duty.

Financing
The national economy began to suffer substantial reverses in the mid-1980s which led to reduction in the relative importance of the health sector in general, and the rural sanitation programme in particular. Health as a proportion of the national budget declined from a high of 8.6 per cent in 1970 to a low of 6.1 per cent in 1980. Whereas the Malaria Service received nearly 16 per cent of the overall Health Ministry budget in 1960, this figure was reduced to only 4 per cent in 1980 (Gali, 1986).

Added to this problem was the progressive impoverishment of the rural population. According to FIDA (1993), the percentage of rural dwellers in Venezuela living below the poverty line rose from 36 per cent in 1965 to 58 per cent in 1988. Thus, at the same time that public investment was declining, the population had less and less financial capacity to solve its own problems.

Paternalism
Oil riches, a marked, cultural affinity for paternalism and an elaborate system of party-based, political patronage, have accustomed the Venezuela population to turn to the government or to the political parties to solve virtually all problems. This has tended to stunt incipient moves toward greater community organization and co-operation which have provided the traditional underpinning for boot-strap programmes throughout the developing world. Thus, both the will and the means for mobilizing self-help schemes to fill the gap left by the retreating public sector have been wanting.

Technology
No sanitation system can be effective without user collaboration. Lack of attention to consumer concerns and preferences in the case of latrine design led to a widespread prejudice against the device which now inhibits its revival in a more appropriate guise.

In the case of water disinfection, a number of technological and human factors came into play. Most village water systems incorporated a mechanism for chlorination based on the use of calcium hypochlorite, although this chemical was not produced in Venezuela.

Importation was not a problem during the years of the oil boom, roughly 1973 to 1982, but in the following period of prolonged economic stagnation, calcium hypochlorite supplies became scarce. There was no provision for the use of sodium hypochlorite, which was available domestically, as an emergency substitute. This weak link in the chain meant that water quality could not be guaranteed. Some consumers responded by applying home remedies, such as boiling water, particularly when there were advertised epidemics of parasitic disease or cholera scares, but most simply adopted a callous, fatalistic attitude toward the risk of waterborne disease.

Even when supplies of disinfectant were adequate there was a problem of dosage control. Modern dossifiers were usually installed initially but the combination of lack of maintenance and timely replacement meant that most had a very short life. The low-level, on-site operator was then left to devise his own, improvised substitute. This usually consisted of a bucket, a piece of plastic tubing and a clothes pin. The crudest solution was to pour chlorine into the water source itself, next to the pump intake, thereby killing all aquatic life in the stream in the immediate vicinity.

Inevitably this kind of improvization produced both overdosing and underdosing. In the former case, consumers usually rejected the water because of its disagreeable taste. In the latter case, which was more common, the amount of residual chlorine was insufficient to provide contingent protection.

An alternative model
One consequence of the rural exodus was that large numbers of unskilled, rural migrants clustered in squatter settlements surrounding oil company installations. In an effort to escape this problem, the companies isolated themselves behind chain link fences, in self-sufficient enclaves, featuring all of the conveniences of modern urban life.

Following nationalization of the industry in 1975, a new policy was promulgated obliging these oil 'camps' to be integrated with the surrounding communities.

It was quickly realized that this integration, if taken literally, would impose on oil workers an unacceptable deterioration in living standards. Therefore, a programme was devised for upgrading basic services in neighbouring communities and rural areas.

When the Orinoco Bitumen Belt was opened for exploration in 1980, the new community assistance model was expanded to include water and basic sanitation for rural villages and towns. This approach was characterized by the use of appropriate technology (improved oxidation ponds, rainwater collection systems, individual, water-monitoring and purification systems), community participation (auto-construction with volunteer, community labour), and technical advice offered by oil company employees resident in the area.

An integrated approach to the problem of parasite infection, reminiscent of Gabaldon's original design, was devised which included four basic elements:

- VIP latrine construction (self-help)
- improved water supplies
- health education
- diagnosis and treatment of infected patients with appropriate drugs

The success of this effort prompted the industry to create, in 1992, the Zumaque Foundation, a private, non-profit-making, NGO to carry on and extend this work to other areas of the country. Accordingly, the Foundation has been helping campesino and indigenous communities in selected areas to take more responsibility for their own welfare and to upgrade sanitary conditions to the level they can afford and maintain, with limited outside assistance from the oil industry and other sources.

Summary and conclusions

Venezuela represents an interesting case of a tropical developing country which was an early pioneer in utilizing modern technology and advances in the science of public health to effect a revolution in rural sanitation. Thanks to these efforts, the country made rapid and even dramatic progress in health and sanitation in its rural areas in the decades following WW II.

This success proved to be a mixed blessing as it contributed to a subsequent, explosive growth of the urban population. Even in the rural areas, these early gains proved to be transitory, with sanitary conditions largely reverting to their earlier state. Helminth and other intestinal parasite infections are still present in the majority of the population. Major infectious diseases, such as malaria, hepatitis and tuberculosis are on the rise and there have been sporadic outbreaks of cholera. Safe water and adequate excrement disposal are still only available to a privileged minority.

Clearly, the obstacles, such as poor communications, illiteracy and lack of infrastructure were of far greater proportions when the programme began back in the 1940s than at a later date when the economic and social development of the country had proceeded to a more advanced stage. Why them was this programme initially so successful?

Much of the credit must go to Arnaldo Gabaldon who almost single-handedly built a rural sanitation empire which was unique in the developing world at that time. The coincident development and commercialization of DDT was also crucial. Oil provided the public sector with the extra resources to finance the programme on the massive scale necessary to produce a genuine impact at the national level. The Rockefeller Foundation and the World Health Organization also provided key outside support and international endorsement.

In hindsight, it is clear that Gabaldon's faith in his own ability to protect the Malaria Service from the normal processes of bureaucratization and politicization was naive. In his haste to produce results, he underestimated the importance of building an adequate base of support for rural sanitation at the community level; a flaw which he recognized late in life (personal communication with the author's wife).

These defects in an otherwise outstanding model can only be corrected by a painstaking effort in health education at the grassroots level, using the services of NGOs, such as the Zumaque Foundation. By diversifying the sources of financing, relying more on international support in the form of soft loans, the risk of interruptions in the programme due to the ups and downs of domestic politics can be minimized. Finally, more attention to the appropriateness of the technology for the particular setting will help guarantee greater user involvement and co-operation.

References

Cutting, W.1993. Deberían controlarse las infecciones por helmintos por medio de medicaciones masivas?Diálogo sobre Diarrea, 42: 4 - 8.

Fondo Internacional de Desarrollo Agrícola (FIDA).1993. El Estado de la Pobreza Rural en el Mundo: La Situación de América Latina y El Caribe, FIDA, Roma.

Galli, A. & H. García.1986. El Sector Salud: Radiografía de sus Males y de sus Rendimientos. En Naim et al, eds., El Caso Venezuela: Una Ilusión de Armonía, Ediciones IESA, Caracas.

Lansdell, M. 1987. The Development of Lagoons in Venezuela. Wt. Sci. Tech., 19 (12) : 55-60.

Maraven, S.A.1990. Estudio de las Parasitosis Intestinales en la Zona Zuata de Maraven, Sur del Estado Anzoátegui. Informe FPO N° 1265, Caracas.

Oficina Central de Estadística e Informática (OCEI).1992. El Censo 90 en Venezuela, Resultados Básicos, Caracas.

Otero, M.1985. Saneamiento Rural: Parasitos Intestinales En Procedimientos, VII Congreso Venezolano de Salud Pública, Caracas.

Ramírez, T. 1987. Historia de la Escuela de Malariología y Saneamiento Ambiental de Venezuela. Imprenta de la Universidad Central de Venezuela, Caracas.

Romero, L.1985. Saneamiento Rural: Programa Nacional de Cloacas y Acueductos Rurales En Procedimientos, VII Congreso Venezolano de Salud Pública, Caracas.

Tanner, M. 1987. Longitudinal study on health status of children in a rural Tanzanian community: parasitosis and nutrition following control measures against intestinal parasites. Acta Tropica, 44 : 137 - 174.

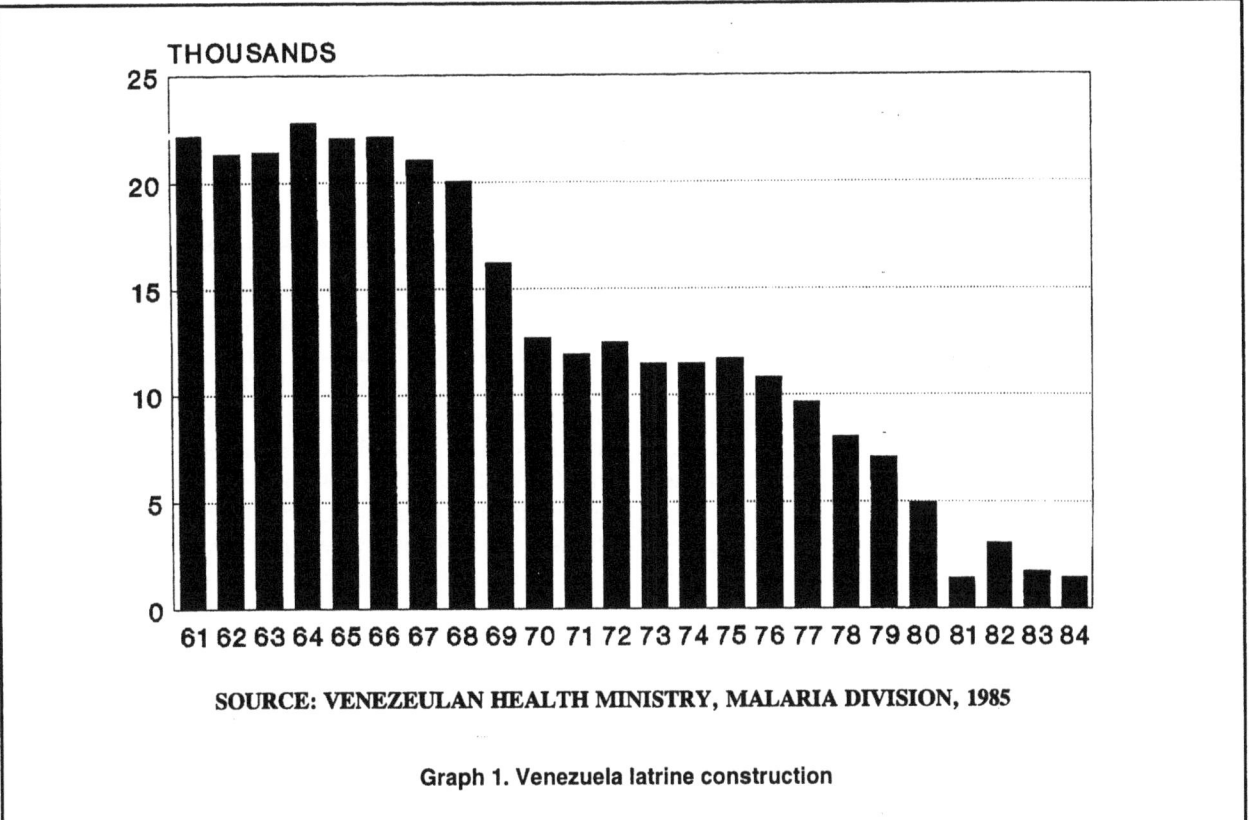

SOURCE: VENEZEULAN HEALTH MINISTRY, MALARIA DIVISION, 1985

Graph 1. Venezuela latrine construction

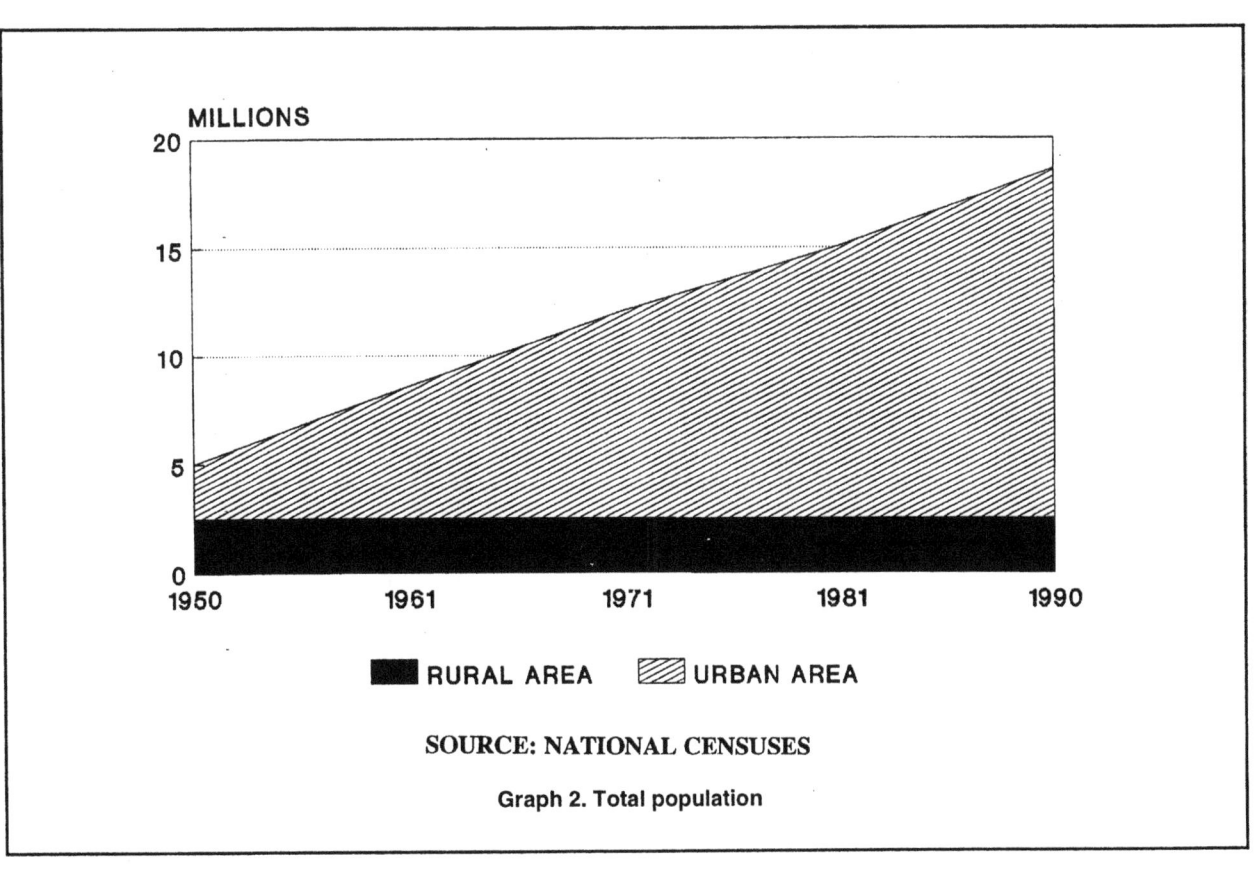

SOURCE: NATIONAL CENSUSES

Graph 2. Total population

Pit-latrine-emptying using motorized equipment

M. Jere, A. Dzotizei and M. Munjoma, Zimbabwe

IN ZIMBABWE, THE provision of sanitation and water supplies has resulted in major health and social changes for many communities, particularly where the intended users are involved in setting goals and defining project objectives. The challenge to researchers, scientists and environmental health officers is the continuity of the technologies implemented.

Zimbabwe's public health policy is based on the principles of primary health care and environmental hygiene is viewed as a fundamental principle of public health policy. In applying these principles, appropriate technologies for the safe disposal of excreta, in the form of an improved ventilated pit latrine, have been designed and implemented in most rural areas of Zimbabwe. The Blair latrine was developed and first implemented in the early 1980s. Thus, many of the early prototype models have been in operation for almost 15 years.

The latrine was originally designed to last for approximately 15 years when serving an average family size of 7-10 people (Morgan, 1990). Therefore, many of the early constructions are full and, the usual practice under such circumstances has been to seal the full pit and build a new latrine. This practice, however, has become prohibitively expensive. Moreover, in peri-urban areas and rural growth points, where rapid population growth is being experienced, available land is decreasing in proportion to population expansion. The net result of these factors coupled with fiscal constraints on the provision of reticulated sewage systems for rapidly expanding peri-urban populations means that desludging already existing pit latrines may be the only option for sustaining a viable excreta disposal system in the short and medium term.

To examine the feasibility and cost effectiveness of desludging pit latrines, a small motorized vacuum tanker was procured and tested in two distinct areas; a large-scale holding camp for translocating populations and a large, well established, peri-urban area.

The research programme was conducted to examine two broad objectives:
i) to assess the feasibility of pit-emptying using the micravac vehicle and,
ii) to estimate the unit cost of emptying a latrine pit and identifying possible areas of environmental impact associated with the procedure.

Study areas

The first phase of the study was conducted at Porta farm, a temporary holding camp for 7000-10 000 people awaiting resettlement. The camp is serviced with 74 communal pit latrines. All the latrines in the camp are unlined versions of the standard VIP latrine, which were not originally intended for long-term use. In contrast, the second phase of the study was conducted in Epworth, a large (N·60 000) and well established peri-urban settlement which has been provided with fully lined latrine pits connected to soakaway tanks. These latrines were designed to last for roughly 15 years with the option of being upgraded into flushable units.

Materials and methods

The vehicle employed was specially constructed for operation in peri-urban areas which have little or no planning regarding the spatial arrangement and distribution of households. The vehicle is compact for easy movement between households and thus is fitted with a 1000 litre capacity tank and a compressor capable of creating a negative or positive pressure (approx. 20 Kpsi) used for filling or emptying the tank respectively.

Before emptying the latrines in the study areas, the distance between the latrine floor and the surface of the sludge was measured and recorded. The latrines at the Porta farm site were not lined and were not recommended for use as bathrooms and thus, the sludge was relatively solid. Therefore, water was added to the pit contents to increase the fluidity of the sludge for ease of extraction. Following dilution the contents of the pits were agitated using ancillary equipment to remove non-faecal solids such as pieces of blankets, sacks and sticks. The pits were then emptied and the distance between the latrine floor and the surface of the sludge again measured. In all, 44 pits were desludged at the Porta farm site. The sludge removed from the pits was disposed of into eight specially constructed disposal pits measuring 4 x 2.4 m^2 in area and 3 m deep with a spatial distribution shown in Figure 1. Sludge was deposited into pits 1, 4, 5, and 8 and the remaining pits were left empty in order to collect effluent from the sludge pits. A disposal pit was considered full when the distance between the ground level and the sludge level was 1 m. The pit would not be used again until the contents subsided substantially below the 1 m mark. The pits were treated with chloride of lime each time sludge was discharged into them and on a daily basis (mornings only) for filled-up pits. Treatment was intended to discourage breeding of flies and to reduce bad odours. Pits which had drained and had semi-solid contents were covered with soil. A similar

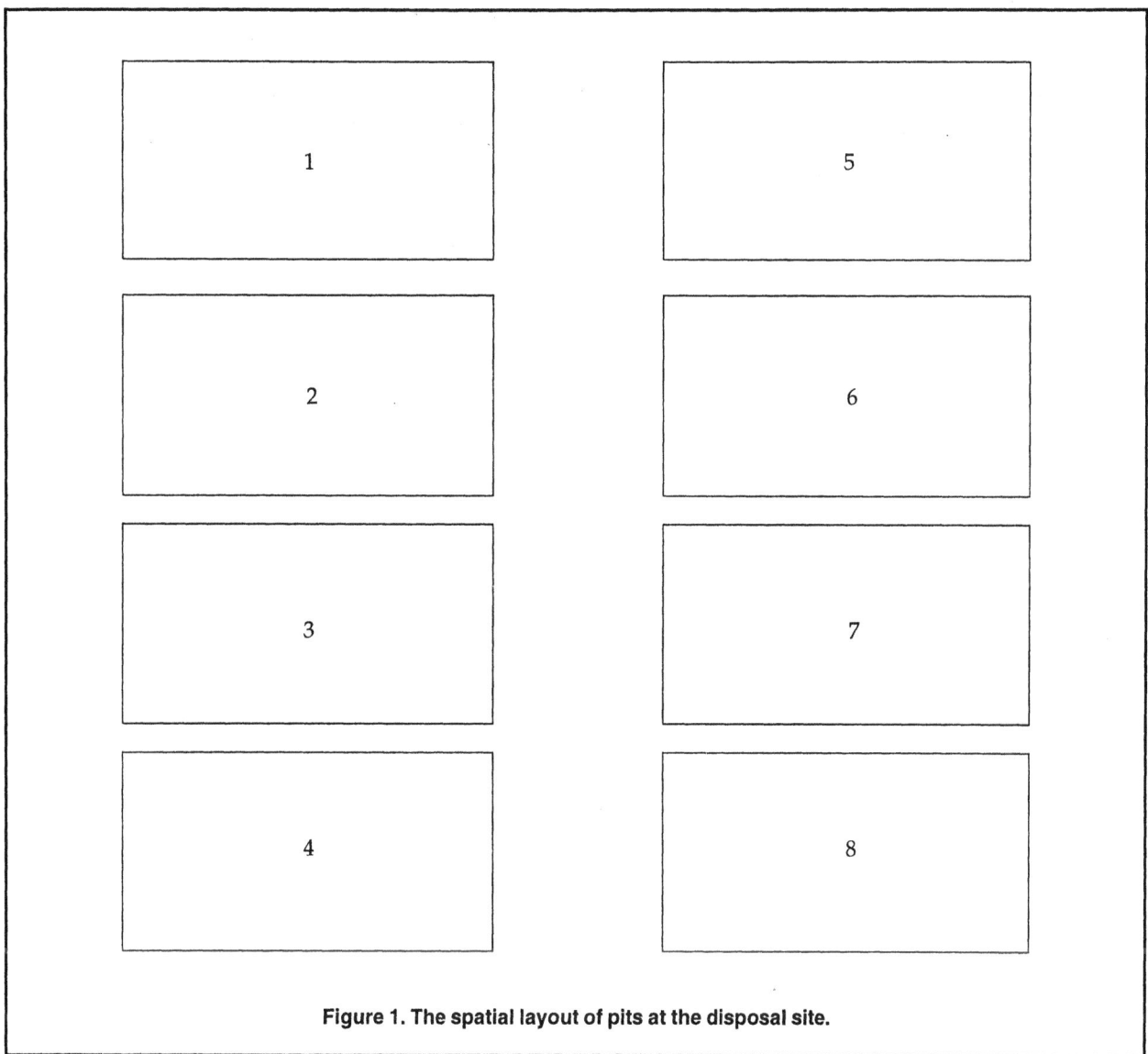

Figure 1. The spatial layout of pits at the disposal site.

procedure was adopted for the disposal of sludge at the Epworth site.

Results and discussion

On inspection, most (70 per cent) of the latrines at the Porta farm site were full; pit latrines in Zimbabwe are considered full when the sludge level is between 30 and 50 cm below the level of the latrine floor. Pit depths following the desludging procedure are shown in Table 1. Originally, the pits were constructed with depth of 3 m, however after emptying, all the pits had a depth of less than 3 m and 36.4 per cent had a depth of less than 1.5 m. The reduction in pit depth is mainly due to an accumulation of soil, resulting from the erosion of the unlined sides of the pit. This erosion process was exacerbated by the desludging process, and on seven occasions, the desludging process resulted in the complete collapse of the latrine. Whilst desludging unlined pits will extend their life span by an average of 1.5 years, it is recommended that the micravac should not be used for these temporary constructions because of the danger of serious erosion of the pits.

The second phase of the study was conducted in Epworth, a peri-urban area on the outskirts of the capital city, Harare. Data were collected during a typical desludging exercise and analyzed to provide an indication of the financial savings which can be achieved through the desludging process.

The great majority of pit latrines constructed in Epworth have fully lined and plastered pits, which are connected to soak-away tanks. The latrines were constructed in this manner to facilitate desludging and upgrading to flushable units.

On average, it took about one hour to desludge 1.0 m^3 of pit contents. This duration includes time spent on fluidization, agitation, stoppage time during the emptying of the pit due to blockages and discharging the contents of the micravac into disposal pits. Because the vehicle has a capacity of only 1m^3, the exercise has to be repeated to gain an effective 2m^3 of empty pit space.

Table 1. Depth of unlined latrines after desludging and the proportion of latrines within each depth range.

Depth Range (x) in metres	Proportion (%)
x > 3	0
2.5 < x < 3	20.5
2.0 < x < 2.5	18.1
1.5 < x < 2.0	25.0
x < 1.5	36.4

During a typical exercise of this nature, two litres of diesel fuel worth Z$ 2.34/litre are used, and the vehicle is hired at an additional cost of Z$3.00 per hour. Therefore, the total cost of removing 2 m^3 of sludge equates to Z$ 10.68.

The average per capita sludge accumulation rate is roughly 0.04 m^3 per person per year (Morgan, 1990). Therefore, it will take a family of seven persons around seven years to refill the 2 m^3 of pit space gained during the desludging exercise. The bonus life span of the latrine will, of course, increase with decreasing family size. The Z$ 10.68 (US$ 1.17)[1] cost of providing a seven-year bonus life span for a latrine is significantly less than the Z$ 1000.00 (US$ 116.84) which would have to be spent to build a new Blair latrine. Desludging not only provides an increased life span for pit latrines, but also reduces markedly the environmental impact of building new latrines, since additional ground space is not required. Neither are additional bricks, which would have to be fired using ever increasingly scarce fuelwood, required.

In conclusion, the small-scale motorized tanker used during this programme proved to be easy to use and efficient in its intended application. We suggest limited use of the vehicle in areas where pit latrines are unlined, to reduce the potential for latrine collapse. On the other hand, we strongly advocate the use of such vehicles in peri-urban and other areas where latrine pits are adequately lined. Desludging of lined pits results in a very significant extension to the life span of the latrine and a minimal cost to the latrine owners. Furthermore, desludging is accompanied by minimal environmental degradation compared to what would be experienced if full latrines were replaced by new units.

Reference

Morgan, P. 1990. Rural Water Supplies and Sanitation. MacMillan Education L.t.d. London and Basingstoke. 358pp.

[1] Current conversion ratio Z$ to US$=8.59 as of 26/05/95

Sanitation and hygiene, Bangladesh's action

Dr (Ms) T.V. Luong, Bangladesh

DURING THE INTERNATIONAL Drinking Water Supply and Sanitation Decade (1981-1990) Bangladesh has already achieved the universal coverage of water supply in the rural areas. Today, 85 per cent of the rural population has access to safe water supply within 150 metres at the average of 115 persons per public operating tubewell. In addition, there are more than 1.6 million of private tubewells (1). Over 97 per cent of the rural people drink tubewell water. Yet, the prevalence of communicable diseases such as diarrhoea and intestinal worm infections remains high. Every day more than 700 children under the age of five die of diarrhoea. It is obvious that improved public health can not be achieved by provision of safe water alone unless people take actions to clean up the environment and adopt good hygiene to break the disease transmission routes.

Promotion of sanitation in rural Bangladesh began in the early 1960s. By 1989 only 10 per cent of the rural population had sanitary latrines after more than two decades of promotion. However, accelerated progress has been made in the last few years. The government's mid-decade goal of 35 per cent sanitation coverage has been achieved during 1994 and a national coverage increased to 41 per cent in January 1995. Also, there has been an improvement in people's hand washing habit after defecation. A national average of 70 per cent people use soap/ash or soil as rubbing agent (2). The recent steady progress made on sanitation and hygiene in rural areas can be attributed to the following key factors:

- intensive social mobilization;
- introduction of a range of low-cost latrine options including 'do-it-yourself' simple pit latrines' and
- high political commitment.

Integrated approach and building up partnership

Until 1987, sanitation received little emphasis compared to the water sector. Realizing the potential of better impact on health, the Department of Public Health Engineering (DPHE), the government rural water supply and sanitation implementing agency, assisted by UNICEF, adopted an integrated approach (IA) using water supply as an 'entry point' to promote sanitation and hygiene. The IA also laid the foundation for social mobilization, as partners from other sectors e.g. education, health, women's affairs, NGOs, scouts and girl guides and religious leaders were involved in promotion at the field level.

Schools, Madrases (religious schools), Expanded Programme on Immunization (EPI) centres and Satellite Clinics for Mother and Child Health (MCH) have been involved as change institutions where promotion on improved sanitation and hygiene started within these institutions and extended to the communities. Sanitary latrines and water supply facilities were provided to selected schools to enhance students' behavioural change. This resulted in about 10 per cent increase in girls attendance (3). Sanitary latrines are being built in selected EPI/MCH centres to benefit mothers who visit these centres and to serve as demonstration models for health workers to promote hygiene and sanitary latrines in the communities.

The widespread demonstration, production and sale of latrines by government centres and NGOs over the years, combined with intensified sanitation and hygiene promotion have stimulated the demand for sanitary latrines. This has created market opportunity for the private producers and led to the further growth of the private sector.

A national survey on latrine producers and market situation in Bangladesh in early 1994 reported that there are a total of 4152 latrine producers in the country. The number of private producers doubled in the last three years reaching more than 2700. It is interesting to know that about 100 potters are currently producing burnt clay rings for sale as latrine pit lining. These burnt clay rings are traditionally used as lining for dug wells (4). All producers are concentrated in 1800 unions and 430 thanas. There are more than 2500 unions and 30 thanas currently without any producer. To meet the demand in the unserved areas, DPHE has already set up 255 mobile centres in places where the demand is high. Actions are being taken up by DPHE and NGOs to set up more production centres in the unserved areas.

Intensive social mobilization communication and hygiene promotion

A national conference on social mobilization for sanitation and hygiene inaugurated by the Prime Minister, Begum Khaleda Zia, in February 1992 added a new dimension to the social mobilization initiative taken up by DPHE and other partners in the country.

Subsequently, a 'National Sanitation Week' was launched by the prime minister in October 1994 to intensify and accelerate the social mobilization efforts. In her inaugural speech, she called for a concerted effort to achieve a new mid-decade goal of 50 per cent sanitation coverage by 1995. The National Sanitation Week has demonstrated the highest level of political commitment on improved sanitation and hygiene.

A three-year social mobilization programme (1994-1996) is being implemented to strengthen the on-going rural sanitation programme. The programme also aims at building up the DPHE's capacities on social mobilization and communication to complement their technical inputs. DPHE is setting up a Social Mobilization Division and a Training Division with communication staff.

The intensive social mobilization programme has marked the turning point for sanitation and hygiene prospects in Bangladesh. Furthermore, the programme also transforms DPHE from a largely technical and 'hardware' organization to one which gives greater focus to software aspects and facilitates partnership-building with other sectors.

To establish a community-based infrastructure at the community level for promotion and monitoring of the sanitation and hygiene activities, a water and sanitation (WATSAN) committee at each union has been formed. The Union Parisad Chairman serves as the WATSAN Committee chairperson and the DPHE sub-assistant engineer, the secretary. The Union WATSAN committee members (40 per cent females) consist of selected ward councillors, teacher, health worker, community leaders, local NGO representative. The functions of the committee and the roles and responsibilities of the members are contained in a set of guidelines developed by DPHE (5).

The need for behavioural change and the role of women as key change agents has placed the hygiene education high on the programme activities. Gender-sensitive promotional materials on hygiene have been developed, used and updated as necessary. Community awareness is created by field motivators through interpersonal communication and courtyard meetings in the villagers. DPHE staff at all levels and fieldworkers have been given training on communication skills.

A recent village-based study (6) focused on women's knowledge, practices and attitudes in water use, sanitation and hygiene reports the following:

- some girls as young as five years old are also water carriers;
- majority of rural women (85/96 per cent) are aware of the health benefits of safe water, sanitary latrines and washing hands;
- more than 90 per cent of rural women wash hands with soap/ash or soil after defecation and after cleaning their baby's bottom and before handling food. In spite of having the knowledge, the rural women are still continuing their traditional practices. In another study, rural women were found to wash their hands more than 12 times a day, but they did not do it in a proper way and they dried their hands with dirty clothes (7).

These studies indicate that rural women are aware of the health implications of unsafe water, an unsanitary environment and dirty hands. However, they need further education and motivation to change their habits and practices for tangible health benefits.

The challenges

Improved sanitation involves not only technology; it hinges on human behaviour and attitudes. The major challenges are:

- sustained behavioural change and durability of the low-cost latrine technology;
- enhanced motivation for women's participation, and
- strong participatory monitoring mechanism at all levels for continuous assessment of behavioural change, use of sanitary latrines and quality of latrine construction.

Research and studies are being carried out to provide necessary information for sustained behavioural change and further improvement of the technology and environmental safety. Maps of top soil conditions and high groundwater level for all districts in the country have been produced. These maps show geological and geographical locations where pit lining is essential. Currently, a study on pit lining technologies using locally available materials is on-going in different areas to determine cost-effective options. Proper application of these simple technical information can further enhance the sustainability of low-cost latrine technologies. For environmental safety, a groundwater monitoring study on pollution risk from pit latrines is being formulated. The results of an on-going anthropological study on men, women and children in the context of water, sanitation and hygiene will provide some basis for further sharpening of promotional activities and messages to change behaviour fundamentally.

Over the years, women's involvement in the programme implementing process, particularly at the community level, is quite visible at various places. In some areas women have successfully taken the lead in promotion of sanitation and hygiene. However, motivation for women's participation at all levels is essential for the acceleration of progress and sustained behavioural change.

Conclusion

Bangladesh has demonstrated the positive and realistic ways of promoting sanitation and hygiene under some of the most difficult situations such as massive poverty and high illiteracy rate. The great strength of the programme is the ability of the DPHE and other partners to adopt various approaches to meet the programme needs at different stages. Furthermore, national commitment supported by various field level organizations is growing. Currently, the Government of Bangladesh is formulating a policy on water supply, sanitation and hygiene programme. The lessons learnt over the years on the promotion of sanitation and hygiene activities should provide the basis to accelerate the programme in the future.

References

1. Mitra and Associates (1992), National Survey on Status of Rural Water Supply and Sanitation, Bangladesh, DPHE-UNICEF.
2. Bangladesh Bureau of Statistics (1995), Progotir Pathey, Ministry of Planning, Government of Bangladesh.
3. Consulting Services and Associates (1994), Evaluation of the use and Maintenance of Water Supply and Sanitation System in Primary School, DPHE-UNICEF.
4. House of Consultant (1994), A National Survey on Latrine Producers and Market Situation, Bangladesh, DPHE-UNICEF.
5. Department of Public Health Engineering (1995), Guidelines on the formation of Union WATSAN Committee, Government of Bangladesh.
6. Voluntary Health Services Society (1995), Women in the context of Sanitation, Water supply and hygiene: a village based study, DPHE-UNICEF.
7. B.A. Hoque and S.A. Ahmed (1995), Handwashing, Home Management of Water and Ingestion of Polluted Water, International Centre for Control of Diarrhoea Research, Bangladesh, DPHE-UNICEF. (draft report)

The water and sanitation programme in Bangladesh is supported by UNICEF through funds from various donor agencies, particular DANIDA and Switzerland Development Cooperation (SDC).

*Bangladesh has a population of 114 million over an area of 147570 sq. km; five administrative divisions, 64 districts, 460 thanas and 4451 unions.

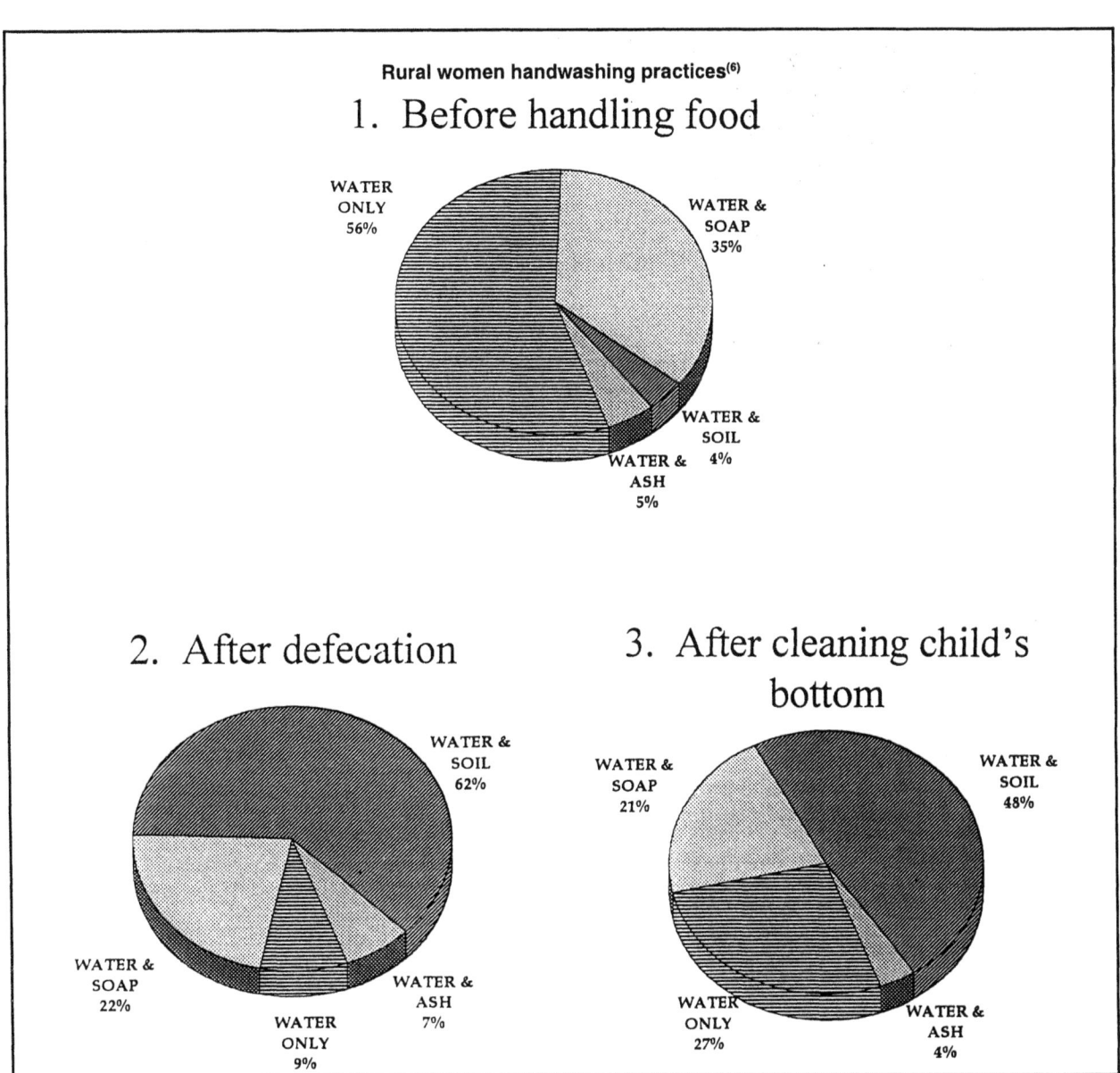

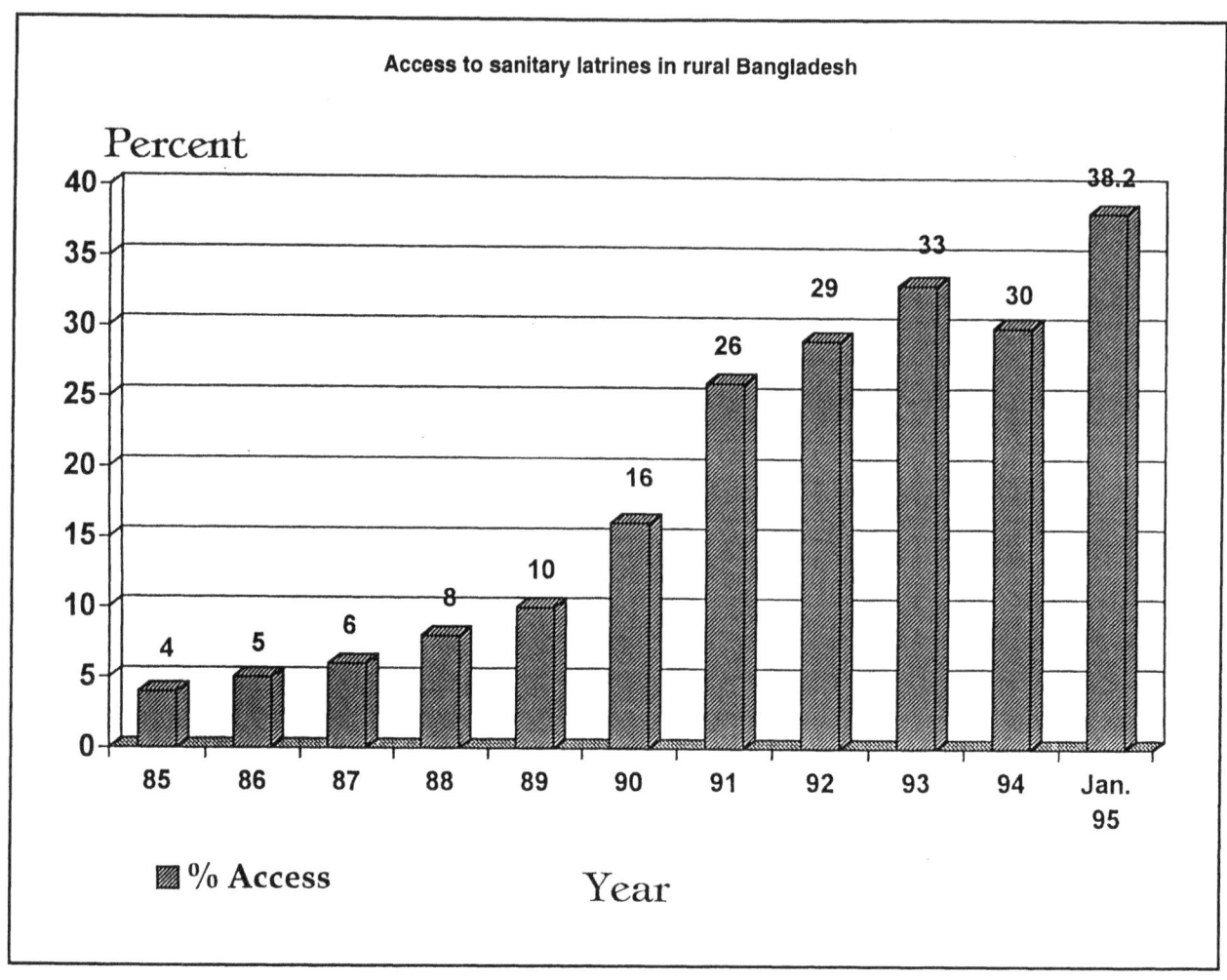

Sustainability of Lusaka sewage works

P.B. Majura and A.F. Banda, Zambia

LUSAKA, THE CAPITAL city of Zambia, has a central waterborne sewerage system which was first constructed in 1956 and expanded upon in 1970 and 1980. It is currently serving more than 400 000 people which represents about 36 per cent of the city's population including trade effluents from industries. No major rehabilitation works have ever been carried out on this ageing system over the past 15 years.

In recent years, the system has experienced both operational and maintenance problems, ranging from poor management, untrained plant operators, lack of motivation among the workers and scarcity of funds. The key technical problems seriously affecting the works include: inoperative equipment such as influent flow meters, mechanical bar screens and grit chambers, reduced sewer and pump capacities, sediment build-up that blocks sewers and interferes with sewage pumps and frequent mechanical and electrical breakdowns.

This paper highlights the main causes of these problems, the efforts that have been made to solve them and a mechanism that has been adopted in order to sustain the existing sewage works.

Background

The sewerage system is of 'separate' type. Originally, it was under the management of the Lusaka City Council. However, in 1988 this was handed over to the Lusaka Water and Sewerage Company, (LWSC). LWSC now owns, operates and maintains seven sewage pumping stations, six of which are standardized with 30kW Flgyt submersible pumps allowing pumps to be interchanged. Two of the stations consist of three pumps arranged in parallel, with the remaining stations configured for two pumps in parallel.

The sewer network of LWSC comprises 90 km of trunk sewer lines and over 230 km of lateral sewers. Sewage is treated in four waste stabilization (oxidation) ponds and in two three-stage conventional treatment plants. The latter, which treats about 70 per cent of the city's wastewater, consists of screening and grit removal, primary sedimentation, filtration through percolating (trickling) filters and final sedimentation in humus tanks. The sludge which is drawn off from the primary sedimentation tanks and humus tanks is treated in anaerobic digesters followed by dewatering on drying beds. The western plant at Chunga area receives wastewater from major industries in the city as well as domestic sewage. The other, the Manchinchi plant treats only domestic sewage including septage delivered by vacuum tankers that service septic tanks.

Oxidation ponds treat domestic sewage only and are located at Ngwerere, Kaunda Square, Chelston and Matero areas within the city boundaries. None of them incorporate anaerobic pretreatment ponds, but each have one primary facultative pond (except the Ngwerere ponds which have two parallel primary facultative ponds) followed by two maturation ponds in series. The total area for all the ponds is 30.5 hectares with the Ngwerere ponds occupying about half of the area.

Constraints on the sewer network

In 1987 German consultants were contracted to investigate the deficiencies of the sewer network and the conditions of the sewers. The main problems that were identified were:

(i) Completely blocked gravity sewer line from the Lumumba Pumping Station to the Chunga treatment works;

(ii) Blocked main sewer to Chelston ponds. The sewage was discharged into a small river beneath the sewer line. All manholes were without covers and the sewage was used for irrigation, which is a health hazard;

(iii) Main sewer line to Ngwerere ponds was blocked by stones, rags, textiles and the sewage was held back. Manholes covers were not properly fixed;

(iv) Frequent sewage overflows during the rainy seasons, particularly along the main south trunk line feeding the Manchichi plant. This was mainly due to the loose sewer network that allowed groundwater to infiltrate the sewers and the absence of manhole covers in many places on the sewer line;

(v) Insufficient pumping capacity, since each of the seven pumping stations operated with only one pump in service. This resulted also in sewage overflows at manholes upstream of the stations. The mechanical and electrical breakdown of the pumps also occurred frequently.

Effeciency of the sewage treatment plants

The treatment efficiency of the two mechanical plants at Chunga and Manchinchi has been seriously reduced over the years due to old and inoperative equipment.

Table 1: Estimated influent BOD₅ and Bacterial Removals in Waste Stabilization Ponds, 1989

Pond Site	BOD -Strength g/m^3	Bacterial Removal FC /100 ml
Ngwerere	350	10 000
Matero	485	2500
Kaunda Sq.	350	81 000
Chelston	300	59 400

Table 2: Design capacities and estimated daily flows of sewage treatment plants

Site	Design Capacity m^3/day	Estimated Daily flows m^3/day
Manchinchi	18 100	25 000
Western	9 050	10 000
Ngwerere	4 320	5 420
Kaunda Sq.	1 690	4 750
Chelston	820	1 700
Matero	2 400	2 300
Total	36 380	49 170

Both plants experience excessive hydraulic and organic overloading and require immediate expansion. At the Manchinchi plant, for example, only two out of 16 trickling filters have functioning distributor arms. Calculations on filter loadings earlier on showed that these were being loaded at the rate of 1400 g BOD_5 /m^3.day compared to the acceptable rate of 125 - 175 g BOD_5/m^3.day (German Environmental Consultants,1987). Alongside with the Chunga plant, the influent flow meters, mechanical bar screens and grit chambers are not operational.

All oxidation ponds require rehabilitation and extension. They are all overloaded and not properly maintained. Flow recorders are absent, inlet structures are broken down and screenings are not properly removed, not even buried. The embankments of all the ponds are presently overgrown with tall grass and the pond sites are not fenced. According to Baird (1993), the treatment efficiency of the oxidation ponds was very poor, except the matero ponds which showed satisfactory results (Table 1).

As seen from Table 1, both the Kaunda and Chelston ponds produce poor quality effluent in terms of bacterial removal. This is quite worrying because the final effluent from both ponds is presently being used by smallholder farmers for irrigating their crops; which is a health hazard.

Overall design capacity of both the conventional plants and oxidation ponds is 36 380 m^3/day; but the estimated total daily flows in all cases far exceeds this by over 49 000 m^3/day; which is more than 35 per cent overloading of the ponds.

It can also be seen from Table 2 that both the Kaunda and Chelston ponds are overloaded by more than twice their intended design capacities.

This is because these ponds serve a potentially large catchment area of the city and at the time they were constructed were located in an undeveloped part of the city and therefore served a much smaller community.

Problems and their causes

The main causes of the problems which have persistently affected the smooth running of the sewage works over the years are:

(i) Absence of preventive maintenance for grit and sand removal from blocked grit chambers.

(ii) Until recently (December, 1994), the sewerage department of LWSC had no drain rods and as such clearing of blocked sewers had become difficult and cumbersome.

(iii) Unskilled operators. While operators for a particular unit in the works are familiar with simple operational skills, this however is not enough to operate and maintain the mechanical structures and facilities that are present at the Manchinchi and Chunga plants. For example, there is only one engineer who was employed in November 1994, responsible for sewer maintenance for the works; but there are still three more vacancies not yet filled to take charge of each of the two mechanical plants and the oxidation ponds.

(iv) Lack of job motivation. Up until May 1994, apart from the low salaries that were paid to the workers, provision of clothing such as uniforms, overalls, gum boots etc. was generally not sufficient. All these seriously affected the job motivation of the workers within the sewerage sector.

(v) Awareness of the importance of the sewerage system particularly by decision makers in the Water and Sanitation Department was very poor. Because of the budget constraints, there was usually not enough money for operation and maintenance purposes and the necessary repairs that were required for servicing technical equipment and other structures.

(v) Abuse of the system. Most manhole covers on the entire sewer network have been vandalized or stolen; and individuals throw stones, rags, plastics, garbage and other solid materials into the uncovered manholes which cause blockages of the system.

Towards sustainability

In order to attain sustainability of the works, the LWSC has already embanked on a rehabilitation project, which it looks at as a first priority rather than construction of new works. External funding for this project was sought in 1993, mainly from the Japanese Government through JICA; but no favourable reply has yet been received. Consequently, tne company is currently carrying out this project using internally generated funds. Funds are obtained through billing households and industries that use this service. Two tariffs are therefore used: a flat fee for households, whether low or high density dwellings; and the volume of wastewater generated by each industry based on the calculated water consumption and BOD-strength of the effluent.

The ongoing activities which are meant to sustain the Lusaka sewage works include the following:

(i) Rehabilitation of the 16 trickling filters at the Manchinchi plant. So far, more than 90 per cent fabrication of the distributor arms and other dilapidated structures has been done. The cost of fabrication and installation is ZK 80 104 000 (ZK 1 is approx. US $ 0.00125).

(ii) Twelve mono pumps have already been bought at ZK 19 000 000; which are to be installed at the Manchinchi and Chunga plants for pumping humus and raw sludge from pump houses. In addition, two stand-by submersible flygt pumps have also been bought at a cost of ZK 3 791 902.92. These are to be stationed at the Manchinchi and Chunga plants as well.

(iii) A total of 800 drain rods including their accessories were bought in December, 1994 from South Africa at cost of SAR 31 928.20. The rods are being used to clear the blocked sewers.

(iv) Desludging of the digesters and oxidation ponds is ongoing work. The desludging of the Matero oxidation ponds was completed at the end of 1994. The contractor also completed desludging the Manchinchi maturation ponds in February, 1994; and is now working on the Kaunda waste stabilization ponds.

(v) The entire Ngwerere sewer line was cleared by the end of October, 1994. Unfortunately, however, the sewer line was again deliberately choked by smallholder farmers who use crude sewage for irrigating their fields.

(vi) Various other tools and safety equipment have also been bought from South Africa at a cost of SAR 78 000. These include a set of hand winches, one Flexian rodder complete with accessories, one safety harness and one Quadalarm personal gas detector.

Conclusion

The main problems of the Lusaka sewage works can be associated to a large extent with inadequate funding that is required to purchase tools, technical equipment and spare parts. Others include: insufficient trained personnel, lack of awareness of the significance of the sewerage system by decision makers which existed before May, 1994 and inadequate routine preventive maintenance.

While actual training of the required workforce has just begun, the company envisages training more workers in the near future on a short-term basis at first, followed later by long-term training for its workers.

Since measures to sustain the sewage works are already under way using internally generated funds, the company is optimistic that external funding for the rehabilitation project through technical support from different organizations will soon be available.

The LWSC is included in the five-year national programme under the water supply and sanitation sector. The ongoing rehabilitation of the Lusaka sewage works is on a priority list and cannot therefore be abandoned.

References

Andrew Baird, (1993)
Short-Term Consultancy on Particular Aspects of Lusaka's Sewerage and Sewage Treatment Facilities, (Draft report).

German Environmental Consultants (1987)
HYDROPLAN: Lusaka Urban District Council Water & Sewerage Department.

Participatory hygiene and sanitation programmes

John K. Odclon, Rural Water and Sanitation East Uganda Project, Uganda

IN OCTOBER 1993, a Regional Participatory Hygiene Education in Methodology Workshop was held in Mukono Uganda. It brought together participants from five countries namely Uganda, Kenya, Eritrea, Ethiopia, Botswana, Zimbabwe and Mozambique. All these are countries piloting the use of Participatory hygiene and sanitation Transformation (PHAST) in the water and sanitation sector.

The major aim of this workshop was to draw experience from existing hygiene education concepts and practice with a view to facilitating the enhancement of human capacities to manage their own lives and their environment.

Why participatory

There have been many approaches used, all intended to involve communities, albeit with varying degrees of success. The underlying issue has been lack of evidence of continuity, sustenance of facilities and replication of activities. The participatory hygiene and sanitation transformation seeks to arouse community spirit for self esteem, associative strengths, resourcefulness, action planning and responsibility which are the motives for community participation and involvement.

The method of application has been through use of participatory tools, pictorial illustrations which depict sequences of all activities as they relate to water and sanitation. These are used to arouse discussions of fundamental issues, for example operation and maintenance (using planning tools), hygiene (using sanitation ladder), monitoring and evaluation, environment, and gender involvement; thereby triggering off interventions to address identified problems.

The RUWASA project experience has largely been a reactivation of the roles of water user committees, extension workers and their supervisors.

This paper will present experiences in RUWASA project as the approach evolved in the last two years or so. It will expose the benefits that are related to community level partners and how these can be used as indicators for success of a water and sanitation project. It will further invite discussion on the way forward for the use of this approach in enhancing demand-driven and sustainable implementation.

Participatory hygiene and sanitation programmes

Hygiene and sanitation have rarely occupied a prominent position on the agenda of water and sanitation programmes. Why?

This is primarily because false assumptions have been used to back up blueprints (plans) for water and sanitation programmes. These assumptions can be taken at two levels — the donor/implementing agency and the beneficiary levels. Some key but false assumptions at the donor/implementing agency level include:

- Improved water supply alone leads to better health
- Health education will automatically create demand for sanitation and change of behaviour
- Sanitation programmes can be made only through the construction of latrines
- People are not willing to pay for sanitation
- Traditional values and knowledge are a barrier to good sanitation practices
- Institutions which have been set up for water supply are also suitable for sanitation development (community versus household tasks)
- The private sector are not interested in sanitation.

At the beneficiary level the false assumptions include:

- There is no immediate benefit in improved sanitation
- Sanitation systems are not reliable
- Responsibility for sanitation lies somewhere else
- Children' faeces are harmless.

The net result of relying on these false assumptions is the aggravation of the sanitation problem both in terms of facility provision and behaviour related to use and maintenance.

The focus of intervention should not be limited to provision of technological options alone but should also be linked to behaviour change. This calls for participation especially at the household and community level. This participation should come about through the enhancement of the community potential to realize their own *self esteem, associative strengths, resourcefulness, action planning,* and *sense of responsibility.* (SARAR).

Participatory techniques using the SARAR methodology have been successfully tried out in the RUWASA east Uganda project, to bring about community level transformation of hygiene practices related to sanitation, and water collection, storage and use.

The findings of the Joint Review Mission 1993 to the RUWASA project, project monitoring reports and studies, as well as observations by project visitors did indicate that concerted efforts by social mobilizers (health assistants and community development assistants) did not bring about desired behaviour especially at the water user committee (WUC) level:

- WUC members could not easily identify who uses their water source
- Sanitation practices among the water users were not accurately known
- There was a tendency on the part of the community to rely heavily on external support e.g. from health workers, RUWASA or NGOs to identify and provide interventions for sanitation, and hygiene problems
- There was hardly any evidence of extensive practice of hygienic behaviour e.g. hand washing after using the latrine.

So what was the problem? Participation of the partners at household and community level had been limited to provision of cheap labour and available materials on the assumption that having been duly instructed on their roles, the WUC would ensure the maintenance of water sources and practice of hygienic behaviour.

A closer look at the mobilization and training techniques revealed that the approach did not adequately equip the mobilizers with the necessary skills to bring about participation and sense of ownership at the community level. Training methodology was mainly didactic interspersed with classroom based discussions, role plays and video shows on operation and maintenance. The result was the WUCs had little contact with the realities of hygiene, sanitation and water use behaviour around them.

On the recommendation of the JRM, and in collaboration with SARAR training experts from the RWSG/WB - Nairobi, the project undertook to develop and try out the use of participatory tools. A Guide for Training Water User Committees using Participatory Tools was developed to assist the social mobilizers in their training activities. A pilot was carried out in Mukono district and on the strength of the success, the participatory training methodology was extended to cover the other districts where RUWASA was active. The subjects covered included community map building, hygiene education, WUC responsibilities, and evaluation. The training which was designed was not limited to hygiene education and sanitation. It covered other areas as well. The tools which were used were:

Mapping, sanitation ladder, faecal routes and barriers, gender task analysis, story with a gap and other planning exercises.

The essential findings in using this methodology were that the WUC and other community members were able to participate actively in discussions related to sanitation, hygiene behaviour, water source maintenance, gender and planning. The use of pictorial illustrations easily facilitated and generated discussion. This was a positive departure from previous didactic approach.

The community members demanded the tools so that they too could train others. This was evidence of a feeling of empowerment to take charge of project activities by community members themselves. It also showed the tools were easy to understand and use at grassroots level. A summary of some lessons learnt are listed below :

(i) The methodology is user friendly and appropriate for use with various (all) categories of people;
(ii) The methodology is interesting, provokes discussion, brings out real life experiences which cannot be accessed using traditional training methods;
(iii) The approach is learner centred, therefore empowering the learner to think, identify and address (find solutions) situations;
(iv) The methodology eases work on the side of the trainer/facilitator;
(v)* The methodology can be used in a structured (RUWASA) or non-structured manner (WaterAid and KUPP). The latter two are using informal community members who are trained to train other community members!
(vi) Training is continuous at the community level;
(vii) The table below shows the tools that were pre-tested and the experiences:

In order to monitor closely the effect of using this methodology for training at grassroots level, the mobilization and training units of the project followed up 19

Table 1.

Tool	Experiences	Adopted
Unserialized posters Photo parade	easy to use as starters	Yes
Community mapping	very good for establishing baseline - sanitation, infrastructure, etc	Yes
Sanitation ladder	easily understood and used also establishes sanitation baseline	Yes
Faecal routes	useful to start off a hygiene education discussion	Yes
Faecal barriers	Enables community members think of solutions to hygiene problems that are within their reach	Yes
Gender task analysis	Evokes lively discussion, brings to light gender roles and distribution and is difficult to halt; ice breaker	Yes
Story with a gap	Eases planning discussions	Yes
Three pile sorting	Useful for hygiene behaviour discussion	Yes
Health case study	Not much used	
Roles and responsibility chart	has been applied in RUWASA area by mobilizers with success	

WUCs in three different sub-counties of Ikumbya (Iganga district), Bussede (Jinja district) and Kauga (Mukono district). A checklist of indicators of good WUC performance was drawn up as follows:

- proper record of water source users
- existence of O&M funds, collection and use
- existence of caretakers (for preventive maintenance and hygiene education)
- good general condition of the water sources (fencing, cut grass, soakaways, drains)
- hygiene education activities (users cleaning containers, posters on hygiene)

Observations:
(a) 79 per cent of WUCs had updated lists of water source users
(b) 64 per cent WUCs had collected and were using O&M funds to pay handpump mechanics, buy grease and spares
(c) 71 per cent WUCs had proper records related to the use of O&M funds
(d) 100 per cent of caretakers had spanners and were carrying out preventive maintenance
(e) 15 per cent of the WUCs renumerated their caretakers with Shs 800 - 2000 (US$ 0.9 - 2.1)
(f) 100 per cent WUCs had hygiene and sanitation messages embedded in their bye-laws e.g. use of clean utensils for collecting water, but there was no indication of direct intervention like meetings on hygienic behaviour.
(g) Five per cent of the WUCs had an updated list of latrine and sanplat coverage of its water users as a basis for follow up on sanitation activities.
18 homes of water users were visited. Of these, latrine coverage was 89 per cent: 72 per cent of the latrines were hygienic (clean floor with sanplats), and six per cent had hand washing facilities. (ref: Internal Project reports CMS)

This data was against a background where it had previously been difficult to obtain accurate information at the water user committee level.

Acceptance of participatory approaches at institutional level

So far the acceptance and use of the participatory methodology has largely been limited to the water and sanitation projects e.g. KUPP, RUWASA and Water Aid. At the policy levels, i.e ministries or agency HQ administrations, the MOH - Uganda supports Uganda Community Based Health Care Association (UCBHCA) which uses a lot of PRA approaches although support is still very limited. The methodology is sometimes thought to be time wasting!

Generally, decision makers who have been exposed to the methodology have shown a lot of interest and implicit support for its use.

Acceptance at community level

The communities appreciate the use of the approach during training. In the RUWASA project area, there have been demands expressed for the tools by water user committee members who would like to use them to mobilize other community members! They have been spurred into action.

Reactions of community members:

- There is full community participation in discussion irrespective of gender, status or educational levels;
- Communities have recommended the use of the tools for all training activities and that all should be trained using this approach;
- attendance during training is consistent throughout the period;
- During community level meetings where this approach has been used, tasks are allocated and sanctions agreed on by community members for non performance;
- Some behaviour changes have been observed e.g. dish washing (Water Aid), hand washing RUWASA), orderly lines at water kiosks (KUPP);
- General level of cleanliness is up!

Constraints experienced

- Lack of support from supervisors and policy makers who have not been exposed to the methodologies;
- Durability of tools (lamination has been tried out with some success);
- Artisans are not always available and need training when present;
- It is expensive to produce materials on a low scale;
- Training costs may be prohibitive as a full-scale workshop requires say 10 working days (administrators' headaches!);
- It a time consuming exercise.

Recommendations

(i) Use of participatory approaches and tools should be encouraged and widely marketed in fields other than water and sanitation, e.g. environment protection, agriculture, income generating. This is to foster sustainability of development initiatives.

(ii) There is need to institutionalize the methodologies (in ministries, agencies) so as to secure future funding. Sensitization of policy makers could be organized nationally or internationally. This will foster sustainability.

(iii) Community level, national and regional exchange visits should be encouraged to foster closer collaboration and capacity building, as well as monitoring and evaluation of the progress of this initiative.

iv) A monitoring and evaluation mechanism be developed/refined for effective assessment of the impact of participatory tools

v) Co-ordination of participatory hygiene and sanitation initiatives at national level should be through an established network supported by participating agencies.

Acronyms

PHAST	Participatory Hygiene and Sanitation Transformation
RUWASA	Rural Water and Sanitation
SHEP	School Health Education Project
SARAR	Self Esteem, Associative strengths, Resourcefulness, Action Planning, Responsibility.
WUC	Water User Committee
JRM	Joint Review Mission
RSWG/WB	Regional Water and Sanitation Group/World Bank
KUPP	Katwe Urban Pilot Project
O&M	Operation and Maintenance
CMS	Community Mobilization and Sanitation
UCBHCA	Uganda Community Based Health Care Association
PRA	Participatory Rural Appraisal

References:

1. A Guide for Training of Water User committees using Participatory Tools, RUWASA, August 1994.
2. Tools for Community Participation, Srinivasan, UNDP/WB.

www.ingramcontent.com/pod-product-compliance
Ingram Content Group UK Ltd.
Pitfield, Milton Keynes, MK11 3LW, UK
UKHW050226150426
5217IPUK00023B/1668